PAULINE AND OTHER STUDIES

PLATE III.

FIG. 8.—Church of St. Amphilochius on the Acropolis
of Iconium.

Frontispiece. *See p.* 170.

PAULINE AND OTHER STUDIES

IN EARLY CHRISTIAN HISTORY

BY

W. M. RAMSAY

BAKER BOOK HOUSE
Grand Rapids, Michigan

Reprinted 1979 by
Baker Book House Company
from the 1906 edition published by
A. C. Armstrong and Son, New York

ISBN: 0-8010-7684-6

This volume is part of the ten-volume
William M. Ramsay Library
ISBN: 0-8010-7685-4

PHOTOLITHOPRINTED BY CUSHING - MALLOY, INC.
ANN ARBOR, MICHIGAN, UNITED STATES OF AMERICA
1 9 7 9

PREFACE

OF the following essays one is entirely new. Six may be called new, as each is worked up anew out of several articles. For example, No. XIV. contains parts of five articles on Pauline Chronology. The rest have been carefully revised and improved in many details.

It has encouraged me greatly to find that even in the oldest articles no change of opinion on Pauline topics has been needed, except to write sometimes more confidently. The object originally was to state facts, not to make daring inferences; and further study during the intervening years has simply been a process of building on the foundation of these old studies. One correction was needed on page 358. About May, A.D. 62, the Jews sent a deputation to meet the new governor of Palestine at Alexandria. Formerly I supposed that he was promoted to

Palestine from a post in Egypt; but in writing on
" Roads and Travel " for Dr. Hastings' *Dictionary* I
learned to correlate this deputation with several other
facts, and thus to recognise a general principle of the
Roman service, which confirms older chronological
arguments.

My best thanks are due to the editors of the
*Contemporary Review, Quarterly Review, Interpreter,
Homiletic Review* and *Expositor* for permission to
use articles published in those magazines.

The papers are not exactly those which at first
I intended to include, but rather a series possessing
a certain unity of character as a survey of important
movements and men in the early Christian centuries.
The eleventh is an experiment how far a lecture with
lantern slides can be put into printed form.

CONTENTS

vii

ILLUSTRATIONS

PLATES

b

CUTS IN THE TEXT

PAGE

MAPS

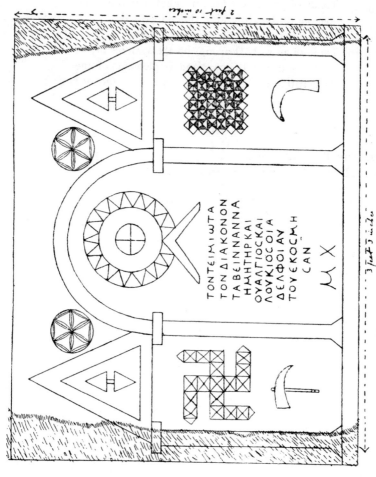

ΤΟΝΤΕΙΜΙΩΤΑ
ΤΟΝΔΙΑΚΟΝΟΝ
ΤΑΘΕΙΝΝΑΝΝΑ
ΗΜΗΤΗΡΚΑΙ
ΟΥΑΓΙΟCΚΑΙ
ΛΟΥΚΙΟCΟΙΑ
ΔΕΛΦΟΙΑΝ
ΤΟΥΕΚΟCΜΗ
CAN
ΜΧ

Fig. 40. Tomb of an early Deacon (symbols of Net, Crown and Swastika, also Implements of Deceased's Occupation).

See page 298.

I

SHALL WE HEAR EVIDENCE OR NOT?

I

SHALL WE HEAR EVIDENCE OR NOT?

IN studying the life of St. Paul everything depends on the
point of view from which one contemplates it, and the pre-
possessions with which one approaches the subject. There
is one preliminary question on which it is absolutely necessary to make up one's mind clearly: Are we open to hear
evidence or shall we rule it out beforehand? In recent
years those who most pride themselves on their " freedom "
of mind have set aside as inadmissible all evidence bearing
on the greatest event of St. Paul's life, *viz.*, his experience
on the road to Damascus. To do so means that they have
made up their mind before they enter on the investigation.

The religion of the Jews from its first beginning to its
fullest development in Christianity was founded on the
belief that human nature can, in certain cases, at certain
moments in the life of certain individuals, come into direct
communion with the Divine Being, and can thus learn the
purpose and will of God. In other words, God occasionally
reveals Himself to man.

St. Paul himself believed unhesitatingly in the frequent
occurrence of such revelations. This belief was part of his
Jewish inheritance, strong with the growth of a hundred
generations, a force driving him on through his whole life.
Hence it demands the attention of every one who studies

(3)

his life. In St. Paul's view all true religion was the direct utterance of the voice and will of God, and all human history was impelled in its course by such utterance. He had been trained from infancy in the Hebrew view, which attributed the whole course of the national religion and fortunes—the latter being simply the measure of national adherence to the religion—to a series of such revelations made by God on various occasions to certain favoured individuals.

In his later years St. Paul did not consider that such revelation had been denied to other nations and confined absolutely to the Jews. On the contrary, it lies at the foundation of his later ideas of history and of life that all nations have some share in the revelation of God, and some capacity for understanding it, that *what can be known of Him is manifest in them, for He manifested it unto them; for His invisible nature,* viz. *His eternal power and Godhead, is clearly seen since the creation of the world, being perceived through the works of creation;* that He has never *left Himself without witness, in that He did good and gave from heaven rains and fruitful seasons, filling men's hearts with food and gladness;* and that, through this revelation, *all men show the work of the law written in their hearts, their conscience bearing witness therewith.*

This revelation, which is granted to all nations, has sometimes been distinguished as "natural" revelation from that which was imparted to the Hebrews, the inference being that the latter was "supernatural". This seems to be an unsatisfactory way of expressing the nature of that undeniable distinction. It is misleading, and even inaccurate, to use the term "supernatural". We hold that revelation of the Divine to the human is a necessary part of the order of

nature, and therefore is in the strictest sense "natural";
and also that all revelation of the Divine to the human
nature must necessarily be "superhuman," being a step in
the gradual elevation of the human nature towards the
Divine.

The nations had one by one rejected that revelation, or,
as we might say in more modern phraseology, their history
had become a process of degeneration. After a beginning
of learning, of comprehension, and of improvement, their
will and desire soon became degraded. In St. Paul's own
words, *after knowing God, they ceased to glorify Him as God,
and to be thankful, but turned to futile philosophic speculations,
and their faculties lost the power of comprehending and became obscured.* The result was a steady process of degradation, folly, vice, crime, which St. Paul paints in terrible
colours (Rom. i.).

History undoubtedly justifies this picture of the nations
over which St. Paul's view extended. Where we can trace
the outlines of their history over a sufficient time, we find
that in an earlier stage, and up to a certain point, their
religious ideas and rites were simpler, higher, purer. Sometimes we can trace a considerable period of development
and advance. But in every case the development turns to
degeneration,[1] and throughout the Græco-Roman world the
belief was general, and thoroughly justified, that the state
of morality in the first century was much more degraded
than it had been several centuries earlier. Society had
become more complex and more vicious. In religion the
number of gods had been multiplied, but its hold on the
belief of men had been weakened and its worst character-

---

[1] This paragraph is a brief statement of the view stated more fully in
" Religion of Greece and Asia Minor " (Hastings' *Dict.*, v.).

istics had been strengthened, while any good features in it had almost wholly disappeared.

It is doubtful how far that principle should be extended in human history, but there are certainly many examples of a similar kind beyond the range of St. Paul's knowledge. The history of Brahminism, of Buddhism, of Islam, of Zoroastrianism, all exemplify the same turn towards degradation and decay, when the power of growth has been exhausted. And, in the light of recent investigations, it must be considered as probable, perhaps almost certain, that many barbarous superstitions which by some modern scientific inquirers in the subject of folklore and primitive custom have been regarded as indications of the character of primitive man, are not really primitive, but merely examples of degeneration.

Some races have degenerated through the influence of war, because they lay too much on the track of armies and armed migration; others deteriorated through unfavourable climatic conditions, either because they were crushed into remote corners among untraversable mountains, or into regions unfit to support life on proper conditions, or because a too enervating and luxurious climate sapped the stamina and energy of the people in the course of generations. Massacre, or the dread of massacre, has been a frequent cause of degeneration. The victors are brutalised. The survivors of the victims deteriorate because the higher qualities of human nature are denied exercise, as entailing the death of those who display them.

Among the Jews alone there was found a long succession of great men who heard and obeyed the Divine voice. Each was, in a sense, the disciple of his predecessor, learning from the past and acquiring fuller comprehension of, and susceptibility to, the Divine nature and revelation. In the process of revelation the religious ideas which they expressed to the people developed and became purer and more elevated. In each new revelation the whole past experience of the race was focussed, and the spark of progress kindled therefrom. Those old Hebrew prophets thus raised the national ideas and the national life, for though the nation always seemed to them to be slipping back into idolatry and the immorality which is its inevitable associate, yet, in reality, the people were being raised, though only very slowly, above the low level of their ancestors. What seemed to the Hebrew prophets to be retrogression was strictly only persistence of old habits.

Yet that apparently favoured nation was not in the long run more responsive than the others had been to the Divine message. It was for a time drawn onwards by the prophets whom it produced. Almost reluctantly, with many slips and many falls, it was raised to a far higher moral level than any of the nations around. The captivity in Babylonia purified it, for it was chiefly the most patriotic and religious who came back, while the more weak-minded and sluggish would not face the difficulties of returning. The Zealots were in the majority, and they held the nation together, resisted the insidious advance of Greek civilisation and education, defeated at last the Syrian armies, and won freedom for their nationality and their religion.

But the hard-won triumph resulted only in unfertile exclusiveness and self-complacency. The people ceased to feel any need and any desire for the Divine guidance, and lost all power of development. The race of the prophets seemed to have come to an end, when John the Baptist appeared with the brief simple message that the Messiah was at hand.

To St. Paul the failure of the Jews to recognise and receive the Christ was the result and the proof of their having ceased to be the favoured nation. They had refused to listen to the Divine voice, and the Divine favour was turned away from them. It had never been part of the Divine purpose to reject the nations. The nations had turned away from God, but they had learned in their consequent degradation and darkness their need of Divine illumination, which the Jews in their self-satisfied exclusiveness had begun to despise.

How far certain germs of his later views already existed in Saul's mind during the early part of his career, it is impossible to say. It is probable that some germs did exist of a wider view than the purely Jewish. But, at any rate, Saul, in his youth, was mainly occupied with the thought of Hebrew progress in the past, and the coming triumph of Hebrew religion. He could not shut his eyes to the fact that the great line of the prophets had for a considerable time been interrupted ; and he must have been firmly convinced that the interruption could not last for ever, and that a new revelation of the Divine power was likely soon to come. There can be no doubt that the feeling to which John the Baptist gave utterance was deep and wide-spread ; and few will doubt that Saul shared it.

With this belief in the reality and frequency of Divine revelation reigning with intense fervour in his mind, Saul must always have been prepared to hear that a prophet had appeared ; and, according to our conception of his character, he must from childhood have been filled with the desire and hope of hearing for himself the Divine voice.

He must have had his mind roused by the message of John ; he may probably have heard him, and believed fervently his announcement of the immediate coming of Christ.

But, further, Saul undoubtedly was eager, and was preparing himself by education, by study, by scrupulous obedience to the Law, by ardent zeal in enforcing it on others, to be in a fit state to hear the voice of God. It may be argued that this eagerness rendered him the more open to self-deception : and there is of course some plausibility in that argument.

The issue was that he did become the recipient of revelation, and that his life was profoundly affected, and his views revolutionised thereby. He repeatedly described himself, or is described by others, as having both seen the Lord and heard His voice.

Now what do we understand by this? The question cannot and ought not to be evaded. Paul's words are too clear and strong to be passed over as inexact or unimportant. He declared emphatically that the revelations made to him, the words spoken to him, and the sights granted to his eyes, were his greatest privilege and honour, constituted the motive power of all his action, and supplied the whole spirit and essence of his life. Those revelations, and especially the first of them, when he saw Jesus on the way, as he was now nigh unto Damascus, were in his view the most real events of his life. In comparison with them, all else was mere shadow and semblance ; in those moments he had come in contact with the truth of the world, the Divine reality. He had been permitted to become aware of the omnipresent God who is everywhere around us and in us.

Various attempts are made to explain away or soften

down his clear and emphatic words by devices of a more or less sophistical kind ; and many people hope in this way to retain all that they like in Paul, while they pretend that he did not mean what they dislike. But all such attempts to close the eyes to plain facts are unreasonable.

In truth that vision near Damascus is the critical point, on which all study of St. Paul's life must turn. On our conception of that event depends the whole interpretation of his life. The question at this stage is not whether that event as he conceived it was true and real, or was distorted and exaggerated in his mind owing to some diseased and unbalanced mental state. That question will come up in its proper place.

The preliminary question alone here concerns us : was that event, in the form that Paul describes it, a possible one, or was it so wholly and absolutely impossible that even to discuss the evidence about it is irrational?

If it be an impossibility that the Divine nature can thus reveal itself to human senses, then the whole life and work of Paul would be a mere piece of self-deception. To those who take that point of view, the only other alternative to self-deception, regarding a man who declared that the Divine nature had manifested itself to his hearing and sight, would be the supposition of imposture. But, in the case of Saul, this alternative is, by common consent, set aside. He was an honest believer in what he said.

Now no amount of evidence can make us believe in what we know to be impossible. One who holds such manifestation to be impossible cannot regard seriously, or even listen to, any evidence of its having occurred. Such evidence is condemned in his mind before it is brought forward, as involving either self-deception and unsound mind or imposture. If he examines at all the so-called "evidence," he does so only as a matter either of curiosity, or of scientific interest in the vagaries of human error.

The view that Paul's experience on the way to Damascus was due to some form of madness has been widely maintained in recent years. It is tacitly held by many who would shrink from explicitly formulating it to their own mind. It is openly and resolutely declared by many learned and honest men. Scientific investigators have discussed and given a name to the precise class of madness to which Paul's delusions must be assigned.

Now there have been many madmen in all times ; but the difficulty which many feel in classing St. Paul among them arises from the fact that not merely did he persuade every one who heard him that he was sane and spoke the truth, but that also he has moved the world, changed the whole course of history, and made us what we are. Is the world moved at the word of a lunatic? To think so would be to abandon all belief in the existence of order and unity in the world and in history ; and therefore we are driven to the conclusion that St. Paul's vision is one of the things about which evidence ought to be scrutinised and examined without any foregone conclusion in one's mind.

Further, it is part of our view that the Divine nature, if it is really existent in our world, must in some way come into relation to man, and affect mankind. The Divine nature is not existent for man, except in so far as he can hope and strive to come into direct relation with it. If he cannot hope to do so, then the Divine nature belongs only to another world, and has no reality, no existence in ours. What is God to us if we cannot come into knowledge of or relation with Him? Either you must say that we know nothing about the existence of any God, or you must admit that man can in some way become aware of the existence, *i.e.* the nature, of God. Now to say that we can become aware of the nature of God is only another way of saying that the Divine nature is revealed to man; and, if it is revealed, that can only be because it reveals itself by coming into direct relation to man. There is nothing that can reveal God except Himself.

It must, therefore, be true that God reveals Himself to man in some way or other. St. Paul claims to have received such revelation; and we ought not to set aside his claim as irrational and necessarily false. Many such claims can easily be put away; but history has decided that his case is one which deserves scrutiny, examination, rigid testing.

St. Paul also claims to have received this revelation in an eminent and unusual degree: in other words, that he was more sensitive to, and more able to learn about, the Divine nature than others.

This claim also is one that deserves to be carefully scrutinised with an open mind. If we admit that the Divine nature reveals itself to men, then there must be inequality and variety in the revelation to different individuals. There is no equality or uniformity in nature.

It is not involved in our view that we must be able to explain clearly in scientific detail exactly what takes place in such a revelation, and by what precise process an individual man becomes cognizant of the Divine nature and purpose. There are powers of acquiring knowledge which are an unintelligible mystery to those who have not possessed and exercised them; and this is a case in which possession implies exercise, and only exists in virtue of being exercised.

Who can gauge, or understand, or describe, the way in which a great mathematical genius hurries on in his sweep of reasoning with easy, unerring rapidity? Even when his reasoning is afterwards explained in detail, few are capable of being educated up to the comprehension of it. To him it is far easier to move on from step to step in his reasoning about the forces that act in the world than to explain his steps so as to bring them within the comprehension even of the few who can be educated to understand. His demonstration of his process of reasoning would be, to all but a handful of exceptional persons, an unintelligible jargon, having no more reality or sense than the ravings of a madman. But to him those words and signs, so meaningless to others, present a vision of order and beauty, of reality and symmetry, which changes the whole aspect and nature of the universe in his thought, and enables him or his successors to understand and direct its forces, and to affect profoundly the life and fortunes of mankind.

Why should we doubt, or hesitate to admit, that there may be even greater differences between different men as regards their power of coming into relation with, and comprehending, the Divine nature, than there is in power of comprehending mathematical truth? Yet all men have some little power of comprehending mathematical reasoning, and similarly all are endowed with some rudimentary power of attaining a knowledge of the Divine nature.

And in both cases, from want of exercise, want of desire, sluggishness, or idleness, the endowment of power may remain undeveloped, and apparently non-existent.

When we speak about recognising the truth of those

great processes of mathematical reasoning which were alluded to, there are two totally different ways and kinds of recognition. The discoverer himself recognises intuitively, but the world takes him on credit: it recognises by faith. This is a case where we believe without understanding. Though we cannot attain anything beyond the vaguest and most rudimentary understanding of what the discoverer has seen and of the way in which he can perceive it, yet we believe unquestioningly and unhesitatingly that he has comprehended a department of external nature which we cannot comprehend.

Now the reason why in that case we believe without understanding and through mere faith is partly because we recognise in him the spirit of truth—we perceive that the man has no reason to deceive us, that his whole credit and in a sense his life is staked on his truth and accuracy—we feel, and all men recognise unhesitatingly, that his is a truthful mind, and one can see the joy and the consciousness of knowledge glorifying and irradiating his personality —and partly because we see the results of the knowledge which he has gained : we believe in his knowledge because it manifests itself in power.

But the original discoverer recognises intuitively and unerringly the truth of his reasoning. To know when one's reasoning is correct is the foundation of mathematical endowment. One sees and feels it, and one cannot shake off the knowledge or free oneself from it. Galileo might, under compulsion, pretend to acknowledge that the earth does not move, but he could not get rid of the knowledge that, in spite of all pretences and confessions, still it does move. This absolute consciousness of knowledge dominates the mind that possesses it, and drives the man on in his career. He must think : he must experiment and test his knowledge in practice, and the test is whether his reasoning realises itself in actual power.

Surely the same principles of belief may fairly and reasonably be applied in respect of the comprehension and discovery of the Divine nature and will and purpose.

To come into direct relation with the Divine nature, what is that except to make a step in the appreciation of the truth that underlies the visible and sensual phenomena, to get a glimpse of the eternal value of things, to see them as they are in reality, not as they appear to the mere individual observation from the purely individual stand-point? Man cannot easily rise above his own selfish and narrow point of view, and in the hurry and pressure of common life he can hardly do so at all; yet he is

> not quite so sunk that moments,
> Sure, though seldom, are denied him,
> When the spirits true endowments
> Stand out plainly from its false ones,
> And apprise it if pursuing,
> Or the right way or the wrong way,
> To its triumph or undoing.

Such moments do not come in the same way, or amid the same surroundings, to all men. The accompaniments are special to the individual. A man can become possessed of knowledge only in such way as he is capable of receiving it, and that is a matter of his habits and education and surroundings.

One who has learned almost entirely through the senses, who lives by reliance on sight and hearing, cannot learn, and could not believe, anything except what comes to him through those senses, or rather is associated with impressions of the senses. The thought is, of course, distinct from the impressions, but it comes with them and seems to come through them, and the reality of the experience lies not in the impressions on the senses, but in the sudden consciousness of the Divine nature animating the world, in which hitherto the man was aware only of the objects that touched his senses.

To one who is accustomed to gain knowledge by contemplation and thought, the revelation of the Divine nature will come through contemplation and thought. Such a one does not connect truth with sense-impressions; rather he distrusts these, knowing that they are mere shadows which his own personality casts on the world, and that reality does not lie that way.

But in either case the perception of the Divine truth is ultimate, final and convincing. He who has seen knows. And he can never again lose the knowledge, nor live unhesitatingly the free unconscious life of previous days. The consciousness of the Divine nature becomes a power within him, driving him on to his destiny, good or evil.

The question whether the physical sensations which are sometimes associated with the perception are real is obviously a superficial and unintelligent one. What sensation is real?

Take here the individual instance. What can we learn from the case of St. Paul, admitting for the moment that he acquired higher and better knowledge of God in those revelations of which he speaks. Those who were with him near Damascus had a vague idea that something was taking place; they were aware of light, and even of sound, but they did not hear any words, nor were they affected in any noteworthy way. Had Paul died there, no one would have known that anything remarkable had occurred.

Such is the clear and unmistakable account in which Paul and Luke agree, though there are some trifling differences between them about details.

On the one hand, it is plain that Paul's companions did not see what he saw. On the other hand, it is equally plain that they learned nothing there, whereas Paul obtained an insight into truth and reality which revolutionised his aims and changed the world's history. If the test of reality lies in the capacity of all sentient beings to experience the same sensations when placed in the same position, then Paul's sensations were not real. But is that a fair test? Are there not phenomena in the world where that test fails? Are there not more things in the world than those which everybody can see and hear? Is this not one of the things which we may and must take on credit and believe without understanding? The question is surely worth putting and carefully considering in the light of Paul's whole career.

There is nothing but scholastic pedantry in debating the question as to the reality of Paul's sensations of sight and hearing on that occasion. There is no standard accepted by the opposing parties, there is no agreement as to the meaning of the terms ; each side discusses with its mind made up beforehand, and its eyes closed to the intention of its opponents. There can be no issue and no result ; the question is as barren as that older question about the number of angels who can stand on the point of a needle. The problem should be approached otherwise.

The lesson which Saul had to learn before he could make any progress in knowledge of the Divine nature was that the actual Jesus of recent notoriety in Palestine—the Jesus whom he had seen and known, as I believe—was still

2

living, and not, as he had fancied, dead. His was not a soul disciplined, eager to learn, ready to obey. It was a soul firm in its own false opinion—not even possessed of "true opinion"—resolute and hardened in perfect self-satisfaction, proud of what it believed to be its knowledge, strong in its high principle and its sense of duty. There was no possibility that he should by any process of mere thinking come to realise the truth. Nothing could appeal to him in this question except through the senses of hearing and sight.

Such we see to be the general conditions of the situation. St. Paul tells us the result. He heard, he saw, he was convinced, he was a witness to the world that the Jesus who had lived and been crucified was still living. But those who were with him did not learn, did not see, did not hear. They were not capable of gaining the knowledge which Saul acquired, nor should we be capable if we could be put in the same situation now. They were not, and we are not, able to respond as Saul was to the impulse of the Divine nature. The same experience would not convince them or us. Saul knew that this was Jesus, and his plans of life, his aspirations after the Divine life, his conceptions of the possibilities of work in the existing condition of the world, his longing for the Messiah who was to make Judaism the conquering faith of the civilised world, his whole fabric of thought and religion and belief, were in such a position that this sudden perception of the truth about Jesus recreated and invigorated all his mental and moral frame.

That perception, then, was the real part of the experience which came to Saul. But that perception could not be gained by him except in a certain way, with certain

physical accompaniments and certain affection of the
senses, and those accompaniments acquire reality from
being the vehicle of a real perception of truth in one
special and peculiar case.

That brief experience in which Saul learned so much
was the outcome of his whole past career, the crystallisa-
tion into a new form of all the loose elements of will and
thought and emotion which his life and education had
given him, under the impulse of the sudden imparting to
his mind of the decisive factor ; and the physical accompaniments conveyed the spark or the impulse which set the
process in motion.

If then it be asserted that the sensations which Paul
experienced were in themselves a necessary part of the
knowledge which he acquired, one must denounce the
assertion as false and irrational.   The sensations were only
a proof of the weakness of nature, the insensibility to
purer and higher ways of acquiring truth, in which Paul
was as yet involved : they were the measure of his *ignorance*, not the necessary vehicle of his knowledge.   As he
became more sensitive to the Divine nature, and more
capable of apprehending the Divine message, he rose superior to the grosser method of communication through the
senses.

That St. Paul was conscious of a growth and elevation
of his own powers of perception in regard to the Divine
nature seems implied clearly in 2 Corinthians v. 16, *even
though we have known Christ after the flesh, yet now we
know Him so no more.*

Standing on this point of view one sees that the variation between Luke (*these men, hearing a voice, but seeing
no man*, Acts ix. 7) and Paul (*they saw indeed the light,*

but heard not the voice, Acts xxii. 9) with regard to the degree to which Paul's sensations were shared in by his companions, stamps the sensations as being accidental and secondary, the encumbrances rather than an essential accompaniment of his perception of truth.

So also the older disciples learned the truth through sight and hearing ; they had known the Man, and they must hear and see before they could realise that He was not dead. But there is in the mind of the Evangelist who saw and heard a consciousness that those sensations are mere accidents of the individual, personally incidental to their peculiar experience and condition, merely ways by which the truth was made clear to their duller minds : *Because thou hast seen Me, thou hast believed. Blessed are they that have not seen and yet have believed.*

What would it have meant to those companions of Paul then, what would it mean to us now, if the information could have been suddenly flashed on them or on us that Jesus was living? It would mean little or nothing. We should dine and sleep as usual. Those men would have proceeded quietly to Damascus, and reported that they had an odd experience by the way, but whether it was real or a phantasm, true or untrue, they did not know.

There lies the difference. The man to whom the Divine reveals itself recognises inevitably. He cannot doubt or hesitate : he knows at once and for ever.

The Divine never reveals itself in vain. Or perhaps one should rather say that the Divine is always ready to reveal itself, but we do not perceive it except when we are in such a state that we are convinced by it, and recognise it. There rises to memory here a wonderful passage in T. H. Green's Essay on " The Philosophy of Aristotle " :—

" If in any true sense man can commune with the spirit within him, in the same he may approach God, as one who, according to the highest Christian idea, ' liveth in him '. Man however is slow to recognise the divinity that is within himself in his relation to the world. He will find the spiritual somewhere, but cannot believe that it is the natural rightly understood. What is under his feet and between his hands is too cheap and trivial to be the mask of eternal beauty. But half aware of the blindness of sense which he confesses, he fancies that it shows him the every-day world, from which he must turn away if he would attain true vision. If a prophet tell him to do some great thing, he will obey. He will draw up ' ideal truth ' from the deep, or bring it down from heaven, but cannot believe that it is within and around him. Stretching out his hands to an unknown God, he heeds not the God in whom he lives and moves and has his being. He cries for a revelation of Him, yet will not be persuaded that His hiding-place is the intelligible world, and that He is incarnate in the Son of Man, who through the communicated strength of thought is Lord also of that world."

But the human being who is to become sensitive to the Divine presence and voice must be able to do his part. The manifestation cannot be wholly one-sided : there must be the proper condition of mind and body, and intellect, and will in the man. What all the conditions are no one can say, except perhaps one to whom the manifestation has been granted. But one thing is sure : a certain state of mental receptivity is needed, and a certain long preparation of the whole nature of the recipient must have occurred.

Such preparation was, in several forms of ancient religion, described as purification ; and formal rules were prescribed, as regards time and rites. In such a state of things the preparation of the mind, the emotions and the will, soon become almost a secondary matter, and purification was mainly ceremonial, though even in the most formal and vulgar religious prescriptions the proper moral and mental state was never entirely lost sight of.

But, it will be objected, when we speak of the Divine nature as revealing itself to man through the senses, we are introducing an element of the supernatural, and asking men to believe what no rational being can accept, inasmuch as it is contrary to reason.

This objection is merely verbal, it shows not even a faint glimmering conception of the real situation, it belongs to a stage and a way of thinking that rational men ought now to have left behind them.

If the Divine reveals itself to the human nature, the latter must in receiving the knowledge rise above its ordinary plane of mere individual existence, it must rise superior to the limitations of time and space, and contemplate truth, and eternity, and reality. Its momentary elevation to the plane of the Divine view is necessarily and inevitably a superhuman fact, but why call it supernatural? It is surely a part of the order of nature that man should reach out towards God; if that, or anything involved in that, is supernatural or marvellous or miraculous, then everything in the life of man beyond the mere reception of impressions and action under their stimulus, every step in the progress of knowledge, every widening of the outlook of man over and beyond the single successive phenomena of the world, is equally marvellous and supernatural. But the order of nature is that man should strive to rise, and should succeed in rising above the level from which he starts. Nothing in his life is real except the advance that he makes above himself. He cannot attain to knowledge and truth, but yet he does attain to them in so far as he struggles a little way towards them. He lives at all only in so far as he moves onward : stagnation is death. All that is real is superhuman : what is *only* human is mere negation and unreality, the expression of our ignorance and our remoteness from truth and knowledge and God.

In truth the stigmatising of anything in the revelation to man of the Divine nature as supernatural or contrary to reason is simply the arbitrary and unreasoning attempt to establish that our ignorance is the real element in the world, and to bound the possibilities of the universe by our own acquisitions and perceptions.

The only proper attitude before such questions is that of inquiry and of open-mindedness—surely that is a truism, and yet it is to the so-called free and critical mind that we have to address this remonstrance !

The investigator in every department of science and study knows that it is half the battle to succeed in putting the right question. In this case the right question is, What can we learn from Paul's experience ? And not how was Paul's evidence falsified ? nor what insanity misled him ?

II

THE CHARM OF PAUL

II

THE CHARM OF PAUL

THE life and the nature of one who has influenced human history so profoundly as St. Paul must be studied afresh by every successive age. His character is far too wide and all-embracing to be comprehended by the age in which he lives and on which he exercised his immediate influence. He is at once outside and inside it: he works on it both from without and from within. He has caught in some degree the eternal principles which sweep through all time, and express themselves in momentary, passing form in each successive age. Thus he transcends the limits of time and speaks to all ages; and his words will be differently understood in different ages, for every age finds that they respond to its peculiar questions. Hence every age must write afresh for itself—one might almost say, every man must write for himself—the life of St. Paul; and the words in which he strove to make his thoughts comprehensible to the raw converts, who needed to be trained in power of thinking as well as in the elementary principles of morality and conduct, must be rendered into the form which will be more easily understood in present circumstances. The attempts to do this must always be imperfect and inadequate, and yet they may make it easier to penetrate to the heart which beats in all his writings. But the aim of the historian should always be to induce the reader to study for himself the writings and work of St. Paul.

In venturing to lay before the readers a study of that character, it is not necessary to claim, in justification of the attempt, peculiar qualifications or insight : it is a sufficient excuse, if one can claim to be putting the same questions that others are putting, and to be one among many students animated by a similar spirit and the same needs.

In the case of St. Paul most readers are already familiar with the events of his life, with the original authorities on which every biographer and student must depend, and with some modern presentation of the facts. But opinion has varied much in recent years as regards the bearing of these facts, and the estimate which should be set on them as indications of the character and aims of the Apostle. Hence, in the present state of the subject, the most important feature of a new study of his career consists in the general interpretation which is to be placed on the facts, and in the spirit with which the work is undertaken ; and it is advisable for the writer in the outset to make clear his general attitude towards the critical points on which the difference in opinion turns.

The fascination of St. Paul's personality lies in his humanity. He is the most human of all the Apostles.

That he was in many ways the ablest and the greatest, the most creative mind, the boldest originator, the most skilful organiser and administrator, the most impressive and outstanding personage in the whole Apostolic circle— that will be admitted by most readers. That he was the most clever and the most brilliant of the Apostles every one must feel. But all that might be granted, without bringing us any nearer an explanation of the undying

interest and charm he possesses for us. Those are not the
qualities which make a man really interesting, which catch
the heart of the world as Paul has caught it. The clever
man is, on the whole, rather repellent to the mass of mankind, though he will find his own circle of friends who can
at once admire his ability and penetrate to the real nature
underneath his cleverness. But St. Paul lies closer to the
heart of the great mass of readers than any other of the
Apostles ; and the reason is that he impresses us as the most
intensely human of them all.

The career of St. Paul can easily and truthfully be described as a series of brilliant achievements and marvellous successes. But it is not through his achievements and
his success that he has seized and possessed the hearts of
men. It is because behind the achievements we can see the
trials and the failures. To others his life might seem like
the triumphal progress of a conqueror. But we can look
through his eyes and watch the toil and the stress ; we can
see him always on the point of failure, always guarding
against the ceaseless dangers that threatened him, *pressed
on every side, yet not straitened, perplexed but not in despair,
persecuted but not forsaken, cast down, but not destroyed.*

We follow his fortunes with the keenest interest, because
we feel that he was thoroughly representative of the eager,
strenuous, toiling man, and his career was full of situations
and difficulties such as the ordinary man has to face in the
world. The life of St. Paul, as it stands before us in his
letters and his biography, was one constant struggle against
difficult circumstances. He was always suspected, always
misunderstood, by some ; and he always found a friend to
stand by him in his difficulties, to believe in him in spite
of appearances, and to be his champion and guarantee.

That is the daily lot of the men who work, of all who try to do anything good or great, of all men who strive towards an ideal of any kind, in patriotism, or in loyalty, or in honour, or in religion; and it is only such men who are interested in the life of Paul. They must be prepared to face misconception, suspicion, blame greater than they deserve; and they may hope to find in every case some friend such as Paul always found.

The description of his first entry into the Christian world of Jerusalem is typical. *When he was come to Jerusalem, he assayed to join himself to the disciples; but they were all afraid of him, and believed not that he was a disciple. But Barnabas took him and brought him to the Apostles, and declared unto them how he had seen the Lord in the way. . . . And he was with them coming and going out of Jerusalem. . . . And he disputed against the Hellenist Jews; but they went about to slay him.* All the rest of his career is similar to that. His past life, with its passions and its struggles, its attempts and its failures, always impeded him in every new enterprise. No one could *deliver him from this body of death.*

We see, too, that—as is the case with all men—his difficulties and his failures almost always were the result of his own nature. It was his own faults and errors that caused the misconceptions and suspicions, by which he was continually pressed and perplexed. In the intense enthusiasm of his nature he often failed to recognise the proper limitations, and erred in the way of overstraining the present emotion. He was carried too far in act and in word; and at a later moment he became conscious that he had been over-enthusiastic, and had not been sufficiently mindful of all the complex conditions.

When we say that he failed to recognise the proper limitations, we feel that the phrase is unsatisfactory ; and we must try to express what we aim at in another way. Let us compare him with the greatest of his contemporaries, the Apostles John and Peter. When we are in contact with them, at least in their later life, we are impressed always with the completeness of statement and the perfectness of vision that are implied in everything recorded of them. They had lived in company with Him who, in a sense far truer than Matthew Arnold meant,

> saw life steadily and saw it whole ;

and they had caught from Him something of that faculty of calm steady completeness of vision.

In all the words of Jesus the reader is impressed with that completeness of statement : the truth stands there whole and entire. You never require to look at the language from some special point of view, to make allowances for the circumstances and the intention of the speaker, before you recognise the truth of the words. You do not feel that there are other justifiable points of view which are left out of account, and that from those points the saying must be considered inadequate. The word is never one-sided.

Take any one of the sayings, such as, *Render unto Cæsar the things that are Cæsar's, and unto God the things that are God's*, or *Wisdom is justified of all her children*, or *The Son of Man is Lord of the Sabbath*. Each of them is a complete and rounded whole, perfect from every point of view. There is nothing more to be said. The true commentator may expound laboriously from various points of view the truth of those matchless expressions, and thereby render a real service to the reader. You must look at each saying first in one light, then in another, analyse it, explain it, and you will better appreciate all that lies in it ; but you cannot add to it, or make it more complete than it is. It stands there once for all. It is the final statement.

Something of that perfection of vision and of expression —that calm serene insight into the essential truth beneath the flow and change of things—that power of contemplating the world upon the plane of eternity—had passed into the mind of John and of Peter. Their acts and their words alike are on that plane of perfectness and finality. Their words were so, because their life and minds were so. *We cannot but speak the things which we saw and heard.* They had looked on the Truth : they had lived with the Truth. Never again could they live on the plane of ordinary humanity or see things exactly as men see them, for they had gazed upon eternity, and the glory was always in their eyes.

Something too of the same steadiness and completeness of vision belongs, and must belong, to the great prophets of the world. They were prophets because they had come into relations with the Divine nature and had seen the Truth. They too could not but speak the things which they had seen and heard.

Let us try another illustration—a modern one, drawn from Hegel's brief essay, entitled Who is the abstract thinker? in which he distinguishes the analytic method of scientific and abstract reasoning from the direct contemplation of the concrete truth of the eternal world. The great German philosopher in a few sentences hits off the various points of view from which a murderer on the scaffold is regarded by different persons.[1] The sociologists trace the conditions of society and education that led him to his crime : the moralists or the priests make him the text of a sermon on the corruption of the class to which he belongs. They see the murderer : they have no eyes for the man as part of the eternal world, as an item in the Divine plan. Sentimental ladies, as they look on, are struck with his handsome and interesting figure : they see another side, and there they are content : if they do not perhaps carry their words of admiration into action by throwing flowers to him on the scaffold. But one person, a poor old woman in the crowd, beheld the scene as a whole, as an act in the drama of eternity : *The severed head was laid on the scaffold ; and there was sunshine. " But how beautifully," said she, " does God's sun of grace lighten up his head ! " The most contemptuous word we can use in anger is, " You are not worth the sun shining on you". The woman saw the sun shining on the murderer's head, and knew that he was still worth something in the eye of God.* She uttered in a flash of intuition a whole concrete truth, while the learned, the educated, and the fashionable world saw only one side or another, abstract and incomplete.

Now with Paul we feel ourselves in contact with a more simply human character than when we study the great Apostles John and Peter. It is not that he never moves and thinks and speaks on the plane of eternity. He often stands, or almost stands upon it, and sees accordingly. But he does not live on it. He only strives towards it.

---

[1] *Vermischte Schriften*, ii., p. 403 (*Werke*, vol. xvii.). A fine page in the late Prof. Wallace's *Logic of Hegel* (Proleg. lxxix.) directed my attention to it in undergraduate days, and fixed it in my mind for ever.

He is the typical, the representative man, who attains in moments of higher vision and inspiration to behold the truth, to commune with the Divine nature. He has, too, far more of such visions than other men. They are the greatest glory of his life, in which he might reasonably take pride.

But one feels that with Paul the vision lasted no long time. It was present with him only for a moment; and then he was once more on the level of humanity.

Yet that, after all, is why Paul is so close to us. We too can sometimes attain to a momentary glimpse of Truth when the veil seems for an instant to be withdrawn from her face;

> I will go forward, sayest thou,
> I shall not fail to find her now ;
> Look up, the fold is on her brow.

Throughout his life, we have to study Paul in this spirit. He sees like a man. He sees one side at a time. He emphasises that—not indeed more than it deserves—but in a way that is open to misconception, because he expresses the side of the case which he has in view, and expects the audience to catch his enthusiasm, to sympathise with his point of view, to supply for themselves the qualifications and the conditions and the reservations which are necessary in the concrete facts of actual life.

Alike in his acts and his words we notice the same tendency. When, after the agreement with the Judaic party in the Church, he went out on his second journey, he was ready, in his unhesitating and hearty acceptance of the arrangement, to do a very great deal in compliance with the Jew's natural and not unjustifiable prejudices. He even made the half-Jew Timothy comply with the Jewish law. No act of his whole life is more difficult to sympathise with : none cost him dearer. It was misunderstood by his own Galatian converts, as Bishop Lightfoot well explains ; and the Epistle which he afterwards addressed to them was intended to bring home to them the whole truth respecting their position in the Church. But, as his act had given dangerous emphasis to one side of the case, the Epistle can restore the equilibrium and give concreteness and wholeness to the truth only by emphasising the other side.

We on our part have to keep the two sides in mind in estimating the historical situation; and we must both take into consideration the later words when we judge the act as an indication of Paul's mind, and remember the earlier act when we estimate the meaning of certain very strong statements in the Epistle, such as *if ye receive circumcision, Christ will profit you nothing*, or *ye are severed from Christ, ye who would be justified by the Law.* Those words are one-sided, and not the whole many-sided truth. They are over-strained ; and it needs much sympathy, and much allowance for the unexpressed but necessary conditions, in order to read in them the Pauline gospel.

Similarly, time after time, we find in the Epistles that Paul has laid himself open to misconstruction in the minds of his converts by emphasising one side of the case, and has to give completeness to his teaching by stating another aspect. For example, he had written to the Corinthians, forbidding them in too general terms to come into social relations with immoral persons ; but he feels afterwards that this, taken literally, would be equivalent to an order to go out of the world and to cut themselves off absolutely from the city in which they lived, inasmuch as all pagan society was maintained on an immoral basis ; and therefore conditions and qualifications and explanations have to be added in 1 Cor. v. 9-13. The first message was not a complete and perfect truth : it was a law that needed a supplement and a restriction.

Again the second letter to the people of Thessalonica is to a great extent an attempt to guard against a misconception of his teaching ; and the misconception was evidently due to the strong emphasis which he had laid on such ideas as the coming of the Kingdom.

But that is the way of mankind. If we would do anything we must strive and struggle along the difficult path of the world, making mistakes often, over-emphasising often the side which we see, afterwards correcting our errors, completing our deficiencies ; and worn out at last and spent with the heat and dust and fatigue of the toilsome road, we may need a friendly voice to tell us that we have not worked in vain, while we are ourselves too conscious of the failures to have any sense of the actual measure of achievement. In the life of Paul we read the life of man ; and thus his story never grows old and never loses its fascination.

But the human character alone, even in conjunction with his great achievements, is not sufficient to explain the fascination that St. Paul exerts on us. I should not reckon even his power of sympathising with and understanding the nature and needs of his followers in so many different lands as furnishing the full explanation. The reason seems to lie in that combination of qualities which made him representative of human nature at its best : intensely human in his undeniable faults, he shows a real nobility and loftiness of spirit in which every man recognises his own best self.

The part which he had to play in Christian society was a difficult one. He came into it much junior in standing and inferior in influence to all the great men of the company. Yet he was conscious that in insight, in practical sense, in power of directing the development of their young society, he was superior to them. He saw what they did not at first recognise, the true line of development for their cause. He carried them with him, as their *de facto* leader. He had on one occasion to rebuke for his wavering and inconsistent conduct the one who at first had been the most enterprising and directing spirit among them. Moreover, he was of higher rank among his own people, sprung from an influential family which could not be ignored even in Jerusalem, marked out from youth as a person of consequence by his education and ability and energy, taking a prominent part among the leaders of his people from the day that he entered on public life. Finally, he was in all probability older than several, perhaps even than many of the Apostles.

All these causes conspired to render the position of Paul among the Christians of Jerusalem a very delicate one. Only the most perfect courtesy and respect for the rights and feelings of others, founded on the truest self-respect, could have carried him safely through the difficulties of the situation. He dared not yield to them, or sink his own personality in respect for their well-deserved authority, for he was strong in the mandate of revelation. Yet he would forfeit our love and respect if he ever obtruded his policy and his claims on them, or failed in the respect and reverence which was due from a neophyte to those whose eyes and minds were quickened with the glory of long communion with Jesus.

In that difficult situation the world of readers and thinkers has decided that Paul never seriously erred. He never failed in reverence to the great men, and he never failed in the courage and self-reliance needed to press his policy on their joint councils. That is why we are still under his fascination, just as much as those who beheld his face and listened to his words and thought it was an angel that spoke. He stands before us not merely as a representative of simple human nature, but also as typical of the highest and best in human nature. We never understand him rightly, unless we conceive his action on the highest plane that mere humanity is capable of occupying.

It must be acknowledged that this description of St. Paul's relations to the older Apostles is very different from that which is commonly given by modern scholars. In the pages of most of them we find the picture of Paul as a man actuated always by jealousy of the great Apostles, continually trying to undermine their authority and to set himself in their place, driven on by the feeling that he could prove his own position only by picking faults in and criticising his seniors, and that he could rise in the Church only by getting them turned out of their place. They set him before us as ambitious, envious, almost selfish, a carping critic of others, yet not himself always very scrupulous in his methods, the least lovable and the most unlovely character in early Christian history. This picture is most characteristic of what is wrongly called the "critical" school, but is far from being confined to it, for the most extreme example is found in a Study of St. Paul, which takes the most "orthodox" view in all matters of criticism (Art. XIII.).

The view which we take, then, is open to the charge of being old-fashioned, because it was held by the men and women of an older time ; and there is a prejudice against a view which, like this, is most characteristic of an older generation and has been rejected by many learned and highly respected scholars in more recent times, a view which is distinctly less fashionable among those of the younger generation who most pride themselves on their open-mindedness and freedom from prejudice.

In Scotland, particularly, many of us remember the light in which Paul was held up to us in our childhood : to our mothers Paul was not a mere name in a book, but a real man held up before us as a model to imitate. He, more than any other character in the New Testament, was considered as the embodiment in actual life of the qualities that made the true "gentleman" (to use the old-fashioned term in the old-fashioned sense)—loftiness of motive, the abnegation of self under the influence of nobler considerations, the tendency to look at all things in life from a generous point of view, the frankness to speak out straight and emphatically against wrong doing and wrong thinking, combined with that courtesy, that delicate consideration for the feelings of others, that instinctive and inevitable respect for others which rise from true respect for self.

It may be considered by some that the greater space which St. Paul fills in the pages of the New Testament explains the reason why he bulked so much more largely in the estimation of our parents ; but this is a superficial way of judging. Paul occupies this space in the original authorities because of his personal qualities and historical importance ; and the older generation, which thought so highly of him, had a very sound and healthy appreciation of the character and personality of the various figures whose action is set before us in the New Testament.

That old-fashioned view was held in an old-fashioned way. There were scenes and events in Paul's life which were acknowledged to be difficult to understand ; but then the difficulty was met by a plain confession of inability to fully comprehend the situation and the reason why Paul acted as he did. It was in such cases considered sufficient to say, that the position of affairs was obscure, and the motives involved were complex and difficult to understand fully, but that Paul could not fall below the standard of his own nature : " once a gentleman, always a gentleman : " and that there must be an explanation of his motives and conduct which was true to his character, and no explanation that was not could be correct.

But, as is natural and right, men cannot remain contented to set aside in that way parts of the life of Paul as too difficult to understand. The robust and simple faith that there must be an explanation which conforms to that lofty conception of his character is not sufficient for the historian and the biographer : it is their duty to understand and to explain.

The idea was a natural one, deserving of careful examination, that the difficulty in regard to those parts and incidents in the life of St. Paul arose from the incorrectness of the general estimate put upon his character. It is quite true that it is the difficulties which are most instructive ; and that on them the attention of the investigator must especially be concentrated. Thus arose the theory, that the standard of judgment must be taken from the great, yet as it seemed difficult, scene in which St. Paul was brought into direct relations with the older Apostles ; that scene was universally understood to be described by St. Paul himself in writing to the Galatians, chap. ii., and also by the historian in the

Acts, chap. xv. : the obvious and undeniable differences between the two accounts, as regards both facts and still more, spirit, were accounted for by the theory that there was something to conceal, and that each account omitted something that the other recounted, and that the full story could only be got by uniting the two narratives.

The innuendo here lies in the idea that there was something to conceal ; and this was worked out in a remorseless and rigorous train of inference throughout not only that scene, but the whole of St. Paul's later life. The thought in the investigator's mind at every point was of this supposed concealment : his aim at every point was to disclose the latent facts which the narrator had been ashamed to make public. This was a canker that vitiated the whole investigation. The conclusion was imported by the investigator at the outset ; and was therefore easily established at every point, as the method was simply to insert the lacking element, which had been omitted by the narrator.

That method of writing history is a seductive, though a dangerous one. It gives infinite scope for ingenuity, brilliant suggestion and feats of skill. The reader is dazzled by the blaze of artificial fire, with which each scene is illumined, and by which the strongest and deepest shadows are thrown on the facts, in picturesque but distorting effects. But life is lived, and history should be studied, not in limelight but in the light of day.

The application of that method to the New Testament was at first mainly the work of the Tübingen school of critics ; and from that school there has sprung a whole class of theories differing in many details, but agreeing in the general principle that the books of the New Testament were mostly or entirely forgeries of a later age, composed not with a view to set forth the simple truth but with the intention of inculcating certain views and doctrinal opinions held by the writers in common with the particular party or section of the Christian Church to which each belonged.

The Tübingen school did not confine their demonstration of their method to New Testament history. They used it elsewhere, as, *e.g.*, in Schwegler's *History of Rome;* and the issue is manifest. Not merely has it been rejected by other scholars on the ground of being merely theoretical and imaginative, it has been disproved, root and branch, in idea and in method and in results, by the progress of discovery.

The reply to the Tübingen theories for a long time took the form of denying that any discrepancies existed between the accounts in Gal. ii. and Acts xv. ; and many laboured demonstrations of that kind were published. The ordinary student could not rest satisfied with this: he felt the discrepancies. We know now that Gal. ii. and Acts xv. describe two different events, and that discrepancies are natural.

Then the young student was placed in a serious dilemma, between two classes of teachers. The one class as a rule took a nobler and more generous view of Paul ; but they failed to apply their theory logically and convincingly to the details ; and their solution could only repel the logical mind, and therefore strengthened the position of the opposing school. One seemed always driven back to the skilful logic of the Tübingen theorists, who carried their readers on in an unerring train of inference from their first assumptions: the discrepancies were due to the attempt to conceal facts that were discreditable.

Yet those Tübingen theorists were involved in an equally

serious difficulty. When one faced the practical facts of history and life, one could find no answer to the question how that Paul whom they imagined could achieve what he did. How was he able to move the hearts of men and touch their feelings? His work is simply unintelligible unless we assume that he had a boundless power of sympathising with others and taking them to himself, such as is inconsistent with censorious, self-seeking ambition. When one sought the answer to these questions, one found that every critic was at variance with himself. In one page they recognised in Paul the qualities which in another they denied him. It was never possible to find a man in the critics' Paul. They set before their readers no unity or reality, but a many-natured bundle of qualities like Frankenstein's artificial man. While the critics praised Paul in the general view, and admired his marvellous influence, they had little but blame for him in detail ; their admiration seemed only theoretical, but, whenever it came to a question of fact or action, it was only faults in him that they saw and emphasised.

But the student who has too exclusive an acquaintance with theories and too little practical experience of life does not easily realise how essentially self-contradictory and impossible that conception of Paul is : one who *lives with shadows for his company instead of men and women*, who knows books, not the facts of life or the natural development of human conduct, can easily be blind to the inconsistency, or, if dimly conscious of it, can yet keep his eyes shut. This weakness of judgment is intensified by a deep-seated vice in the modern methods of scholarship.

The student finds that there is so much to learn that he rarely has time even to begin to know. It is inexorably required of him that he shall be familiar with the opinions of many teachers dead and living, and it is not often sufficiently impressed on him that mere ability to set forth in fluent and polished language the thoughts of others— assuming that he can acquire that power at which he aims, and towards which he struggles with all his energy—is not real " knowledge ".   He does not learn that learning must be thought out afresh by him from first principles, and tested in actual experience, before it becomes really his own.   In Plato's words, he gets at college much " true opinion " (let us hope not " false opinion "), but little " knowledge ".   He must *live* his opinions before they become knowledge, and he is fortunate if he is not compelled prematurely to express them too frequently and too publicly, so that they become hardened and fixed before he has had the opportunity of trying them and moulding them in real life and experience.

Yet, if one's experiences are not too unfavourable to permit due growth, if one is not too soon hardened by pre- mature success or any other cause into perfect self-satisfaction and contentment, one must gradually become convinced that the Paul of real life was a very different character from the theorist's Paul ; and the man who gradually takes form before one's mind, in the vivid comprehension of his words and actions, is (as one then finds) the same Paul whom the author of Acts had in his view.   Then one recognises and knows, absolutely and irresistibly and for ever, that Luke had known the man, had been his friend and confidant and coadjutor, and was not an impostor of the second century who was wholly dependent on written sources of information, which he barely understood and frequently mangled.   Thus Paul and Luke stand together. If the theorist's Paul be the true one, then the writer of

Acts had never known him, for he describes a different person—the generous and lovable Paul. But when you think of this other Paul, then you feel the deep, intimate, personal love and admiration that Luke entertained for him, giving life and reality to every sentence that he writes.

Thus after all one comes back to the old-fashioned view, but not in the old-fashioned way. One has acquired also the virtues of modern scholarship, the resolution to be slave to no authority, to test every opinion, and never to remain contented in the presence of any difficulty. One is resolved to understand Paul's action throughout, and not to rest content with the assumptions in which general opinion has acquiesced. Then one learns that current conceptions must be corrected in important respects, and that, when the needed corrections are made, the difficulties turn out to be due to errors in regard to the general framework and surroundings amid which Paul's work was done. In the belief that most of the difficulties are thus solved, the following Study of the practical life, the Statesmanship, of Paul is written.

III

THE STATESMANSHIP OF PAUL

III

THE STATESMANSHIP OF PAUL

To the scholars of the "Tübingen School" belongs the credit of inaugurating, as a practical reality, the free, unbiased study of early Christian history, with the single aim of reaching the truth, instead of assuming it. But from this splendid merit much must be detracted, when we observe how they carried out their attempt. In a task which demanded intimate familiarity with the life and spirit of the Roman Empire, they showed a singular absence of special knowledge (combined with unhesitating confidence in the perfection of their knowledge), and an extraordinary incapacity to gauge the proper meaning of a Greek or Latin paragraph. Thus they evolved a history of early Christian times which was in contradiction to many of the authorities whom they quoted and misunderstood.

It was a great thing to substitute freedom of spirit for blind following of authority; but we shall do away with all the value of their teaching if we allow the glamour of a modern to be substituted for the sacredness of an ancient authority. If we remain true to the spirit which impelled them, disregarding authority and seeking only for truth, we must set them aside and start anew. And, above all, we shall rebel against the tyrannous spirit of their pupils, who in the name of freedom would stifle investigation, and limit by *a priori* rules the conclusions which a scholar may express as the result of his studies.

Especially in the case of the Apostle Paul, subsequent scholars have been too much under the spell of that school, and even those who recognised that the Tübingen opinions were incorrect, too readily admitted that the mistake lay only in pressing too far a correct method, whereas, in reality, the premises were erroneous and fictitious. We believe that a seriously incorrect picture of that great man has been commonly set before the world by modern scholars; and we would venture to plead for a reconsideration of the case.

We shall treat our subject as an episode in Roman history. It is, of course, impossible to ignore the religious aspect of any Pauline question, but so far as possible we concentrate attention on the work of Paul as a social influence on the Roman world.

I

In the first century of our era the Mediterranean world was full of the mixing and clashing of nations—not simply in the way of war, which belongs to all centuries and is specially characteristic of none, but far more in the way of peace and conscious effort at amalgamation. The attempt was being made on a great scale to forge the nations into an articulated organism of provinces, looking to a single Imperial central heart and brain for order and unity. The ruling power was Rome. The motive force to set in motion all that seething mass of materials, so that they might coalesce in new unions, as provinces of one fatherland, was the Imperial policy—that marvellously wise and far-sighted creation of the genius of Julius Cæsar, shaped further by the skill and prudence of Augustus and his great minister Agrippa. Maecenas, whom the historians add as a third to make the pair a trio, or even mention to the exclusion of Agrippa, is an overrated person : the supposed contrast between his great but hidden importance and his apparent indolence and luxury and self-effacement tempted the old historians to attribute to him much to which he has no real claim. He was simply a very clever manipulator of the party machine in the city, an able political wire-puller, who was exceedingly important in the earlier stages of Augustus's struggle for power, but who lost all his importance and sank into insignificance and oblivion in B.C. 23, when the era of constructive Imperial statesmanship began.

The attempt was, at first, too far-reaching. It was sought to obliterate the old national lines of separation. The provincial boundaries were so drawn as sometimes to break up single nations between several provinces, and sometimes to include several nations in one province. Each province was treated as a unity, and the Greek rendering of the Roman term "*province*" was actually *nation :* "the province Asia" is expressed in the political Greek of the time as "Asia the nation". But to belong to a nation in the old sense was non-Roman and anti-Roman, and was reckoned as the mark either of slave origin or of disloyalty. The loyal subject of the Empire was reckoned and designated by his province and city, not by his nation ; though the real nature of the designation has often been concealed from modern scholars by the fact that a provincial name was in many cases identical with some national name. Especially the New Testament scholars have rarely showed any knowledge of this principle; and have often contemned, with the licence of ignorance, those English scholars who wrote from a higher and truer point of

view.[1] Like most of the fruitful principles in Roman Imperial history, this was first observed and worked into the
study of the subject by Mommsen. When Paul called himself "a Tarsian of Cilicia," he was not speaking of the country
Cilicia, great part of which was under the rule of kings. He
was describing himself by his city and his province; and he
was so understood by the Roman officer to whom he spoke.

For a time the attempt to destroy the old national lines
of separation seemed likely to prove successful. The Roman
Imperial policy was aided and supported both by the enthusiastic loyalty of the subject peoples and by the almost
universal fashion of regarding as vulgar and contemptible
everything that differed from the Greek or the Roman
standard. But nature was too strong. National character
could not be ejected either by fashion or by loyalty. In
the second century Hadrian recognised frankly that the
former policy had been pressed too far, and inaugurated a
new policy of respecting national ideas and enlisting them
in the service of the Empire.

In the first century, however, that earlier policy was
strong and popular, and the history of the time must be
studied according to it. We must remember that the loyal
population thought and classified according to provinces,
that national designations were used only as a necessity to
express geographical facts, and not political relations, that
a horse or a slave or a foreigner was called "Phrygian" or
"Lycaonian"; but a citizen of a Phrygian city was called
by his province (either Asia or Galatia), except that the
national designation was applied to him sometimes in jest

---

[1] I may quote, as one of the best examples of the true spirit in treating
early Christian history, the Rev. F. Rendall's article in the *Expositor*, Nov.,
1893, p. 321 ff., on "The Pauline Collection for the Saints".

and raillery as a nickname, or in contempt, or from geographical necessity to define more precisely his locality.

Of all the men of the first century, incomparably the most influential was the Apostle Paul. No other man exercised anything like so much power as he did in moulding the future of the Empire. Among the Imperial ministers of the period there appeared none that had any claim to the name of statesman except Seneca; and Seneca fell as far short of Paul in practical influence and intellectual insight as he did in moral character.

We cannot suppose that Paul was entirely unconscious of the social and political side of his schemes and ideals, or that he was simply pushed forward as a blind, unthinking agent, an impotent piece in the game that God was playing "upon this chequer-board of nights and days". That is not the theory of the Christian thinker. We propose to examine what evidence there is of any definite idea and principle— purely on the external and non-religious side—in the action and the teaching of Paul. What creative and guiding idea —if any—did he throw into the melting-pot, in which Roman policy was stirring and mixing the nations?

If there was no idea guiding his action, he would have to be ranked as a religious enthusiast of marvellous energy and vigour, but not as a religious statesman—as a rousing and stimulative force, but not an organising and creative force. But it seems beyond question that his creative and organising power was immense, that the forms and methods of the Christian Church were originated mainly by him, and that almost every fruitful idea in the early history of the Church must be traced back to his suggestive and formative impulse. He was a maker and a statesman, not a religious enthusiast. He must therefore have had in his mind some ideal, some guiding conception, which he worked to realise.

Bearing in mind the limits we have imposed on our investigation, we look to see what was his attitude towards the political ideas and divisions and classification amid which he lived. We shall not stop, except for a moment, to allude to the familiar principle which he expresses, in the writings preserved to us, regarding the facts of Imperial organisation. He always acts upon the principle, and impresses it on his own churches, that existing authorities and government should be respected, not as right, but as indifferent.

Such are the sentiments and advice in his later and Christian stage. But his ideas as a Christian were developed out of his pre-Christian ideas and experiences. What did he think before he was a Christian? We go back to his early years. We ask what had been his attitude towards the Roman world in his earlier stage? What was the tone and character impressed on him by his surroundings as a child? Let us try to estimate in a practical way the conditions amid which his family and himself were placed in Tarsus, and the necessary effect of them.

II

In his own writings or speeches, Paul gives some important evidence bearing on the question as to his sentiments in childhood and youth.

In the first place, we note what he writes to the Galatians: " It pleased God, who separated me even from my mother's womb, and called me through His grace, to reveal His Son in me that I might preach Him among the nations ". Even before his birth, God had chosen him and set him apart to be the man that should preach Christ to the nations; but a special revelation of Christ was needed before he awakened to full consciousness of the purpose.

That statement is couched in the simple, concrete form in which ancient thought uttered itself; and it expresses what we should put in more abstract and scientific terms— that heredity and environment had determined his bent of mind, that his family and his early surroundings had been so arranged by an overruling power that he was made to be the person that should preach to the Gentiles; but that the truth which ultimately he should preach had to be awakened to consciousness in him at the proper time.

Secondly, he writes to the Romans, strangers to him personally, and explains his deep interest in them: " I am debtor both to Greeks and to barbarians, both to the educated and the uneducated classes ". He had got something from them all, and he was bound to repay. He had learned good from them all, and he must teach them all good in return. He fully recognised that, in his position as a Tarsian and a Roman citizen, he owed certain duties to Tarsus and to Rome; and he was a man that never ignored or neglected any duty.

Looking at the situation broadly, we see that the greatest fact in the worldly position of the Jews at this time was their relation to the Roman rule. It was difficult even for a Jew who lived in Palestine to restrict himself so completely to Jewish surroundings that he was not frequently brought into contact with the Roman world. The soldiers, the officers, the tax-gatherers, the traders of Rome were around him. The justice, the laws, the organisation of Rome were constantly pressing upon him.

If it was difficult for the Jew to isolate himself in Palestine, it was impossible for the many thousands of Jews who lived in the great cities of Asia Minor and in Rome to do so. Still more was it impossible for the Jew who had acquired the rights of Roman citizenship to remain blind to the question, what was the relationship between his position as a Jew and his position as a Roman? This was the situation in which Paul spent his early years : son of a Jew, who was also a citizen of the great Greek-speaking city of Tarsus, and who possessed the honours and rights—very important honours and rights—of a Roman. Every day of his life Paul's father was necessarily brought face to face with the world of Tarsus. As a Roman, he was a person of rank and consequence. Few people can be blind (none ought to be blind) to what gives them rank and influence in their city ; few can be blind to the claims of their own city, in which they possess rank and influence. It was not necessary for the Jew to forget or ignore his Jewish birth and religion and people, while he recognised his position and opportunities as a Tarsian and a Roman. There was no opposition between them. Both Tarsian and Roman law fully admitted that Jews were never to be compelled to do anything contrary to their religious principles ; they had full liberty to observe every religious duty, to go and come freely to Jerusalem, and any interference with their privileges was punished by the law. These privileges really gave the Jews superior advantages over their fellow-citizens ; and the consequent jealousy of the Greeks in the Asiatic cities often broke out into quarrel, complaint, and even riot.

Such had been the favoured position of the Jews in those great cities of Asia Minor like Tarsus from the third or second century before Christ. Their advantages were increased after the Roman Empire became the ruling power. The peace, the order, the security of property, the ease and regularity and certainty of intercourse by ship and by land between the different provinces of the Empire, the absence of vexatious restrictions and oppressive dues on articles of commerce,[1] the abundance of money, the almost perfect " Free Trade within the Empire," resulted in a development of commerce and finance on a vast scale. This was eminently favourable to the Jews with their financial genius ; and there was opened up before them a dazzling prospect of wealth and power. They had merely to accommodate themselves to their situation, and the world was at their feet. To utilise those splendid prospects it was not required that they should do any violence to their religion. All that was needed was that they should cease to hold aloof from the surrounding world, that they should, to a certain degree, mix with it, speak its language, learn its ways, profit by the education it could offer, use its resources, and conquer it with its own weapons.

And it was not only in respect of wealth and material success that this glorious prospect was open to the Jews in the Roman Empire. It was equally the case in religion. The Jewish faith, so strange and mysterious and incomprehensible to pagan society, with its proud isolation, its lofty morality, its absolute superiority to pagan ideas of life, its unhesitating confidence in its superiority—that religion exercised an extraordinary fascination on the Roman world, not so much on the purely Greek cities, but more on Rome and on Central Asia Minor. Every synagogue had a surrounding of persons interested in this religion, affected in varying degrees by it, desirous to hear more of it—persons who were called " the devout " or " the God-fearing," and are often

---

[1] The customs dues were not heavy, but only a quite fair return for the advantages which the Imperial peace afforded to trade.

mentioned by Luke under those names. That large circle of persons added to the importance, the dignity, the weight of the Jews in the pagan world. The "devout" pagans formed, as it were, an intermediate stage or step between the Jews and the common pagan—which brought home all the more vividly to both Jew and pagan the interval between them. It is even highly probable that "the devout" added to the wealth of the Jewish communities, both by payment of formal dues and by voluntary gifts (as was the case with the centurion—Luke vii. 5—who built a synagogue at Capernaum). One great reason why the Jews so bitterly resented the attraction which Paul exercised on "the devout" was that he drew them and their gifts away from the synagogues : hence the frequent declarations made by Paul that he has accepted no money from his converts, declarations which imply and reply to frequent accusations.[1]

There was, therefore, opened to the Jews as dazzling a prospect of religious and spiritual influence in the Roman world as of material wealth and prosperity. There have never been wholly wanting Jews whose vision was concentrated on the spiritual prospects of their race, whose imagination was filled with visions of religious progress. These have been the great prophets and leaders and elevators of the people, preventing the mass of Jews from losing hold on the spiritual side of life, from becoming absorbed entirely in the pursuit of wealth, and from sinking amid that pursuit down to the level of pagan society. Such a prophet and leader of his people was Saul of Tarsus destined to be, according to our view.

[1] Mr. Baring Gould, in his *Study of St. Paul*, has the merit of properly emphasising this fact. I am the more bound to say this, as I think that he takes far too low a view of Paul's character and action. See Art.

Now consider what are the possibilities of the situation in which Paul was nurtured at Tarsus. It might be possible for a dull and narrow, but intense and fanatical nature to grow up in Tarsus in a reaction and revolt against pagan surroundings, to revert by a sort of atavism to the type of his ancestors before they were settled as part of the Jewish colony there, to reject and despise and abhor all contact and participation with the Tarsian world. But Paul was not such a hard and narrow nature : he could not grow up as a citizen of Rome and of Tarsus, and yet remain blind to the power and the spiritual opportunities of Jews and Judaism in the Empire ; for Paul was as absolutely free from mere blind bigotry as he was from all sordid and vulgar motives. As he grew up, he felt himself to be a strict law-abiding Pharisee ; yet he was also a Roman, speaking Latin in order to assert his Roman rights ; he was also a Tarsian, *i.e.* a Hellene, and he had to speak Greek in ordinary life.

Clear evidence of Paul's feeling for his Tarsian home may be seen in the account which Luke gives of one of the most terrible scenes in his life, when, bruised and at the point of death, he was rescued from the clutches of a fanatical and exasperated Jewish crowd by the Roman soldiers. If we imagine what his condition must have been—sore from the blows and the pulling asunder of his rescuers and of the mob, probably bleeding, certainly excited and breathless, the shouts of the crowd still dinning his ears, " Away with him," as they strove to get hold of him again, his life hanging on the steadfast discipline of the soldiers and the goodwill of their commander—we must feel that he would not waste his words at that supreme moment, when the Roman tribune hurriedly questioned him as to his race and language, in stating mere picturesque details : anything that rose to his lips in that moment must have been something that lay near his heart, or something that was calculated to determine his rescuer's conduct. He said : " I am a Jew, Tarsian of Cilicia, citizen of no mean city ". This was not his strict legal designation in the Roman Empire, for he was a Roman citizen, and that proud description superseded all humbler characteristics. Nor was the Tarsian designation the one best calculated to move the Roman tribune to grant the request which Paul was about to make : that officer was far more likely to grant the request of a Roman than of a Tarsian Jew. Nor had Paul any objection to claiming his Roman rights, for he shortly afterwards claimed them at the tribune's hand.

A critical friend questions my opinion that Paul was excited on that occasion, and argues that he was cool, pointing out that his first request was to be allowed to speak to the mob. I cannot see reason to change. That Paul was marvellously cool and collected and courageous in a most perilous scene has always been one of the reasons why I admire him so much ; but I do not think that he was in the same state of mind as if he had been walking through quiet streets quietly with a sympathetic friend. In such a scene of hairbreadth escape from being torn to pieces by his own countrymen, Paul's mind was inevitably affected in a certain way and degree. Any one who has ever been in a position of serious danger knows that, however cool and self-possessed one may be, there is a certain affection of the mind, which for want of a better name I have called excitement. The thoroughly brave man is never so collected, so capable and so dangerous to his enemies as in the moment of danger ; but I do not think he is free from excitement ;

he is strung up to exert all the best powers of mind and body to their highest degree.

My friend also points out that the Roman officer had mistaken Paul for an Egyptian outlaw, whom he was rescuing from the mob in order to deliver over to justice; and that Paul replied: "I am (not an Egyptian, but) a Jew of Tarsus". That is quite true; but it is not the whole truth. If Paul had merely sought to impress the officer with his respectability, the best way obviously was to tell that he was a Roman. A Roman centurion would have shown far more respect to a Roman than to a Tarsian citizen.

It seems impossible to explain Paul's reply on this occasion except on the supposition that "Tarsian" was the description of himself which lay closest to his heart. And, especially, the praise of Tarsus as a famous city is hardly capable of any other interpretation than that, in his deeply stirred emotional condition, he gave expression to the patriotic love which he really felt for his fatherland and the home of his early years.

It is not impossible now, and there is no reason to think it was impossible then, for a Jew of the Diaspora to entertain a distinct and strong feeling of loyalty towards the city where he was born and in which he possessed the rights of citizenship. It must be remembered that the feeling of an ancient citizen to his own city was much stronger than that which is in modern times entertained usually toward one's native town. All the feeling of patriotism which now binds us to our country, irrespective of the town to which we belong, was in ancient times directed toward one's city. "Fatherland" denoted one's city, and not one's country. Both *Patria* in Latin, and *Patris* in Greek, were applied to the city of one's home.[1]   It was only to a small degree, and among the most educated Greeks, that Hellas, as a country, was an idea of power.   The educated native of a Cilician city like Tarsus regarded the country Cilicia as implying rudeness and barbarism, and prided himself on being a Hellene rather than a Cilician ; but Hellas to him meant a certain standard and ideal of culture and municipal freedom. He was a "Tarsian," but Tarsus was, and had long been, a Hellenic city; and the Greek-speaking Tarsians were either Hellenes or Jews, but not "Cilicians" in the sense of nationality, only "Cilicians" as members of the province.

Moreover, citizenship implied much more in ancient times than it means now.   We can now migrate to a new city, and almost immediately acquire citizenship there, losing it in our former home.   But in ancient days the Tarsian who migrated to another city continued to rank as a Tarsian, and Tarsus was still his Fatherland, while in his new home he was merely a resident alien.   His descendants, too, continued to be mere resident aliens.   Occasionally, and as a special compliment, a resident alien was granted the citizenship with his descendants ; but a special enactment was needed in each individual case and family.

The city that was his Fatherland and his home mattered much to Paul.   It had a place in his heart.

III

And how perfectly natural is it that this should be so! How unnecessary it seems to prove so laboriously that Paul had a warm feeling for the home of his childhood!   He

[1] To a certain degree the Roman Imperial régime succeeded in widening the scope of the term *patria*.   That is one of the many advances which it enabled the world to make.   It gave to men the power to feel that their Fatherland was their country and not their narrow township.

was a man, a natural, warm-hearted man, not the emotion-
less ideal philosophic prig whom his contemporary, Seneca,
described as the perfect hero. That alone ought to be proof
enough. And it would be proof enough were it not for two
obstinate and most mischievous prejudices.

The first is that deep-rooted idea among many scholars
that the "early Christians" could never be natural human
beings, but were perverted into some unnatural frame of
mind in which ordinary human ties and affections ceased to
have much force for them, and the world and its fashions
and relations appeared to them as their enemy, while they
hesitated at no outrage upon established social conventions,
and recked so little of truth in their efforts to glorify and
propagate their religion that no statement which they make
can be trusted, unless it is corroborated by non-Christian
evidence. That there were such Christians, is doubtless
quite true. There are many individuals who are capable
of seizing a great idea only in a one-sided and narrow, but
intense, way. They have their use; and their limitations
give them in some directions increased strength. But these
did not give the tone to the Church in the first or second
century. Read the Letter of the Smyrnæans about Polycarp: and observe how the writer contrasts his gentle dignity
and undisturbed calm with the nervous and hysterical conduct of some Christian martyrs—those, for example, who
went to extremes in showing their contempt and hatred for
their judges, rousing the indignation even of the humane
and law-abiding Pliny, while they returned evasive answers
to simple questions, lectured Roman dignitaries as if the
latter were the criminals and they themselves the judges,
and even used offensive and insulting gestures in their eagerness to gain the crown of martyrdom. But to the writer of

that letter, it is the conduct of Polycarp that seems to be on the same plane of feeling as the action of Jesus, while he distrusts the abiding strength of the violent and outrageous.

The second prejudice is that Paul was a narrow, one-sided, bigoted, Pharisaic Jew, ignorant of, and hostile to, all higher Hellenic education, literature and philosophy, brought up by his father according to the principle "Cursed be he that shall teach Greek science to his son".

In contrast to these poor and barren opinions, we see that Paul was far more than a Jew. His Jewish inheritance in religious and moral conceptions was, of course, by far the most important part of his equipment for the work that lay before him. But his experience as a Tarsian and as a Roman was also indispensable to him; and, as we have seen, he was himself quite aware of the debt he had incurred to the Gentile world. "Tarsian," to him, expressed a thought that lay very deep in his heart; whereas the name "Roman" expressed an idea more intellectual than emotional, more a matter of practical value than of kindly sentiment. But the Roman idea was a very important part of his qualification as a statesman, and a moulder of the future of the Empire. There had passed into his nature something of the Roman constructiveness, the practical sense for economic facts, the power of seeing the means to reach an end in the world of reality and humanity, the quickness to catch and use and mould the ideas and ideals of the citizens of the Empire.

The two scholars who have best perceived the Greek side of Paul's thought are the only two, so far as I know, who have studied him in the light of real familiarity with the life of the Greek cities—Professor Ernst Curtius in Germany and Canon Hicks in England. Some have dipped into Greek life in search of illustrations of Christian history; and some have studied it deeply for that purpose. Those two scholars have studied the Greek life of that period for its own sake, with professional thoroughness; and then studied Paul in the light of full knowledge. The Roman side has never, so far as I know, been sufficiently estimated.

There is much in a name; and it is peculiarly unfortunate—it has blinded and narrowed the modern view of that extraordinary man—that no one ever thinks of Paul by his Roman name. But it is as certain that he had a Roman name and spoke the Latin language, as it is that he was a Roman citizen. If, for example's sake, we could think of him sometimes as Gaius Julius Paulus—to give him a possible and even not improbable name—how completely would our view of him be transformed. Much of what has been written about him would never have been written if Luke had mentioned his full name. But Luke was a Greek; and the Greeks had never any interest in, or any comprehension of, the Roman name, with all that it implied. Just as, true Greek that he was, he never liked or understood the Jews, so he could, indeed, respect, but never appreciate and comprehend, the Roman talent and method in administration. Fortunately, it was not essential for the historian of the early Church to fully understand the old Roman nature. But still there are places where we feel his limitations.

Thus Paul grew up at once a Roman and a Tarsian and a Jew. The constant presence of those opposite facts before his eyes, the constant pressure of those opposing duties upon his attention, would set almost any boy a-thinking; and out of Paul's thinking grew his ideals and plans of life.

Before his mind, as he grew up, there lay always outspread that double prospect—the lofty, stern purity of the

true Judaism among the pagan world, and the danger that
the Jews might slip back towards the pagan level. This
last was a real danger in the Jewish colonies of Asia Minor.
Many Jews had become strongly affected by pagan surroundings; they had formed eclectic systems, a syncretism
of Jewish and pagan elements, sometimes in the way of
philosophic religion, sometimes in mere vulgar magical arts
for practising on the superstition and emptying the pockets
of pagan devotees in the outer fringe of "the devout," as we
see at Colossæ, Ephesus, Thyatira ; they intermarried with
the pagans, and the children of the mixed race, sometimes
at least, were not subject to the Jewish law, as at Lystra; in
the words of the Talmud, "the baths and wines of Phrygia
had divided the Ten Tribes from their brethren".[1]

In view of that danger, ever present before his eyes in
Tarsus, a danger which he had clearly comprehended—as
we see in his emphatic warnings to the congregations in
Galatia, Corinth, etc., who were exposed to it as much, and
in the same way, as the Jews—what was Paul to do ? How
should he act? What was the remedy which he must press
upon the minds of his own people, as the great prophets
of old had done in the face of the dangers in their time?
There was but one remedy. Judaism in the midst of
Roman society must assimilate that society and raise it to
a higher level, or it must perish. Had Judaism been persecuted, it might have preserved its purity by remaining
separate. But it was not persecuted; it was treated fairly;
it was even favoured in some considerable degree by the
Imperial policy. The temptations for Jews to assimilate
themselves to the society of the cities in which they lived

---

[1] M. Isidore Levi rejects Neubauer's translation as given in the text.
The fact remains, whether or not the Talmud states it.

were irresistible to mere human nature, for the most brilliant prospects were open to them if they did so. There were, therefore, only two alternatives open to Judaism in the Empire : either it must conquer the Empire or be conquered by it ; either it must be a power to raise Græco-Roman society to its own level, or it must sink to the level of that society.

We can see that clearly now. But did Paul see it at the time? The truth is that at that time it was far clearer to the thinking mind than it is now. It was the great fact of the time : it must have been obvious to any Jew with insight to pierce below the surface of things. To the prophet's eye the situation was clear. The time for the Messiah was arrived. It was impossible that God should suffer His worship to perish. That worship must conquer the Roman world, or it must perish ; but victory with the Messiah was at hand.

IV

At a certain point in his early life Paul went up to Jerusalem to begin the proper course of study of the law, under the charge of one of the greatest and most famous Jewish teachers, Gamaliel. Such was the natural, almost the necessary, course for a Jew who felt strongly the religious needs and prospects of his nation.

It does not, however, appear that he went to Jerusalem very young. His life had been spent at Jerusalem from his youth up ; but the word "youth," in the strictest Greek usage, begins about twenty and ends with the approach of old age (Acts xxvi. 4); and though we cannot assert that Paul used the term in this strict sense, yet we ought not to assume that he meant it to indicate a much earlier age than

twenty, inasmuch as he does not use the word " childhood ".
He distinctly implies that his conduct, as it was shown at
Jerusalem, was that of a young man, not of a child; and
the fair interpretation is that he came to Jerusalem after,
not before, he was of age to assume the *toga virilis*, which
was usually in the fifteenth year. But then he chose the
religious life, and came to Jerusalem over, not under, the age
of fifteen. He made his choice at a comparatively mature
age; and it is a perfectly legitimate and practically certain
inference that he was previously brought up in the house of
a Roman citizen, to be ready to take his place in the world.
We know that he could use the Latin language, for he could
claim his rights as a citizen, and he could appeal to the
Emperor; and it is certain that his appeal was allowed on
the ground that he was a Roman whose life was endangered
by Jews.

Another consideration points to the same conclusion.
Paul was never married; and in the *Apologia pro vita sua*,
which he wrote to the Corinthians, when they suggested, as
a cure for the immorality of contemporary society, that all
Christians ought to be ordered or advised to marry,[1] he
makes it quite clear what his view was. There were some
who chose the Divine life, some few who were capable of it:
these would probably not marry, and they were right. A
universal rule, such as the Corinthian philosophers advocated, was an outrage on the freedom to which man was
heir.

One cannot read that passage, 1 Corinthians vii. 9,
without feeling that Paul is defending himself by stating
the reasons which impelled him when young to violate the

---

[1] *Expositor*, October, 1900.

almost universal Jewish custom and remain unmarried.[1]
He had chosen the Divine life; and his resolution was that
expressed afterwards by Rabbi Asai, who took no wife:
"My soul cleaves to the Law: let others see to the up-
building of the world".

This choice points to an age beyond mere childhood.
It is the settled resolution of a man, not the hasty, imma-
ture choice of a boy. Even in the early maturity of a
southern race, we must suppose that Paul made his choice
over, not under, his fifteenth year. On the other hand, his
choice could not be long postponed after that age. A Jew
was expected to marry between fourteen and twenty. Paul
chose the Divine life; and forthwith he went to Jerusalem
where alone the proper course of study could be found.

The change of scene, when Paul went to be educated in
Jerusalem, produced no essential change in his relation to
the Roman world, and is unlikely to have caused any change
in his aims. He had chosen the religious life in preference
to the worldly life; and many years of study in Jerusalem
were needed to fit him for his career. During those years
Jesus appeared, and died.

To a Jew who saw vividly and keenly either the material
or the spiritual position which was open to the Jews in the
Empire, the coming of the Messiah meant the realisation of
that commanding position in the Roman world, of which
they dreamed and to which they looked forward. The
Messiah was to make them the lords over their conquerors.[2]
To all such Jews the death of Jesus was peculiarly offensive.

[1] I may be permitted to refer to the *Expositor*, October, 1900, p. 298 ff.,
where (and in the preceding sections) the passage in question is very fully
treated.

[2] On Paul's interpretation of this idea, see the end of § VI.

That death turned His career into a hateful parody of their Messianic hopes : a life of humility and poverty extinguished in ridicule and shame was set before them, and that impostor they were to worship as the King of the Jews. The more eagerly Paul had thought about the glory that lay before triumphant Judaism in the Empire, the more intensely must he have detested the impostor who had, as he thought, degraded before the Romans the Messiah and the nation.

The intense bitterness with which Paul pursued the Christians was, therefore, the necessary consequence of his anticipated conquest by the Jewish religion of the Roman Empire. They were the enemy : they degraded his ideal, they made a mockery and a farce of it : they must be destroyed, if Judaism was to reach its destined glory in the world.

In the midst of his persecuting career came the event which suddenly transformed his whole life. It did not alter his ideal and his anticipation. He was as true and as enthusiastic a Jew after as before. He still longed for, and looked forward to, Judaism taking its true position in the Roman world. But the way in which Judaism was to reach that position was now changed in his thought.

On our conception of that epoch-making event depends our whole view of Paul's life. As we understand that transforming event, so do we understand, or fail to understand, the man and his work. A fashionable misconception of that event in modern writers is to minimise its suddenness, to represent it as the culmination of a change that had been gradually working itself out in his mind. On that view his old ideas had been slowly loosening and dissolving, and suddenly they assumed, under a slight impulse, a new form.

But he himself has no mercy on that theory. Nothing can exceed the emphasis with which he declares that there was no antecedent change in his views: he was, in the madness of his career, carrying the war into foreign cities, eager to force the Christians to rail against and mock the impostor. But Paul had a clear and philosophic mind. He saw clearly his own position. His whole mind and conduct was based on the certainty that the impostor was dead. If that were not so, the foundation crumbled beneath his feet.

Then suddenly he saw Jesus before him, not dead but living. He could not disbelieve; he saw; he heard; he knew. He says to the Corinthians, "Have I not seen Jesus?"

To examine the circumstances of that wonderful event in a satisfactory way would need a long special article. But fortunately, we need not here, for our present purpose, enter on the somewhat pedantic discussion of the more scholastic critics, who prize words above realities, whether Paul's vision was real or imagined. It is sufficient for our purpose that to Paul himself it was the most real event of his whole life. All else was, in comparison, shadow and semblance. There he had enjoyed a brief vision of the truth, the Divine reality. He had seen God, and spoken with Him. His earthly self had been permitted for a brief space to become aware of the omnipresent God, who is everywhere around us, and who sometimes permits certain mortals of finer mould and more sentient nature, His chosen prophets, to hear His voice, like Samuel and Elijah, or to see Him, like Moses: only by the inadequate and imperfect way of the senses can their human nature become cognisant of the Divine nature.[1]

[1] See the first article in this volume.

What is certain and fundamental is this. On that
vision Paul's future life and work were built. He could
not disbelieve, for he had seen and known. To think of
disbelieving was to deny his own self, his mind, his existence. He had no room in his nature for even the
thought of disbelieving or questioning. He had seen the
Jesus that he had fancied to be a dead impostor: he had
recognised that He was living: he knew that He was God.
There was no more to be said; what remained was—to act.

Further, through that vision the civilised world was conquered, and the whole history of the world was changed.
Those who think that the world's course can be altered by
the figment of a diseased brain may engage in the purely
academic discussion as to the reality of Paul's vision. Those
who were with him could not hear or see what he heard and
saw. That only proved to him how much favoured he was,
and how little able they were to see into the realities of the
world.

An infinitely more important question is, how far that
vision changed Paul's ideal and his nature? Our view, which
is set forth later on in this paper, is that the ultimate result
on Paul's mind was to make him more clearly conscious of
the true nature of his own ideal. The vision and the revelation removed, as it were, an obstruction from the channel of
his life, and in his later career we see the full powers of his
heart and mind sweeping down in free, harmonious, mighty,
irresistible course. He was not, in his later life, treading
laboriously in a path marked out by an overruling power,
contrary to his own instincts. He was enabled to use, with
perfect mastery and absolute concentration of mind, the
marvellous faculties and ideals with which nature had provided him. He was set free from clogging and hampering

associations, which would have made his success impossible, and with which he must inevitably have come into collision as soon as he really began to work. He was a Pharisee; but he had so much clearer and wider an outlook than the Palestinian Pharisees that he could never have acted in agreement with them except in the destructive effort against the Christians.

V

For many years after that crisis, it would almost appear as if Paul had lost hold of his old idea and really turned away from it. This was, for several reasons, a necessary step in his development. For the moment he had lost all confidence in his own aspirations. He would not confer with flesh and blood, if we may turn his phrase to our purposes. He desired only to do what was set before him. It seemed to him that his experience qualified him peculiarly well to appeal to the Jews: he had been so fanatical an opponent of Jesus that his witness must convince them. This work seemed to be given him to do; and to that he devoted himself, abandoning his old dreams and plans.

When in later years he looked back on that epoch-making crisis, he recognised that the Divine, foreordained purpose was then manifestly revealed—that he should go to the Nations. But at the time he did not clearly recognise it. It was not so explicit as to compel intelligence. He was commissioned to both Jews and Greeks, and he went to the Jews of Damascus, of Jerusalem, of Cilicia. At last—after twelve years—in Antioch, under the guidance of Barnabas, and following the previous trend of events there, he began to address the Greeks, but as yet only through the door of the synagogue.

In fact, Paul at first was not ready to go direct to the Nations. He had not yet fully understood his position. He could not speak until he had completely assimilated and formulated his ideas. He must know what was the Kingdom of God as a Christian ideal before he could make it conceivable to the Nations. He had seen with his own eyes that Jesus was living ; and that truth he had preached to the Jews. To them that was sufficient for a message of conversion. They denied that He was living, and the denial was necessary for their position. If He was living, then the whole fabric of their religious platform fell into ruins. But much more was needed to make a message intelligible to the Nations. They had not denied that Jesus was living. They were merely indifferent. Jesus had not crossed their horizon. Whether He were living or dead mattered nought to them. In order to appeal to them, Paul must know how to set before the Nations, in a form intelligible to them, the whole truth, of which part was learned by all Jews at the feet of their fathers, in the family life, in the family celebration of the Passover.

Then, fourteen years after the first revelation of the Divine purpose, Paul became aware of a new message, in a more precise and definite form, when he was in Jerusalem for the second time since his conversion : " Depart ! for I will send thee far hence to the Nations ". Doubt and disobedience were alike impossible, and the work of Paul's life now at last began.

VI

In the first missionary journey, A.D. 47-49, there is no clear proof that Paul had already consciously in his mind a purpose affecting the Roman world. It is not possible to say more than that he went in that direction, and, after some wavering preliminary steps, occupied the frontier province of Galatia, and thus seized on the first great step in the road that led from Syria to the West. But the bare narrative in Acts does not reveal any consciousness of the nature of that step; and Paul's own words seem to imply that it was without any distinct plan in his own mind that he planted his chief work in Galatia. In truth, the sea route along the coasts of Cyprus, Pamphylia and Lycia seems at first to have been before the mind of himself and Barnabas; and they were led out of it and set on the land route through Southern Galatia by unforeseen and incalculable events. Still, that sea-road also led to the West and to the centre of the Empire; and the fact that Paul at first chose the sea-road would be quite consistent with an ultimate Roman purpose. The ordinary way by which travellers went from Syria to Rome was by sea; and the voyages of that period were coasting voyages. Hence, if Paul had already a purpose towards Rome vaguely present in his mind, he would think first of the coasts along which such a voyage lay.

It seems, in truth, rather strange at first sight, that the Lycian and Pamphylian coasts were Christianised only slowly and late. Many Christians travelled back and forwards between Syria and Rome in the first two centuries; and as the prevalence of westerly breezes in the Levant made the voyage very slow along the south coast of Asia Minor, one might have expected that the new religion would have spread rapidly in the coast-lands. But in those coasting voyages the travellers were kept close to the ship by the very uncertainty of the wind. It was never possible to say at what moment the land breeze might arise by whose help the ship might work its way westwards; and the favourable chance must not be lost. Those who were not on the ship when the wind veered lost their passage. Such was once my own experience in a voyage along the Æolic coast. After waiting for hours in the harbour of Phocæa, hoping for a favourable change in the breeze, as the universal opinion was that the wind was settled for the day, I went, after midday, to take a hasty survey of a reported monument about half an hour distant. When I returned, after two hours or less, the small sailing vessel in which I had been offered a passage had gone. The wind had suddenly changed enough to let it get round the promontory; and thus I missed an opportunity which never again fell to my lot. But it was not a valueless experience. It brought vividly home to one the reason why the land roads rather than the coast roads were the lines by which, in ancient days, new thoughts and new religions won their way. Rome was Christianised by sea-travellers, but the intermediate harbours were not affected so early as Rome and Puteoli (where the Roman voyage ended).

The one exception confirms the rule: Crete was early Christianised, and, if we had any information, we should doubtless find that the new religion spread first on the south coast, along which Rome-bound vessels were constantly working their slow course. Crete was a great wintering place for those vessels. They could work their way from point to point thus far along the coast, taking advantage of favourable opportunities. When they reached the harbour of Phœnix, however, near the western end of Crete, they had before them the long sea course over the Ionian waters (or, as sailors called it, Adria) to the Italian or the Sicilian coast; and, if it were late in the season, they must lay up there for the winter. Thus passengers bound for Rome might have four months sure before them in Phœnix, while they never had an hour sure in any other harbour before Puteoli.

In the second missionary journey Paul's purpose and his method are clear. The first stage on the land road had been previously gained. Paul now fixed his eye on Ephesus. That great scholar, Dr. Hort, has said all that need be said on this point in his *Lectures on Ephesians and Colossians*, p. 82 : " On his second journey he was apparently making his way to the province Asia, doubtless specially meaning to preach in its great capital, Ephesus, when he received a Divine warning," which diverted him temporarily from his Ephesian purpose, and led him to the provinces Macedonia and Achaia. But " on his return to the East, though he had little time to spare, it would seem that he could not be satisfied without at least setting foot in Ephesus and making some small beginning of preaching in person there ". And then " he said farewell, with a promise to return again, if God will ". Then, in the third journey from Syria, once more " he followed his old course through Southern Asia Minor, and this time was allowed to follow it right on to its natural goal, Ephesus. . . . The whole story gains in point and clearness, if we suppose that it is essentially a record of the steps by which St. Paul was enabled to carry out a cherished desire, to be himself the founder of a Christian Church in that great metropolis in which the East looked out upon the West."

Now, Ephesus was not a greater city than Alexandria, nor a city so full of intellectual and commercial life as the rich and busy Egyptian metropolis, seat of one of the greatest universities of the world. What, then, did Dr. Hort conceive to be the reason why Paul was so eager to occupy

Ephesus at this early stage of his work? He does not expressly state any reason—he was not at the moment in search of a reason—but it lies in his words ready to our hand. Ephesus was the next step in the conquest of the Roman Empire, for it was the door by "which the East looked out upon the West" in the Roman system of communication. With Galatia already occupied, Asia and Ephesus formed the next stage. We have a right to quote Dr. Hort as a witness, whether consciously or unconsciously, that already in the plan of his second journey Paul was looking forward to the conquest of the Empire.

In the rest of Paul's career, both in the organisation and articulation of his scattered congregations into the great unity of the Church, and in the indications given of his future plans, the same purpose is clear and (one might almost say) unmistakable. He thinks, as it were, in Roman provinces: he uses names for the provinces which were purely Latin and never employed by Greek writers of his time, though later Greek writers of Roman history occasionally used them. As the Roman fashion of naming a province changes, he too changes; and whereas in his earlier writing he speaks of Illyricum (which a Greek would call Illyris), in a later letter he mentions Dalmatia. He classifies his newly founded churches according to the Imperial provinces. He estimates his progress according to provinces —Syria and Cilicia, Galatia, Asia, Macedonia, Achaia, Illyricum—and as he goes forward he plants his steps and his institutions in their capitals. This is the language, these are the thoughts, of a man whose aim is co-extensive with the Empire, "the creation of a unity within the Church as extensive as the Imperial organisation" (to quote Mr. Rendall's words in the article already mentioned).

So, too, he lays his plans for the future. He will go over into Macedonia. He "purposed in the spirit, when he had passed through Macedonia and Achaia, to go to Jerusalem, saying: After I have been there, I must also see Rome". But Rome was already occupied by other founders, and Paul shrank from building upon another man's foundation, "wherefore also," as he writes to the Romans, " I was hindered these many times from coming to you "; but at last, having established the Churches of the East, he resolves to occupy Spain, the extreme limit of the West, the remotest province of the Empire ; and on the way thither he will visit Rome, " for I hope to see you Romans in my journey, and to be brought thitherward by you ". He was eager to visit the capital of the Empire, and to achieve something there, yet his unwillingness to interpose on the work of others made him always shrink from his longed-for goal, until the opportunity offered itself to "see Rome" on his way to Spain. It is strange that this careful and courteous apology for intruding on a field already occupied (by an Apostle) should have been misunderstood by so many modern scholars, who have actually quoted this apology as a proof that the Roman field was unoccupied when Paul went there.

The eagerness to see Rome, the design of going to the West after conquering and organising the East, admit of no other interpretation except through the fully formed plan of conquering the Roman world.

Tradition even stretches his plans into Britain, the northern limit of the Empire ; but it is too uncertain to be used as evidence. He was, however, sending his subordinates at least as far as Gaul in his later years (if Tischendorf is right in accepting the reading of the Sinaitic Manuscript, " Gallia," in 2 Timothy iv. 10).

To follow out this idea in detail would overstep the permissible limits.   These indications, however, may be enough
to show that there lay in Paul's mind from infancy, implanted
in him by inheritance from his Tarsian Jewish parents,
nourished by the surroundings of his childhood, modified
and redirected by the marvellous circumstances of his conversion, the central and guiding and impelling thought that
the religion revealed to the Hebrew race must conquer and
must govern the Roman world (which, ultimately, would
mean the whole world), and that the realisation of this idea
was the Kingdom of God.

This was a very different idea from the idle dream of
the Palestinian Pharisees and Zealots, a barren fancy, born
of ignorance and narrow-mindedness, that the Messiah
would plant their foot on the necks of their enemies and
make them to rule over their Roman conquerors.   Such a
thought was fruitless and useless.   The man who could give
it space in his mind was never chosen by the Divine overruling will to go to the Nations.   We see in Paul a totally
different conception of the Messiah.   After his Christian
days began, that is, of course, obvious.   But even from his
childhood it was a rich and great idea—and therefore an
idea of justice and freedom, bringing with it equality of
rights, equality of citizenship, free participation in the one
conquering religion.   To prevent the Jews from sinking to
the level of the Nations, among whom their lot was cast, the
Nations must be raised to the level of the Jews.

Such an idea naturally developed into Christianity.
The man who entertained it was really quite out of harmony
with the narrow Jewish party, and after a time he must discover this in the ruin of all his earlier plans.   But Nature
and the Divine purpose were inevitably driving him towards

his true party and his true allies, as the ox is driven by the pricks of its driver's goad; and though Paul, for a time, resisted with blind fury, the power of Nature was too strong, and the truth was presented to him on a sudden in an irresistible and compelling way, which seized him in its grasp and dominated his entire mind and being ever afterwards.

The Pauline idea of the Kingdom of God, from the religious point of view, is admirably treated by Professor Sanday in the *Journal of Theological Studies*, i., 481 ff. To speak in Pauline words, "the Kingdom of God," contemplated in its absolute reality, apart from the fetters of space and time, "is righteousness and peace and joy"; "it is not in word but in power". But here, at present, we look only at the external side, as the idea develops itself in existing society and political circumstances, constrained by the conditions of the world in which man lives. The Kingdom of God had to unfold itself in the Roman world, province by province, in the cities of men, in parts and small groups of persons, far separated from one another by sea and land, by language and manners. While Paul never loses sight of the eternal and absolute idea, he is generally engrossed with the task immediately and practically before him, the life of the Church scattered over the provinces of the Empire, "the elect who are sojourners of the dispersion in Pontus, Galatia, etc.," the Church of the Diaspora.

VII

It may be objected to the interpretation of Paul's aims which was stated in the former part of this article, that some more explicit expression of his intention might have been expected in his writings, in addition to the obscure indications of which some instances have been quoted in our pages. But this objection has no force in view of the character of his writings.

In all his letters which have been preserved to us, Paul is absorbed in the needs of the moment, eager to save his readers from some mistake into which they are liable to fall, or have actually fallen—anxious to strengthen them and to move their minds—compelled to answer accusations against himself and misrepresentations of his actions which had endangered his hold on the hearts of his correspondents. He is always, as it were, with his back against a wall, fighting for life against principalities and powers, men and sin. So it must always be with a man who is not an opportunist, but aims at an ideal.   His life must be one long fight, which will not end till he dies, or till he gives up his ideal and falls back into despairing acquiescence in the existing order. But for Paul only one thing was possible.   He could not rest : he could not abandon his ideal : he must fight on to the end.   Accordingly, when we are on the outlook for some expression on the external side, as distinguished from the purely religious expression, of the ideals which underlie and give unity to the storm and stress and constant fighting of his life, the letters, controlled as they are by consideration for the immediate needs of others, are not well calculated to help us in our search, though, as a whole, they become far more luminous and consistent when read on our view.

If we had a defence pronounced by Paul before a great tribunal, where sat a judge of the type of Seneca at his best, we might expect to find in it a survey of his life and work rising above a mere reply to criticism, and expressing his ideals in a form that could be comprehended by the judge. Before a judge like Felix it was useless to pitch his defence

on a higher level than a statement showing that he had not
done the particular act which he was accused of. A judge
of the higher type, such as Rome produced in unusual
numbers, would have sought to understand the deep-lying
motives which had brought about the collision between Paul
and the chiefs of his people; and Paul, with his unerring
instinct, would have given the judge what he desired. What
would we not give to have an account of his defence before
the supreme tribunal of the Empire in Rome, or even that
in Corinth before Gallio, the brother of Seneca?

There is only one case in which Paul's appearance before
a tribunal of a higher class has been described to us, *viz.*,
the Council in Jerusalem. Bitterly prejudiced as the Jewish
Sanhedrin was, still it was composed of the leading men of
the nation, men of experience and standing, men with a
certain reputation which they must maintain, even though
they were already convinced before the trial began that the
defendant was guilty, men who were accustomed and trained
to look a little below the surface, and who were not ready
to accept a mere superficial defence. It was not a tribunal
of the highest kind, but it was the great Council of the
Jewish nation; and a real defence of his life might have
been made before it; but the speech was interrupted at the
outset. Paul saw that he ought to begin his defence with
a brief and pithy sentence, and "he cried out in the Council:
I am a Pharisee, a son of Pharisees: touching the hope
and resurrection of the dead I am called in question". That
was the beginning and the enforced end of his defence in
the great crisis of his life. What can we make of it?

That is one of the greatest scenes of Paul's life. On our
interpretation of his aims, those few words addressed to
the Sanhedrin stand forth as the sharpest and most com-

prehensive statement that has come down to us from him about his work and his plans. But before describing the meaning which we gather from those words, it is necessary to state briefly the meaning which is, and must be, taken from them on the ordinarily accepted view of Paul's ideals —according to which the scene sets him in an unfortunate and disappointing light.

According to that generally accepted view, Paul was snatching a momentary victory by a clever stroke of policy, playing on the passions of his hearers and judges, leading them away from the real point at issue and directing their attention to a different question on which they were sure to quarrel with one another and forget the prisoner. On that view he had been a Jew and a law-abiding Pharisee of the straitest type, brought up strictly within the narrow Jewish circle of thought and custom, ignorant of the teaching of the western schools, who, however, had become a Christian and was being tried for calumniating and bringing contempt on his original faith : in claiming to be a Pharisee he was rather unfairly laying claim to his pre-Christian character, and in saying that the accusation against him turned on his belief in the resurrection of the dead he was raising an unreal issue, with barely enough of justification to save him from falsehood.

A writer to whom we can always turn for a clear and sharp presentation of accepted views in their most reasonable form, Canon Farrar, in his *Life of St. Paul*, finds that "we cannot defend his conduct at that meeting," and explains his action on the ground that "he was a little unhinged, both morally and spiritually, by the wild and awful trials of the day before": "the words suggest a false issue": they show that Paul failed in that " scrupulously inflexible

straightforwardness" which the Canon finds to be characteristic of "the English in particular". "Yet," he proceeds,
"after all these qualifications," after making "every possible
deduction and allowance for a venial infirmity," "we cannot
in this matter wholly see how St. Paul could say without
qualification in such an assembly, ' I am a Pharisee ' ". That
conduct " was hardly worthy of St. Paul ". " Moreover, the
device, besides being questionable, was not even politic. It
added violence to a yet more infuriated reaction in men
who felt that they had been the victims of a successful
stratagem."

On our part, while we acknowledge that the last sentence
which we have quoted describes what must inevitably have
been the result, if Paul's action had been a mere crafty trick,
we fail to see any proof that that result actually occurred,
and that the sympathy which his words created in a portion
of the Sanhedrin turned immediately or at all into redoubled
fury. The Council, certainly, continued to be bitterly
hostile, and even became more bitter, but it was dominated
by the Sadducee priests, who were all the more infuriated
because of the check which Paul's bold words inflicted on
them at the meeting.

We are, in truth, very imperfectly informed as to the
attitude of the Jews towards Paul. Luke, as we shall see,
was strongly prejudiced against the Jews; and yet we
gather from him that there was generally an appreciable
minority of Jews in the cities of the East who were favourable to Paul, that in Berœa a majority of them were on his
side, and that in Rome the leading Jews adopted a guarded
and non-committal attitude, which has been a riddle to
modern scholars, but which seems very significant. The
Roman Jews were well aware how strong was the opposition

to Paul among many of their nation. They must have been well aware of the long prosecution to which he had been subjected in Palestine ; but they were not determined against him ; and this must certainly be due to the fact that a minority of the Jews regarded his policy as being not entirely wrong.

Yet it seems impossible to avoid that unfavourable interpretation of the Council scene on the commonly accepted view of Paul's early life. If he had been only the narrow, hard, bigoted and ignorant Jew whom some modern writers describe, he undoubtedly had completely changed after he became a Christian, and had swung round to the opposite extreme. Beginning, as they say, in early life by opposing and hating everything that was not pure Jewish, he afterwards was all for breaking down and destroying the bar of separation between the Jews and "the Nations". The man whose maturer views are the absolute antithesis of his youthful ideas has no right, when he is challenged in the Council of his people, to pretend and solemnly assert that he still holds his earlier ideas.

But when Paul declared in that great crisis, before the elders and rulers of his nation, that he was "a Pharisee, son of Pharisees," he was obviously claiming to be still what he had been born and bred : he was asserting the continuity of his mental development from first to last. Nor does that assertion stand alone. Paul has left us many other statements to the same effect. Sometimes indeed he seems to say almost the opposite : he speaks in the strongest terms of the complete revolution in his life that was made by his conversion : everything was changed for him : he passed from death to life. Nothing can be more emphatic than his expressions in some places. But in other places he sums up his whole life as a continuous and unbroken process, describable in its entirety by the same words; and he studiously avoids anything which could suggest that any revolution or serious change had occurred in its character. Thus, for example, the first words he uttered in the Council, as he began his defence, before the High-priest interrupted him by ordering an attendant to strike him on the mouth, were these: "Brethren, I have lived before God in all good conscience until this day". The description is not restricted to one half of his life. Before and after his conversion alike he had been equally zealous to serve the God of Israel. That is pretty nearly equivalent to his statement, made a few moments later, that he was still a Pharisee. So again, he claimed in his defence before Felix, a few days later, that as a Christian he was "serving the God of our fathers, believing all things that are according to the Law . . . always exercising myself to have a conscience void of offence towards God and men". His defence was always the same, and therefore had been carefully planned: that his life had been consistently directed from the beginning towards one end, the glorification of the God of Israel by admitting the Nations to be his servants, and that this was true Judaism and true Phariseeism.

Those two groups of statements are in the strongest contrast with one another. But, in our interpretation, there is no contradiction between them. Both assertions are equally true. His life, before and after, was the same, and yet utterly different. The difference was infinite, yet the difference was slight. The whole of the present paper is an attempt to state and make evident the meaning of this apparent contradiction; but to carry out the idea properly requires an entire study of Paul's life. Every incident in his career is affected by this view; some are seen in a totally different aspect.

In the Council scene, then, a plain issue is presented. On the one hand, we find that his claim to be still what he had been from the beginning is simply a brief statement of the view which we have been stating of his life as a whole. On the other hand, those who take the common view are bound to hold that his statement before the Sanhedrin came perilously near being false; and Canon Farrar, in his clear, narrow, logical way, accepts the inevitable inference; but others try to palliate Paul's conduct, and go to far greater extremes than Canon Farrar would permit in making excuses for it.

It may be, and has been, urged that, when a prisoner is, or considers that he is, subjected to undeserved trial on a trumped-up charge, he may justifiably go to considerable lengths in evading the main issue, and in stirring up latent disagreement among his judges. But that question of casuistry does not concern us here. Paul had come up to Jerusalem well aware that he would be seized and accused by the Jews. He elected to take this risk, because his scheme of work pointed the way to him; and he went straight on in the line indicated. In his trial the highest interests were involved; the right of free speech and of liberty to preach hung on the issue. It was not necessary to come to face the trial; but he who chooses to face a trial, who comes voluntarily forward to speak on behalf of his religion and his co-religionists, falls far short of his own beginnings, if, in the crisis, he tries to outwit his opponents and to save himself by a clever trick. Such a victory is not a real victory. It would not strengthen the cause which Paul had at heart; and it would only be a temporary and evanescent advantage. On this occasion Paul was bound to be true to himself, to claim the freedom that he considered was his right, and to have recourse to no subterfuge. He was, however, fully justified in putting his defence in the form which would be most effective with his judges. If one party among his judges was more capable of being brought to a favourable view of his claims than the other, he would naturally and justifiably aim at affecting the minds of the more hopeful party. But he must not stoop to mere trickery, and he must be unswervingly loyal to his cause.

Moreover, it cannot reasonably be maintained that Paul's trial was undeserved, and that the charge against him was trumped up. It was quite fair that he should be tried—provided the trial was justly conducted. It was the best thing for him that he should have the opportunity of stating his own defence before the rulers of his people. Considering what Jewish views and principles were, we do not see that the Council can be blamed for bringing him to trial—provided always that they gave him a fair trial. He had, undoubtedly, done harm to the Judaism which they represented. He had spoken sharply and severely against it. He had drawn away from it many of its admirers and benefactors in many cities of the Empire; and his influence was calculated to lower the prestige of the existing Jewish institutions among "the Nations". He, on his side, claimed to represent the true line of development in which Judaism ought to advance. He held that Judaism was sinking below its true self and becoming dead, because it resisted the forces within itself that were impelling it to advance. It was right for the Council to bring him to trial, and to hear his defence. It was right for him to plead his cause with absolute truth, to refuse to sink below his own highest level, to condescend to no tricks or stratagems. On the one side there must be a charge stated against him : on the other side, there must be a denial of the charge, and an argument in support of the denial. Paul's denial is couched in the form of a statement that he is a Pharisee. The right criticism of the proceedings is, not that there ought to have been no trial, but that, as it was conducted, it came perilously near making the prosecutors the judges.

VIII

Now, according to our view, Paul's career as a Christian was not the negation, but the completion, of his early ideals ; it turned his youthful dreams into realities. He was not less of a Jew after he became a Christian : he only came to know better what Judaism really was. He began, at his conversion, to obey the law of his own character, inherent in him from his birth, and developed by his education. Henceforth, he recognised and obeyed the guidance of Nature, or, as he would say, of God, which previously he had stupidly, blindly, ignorantly resisted. But he lived in all good conscience before the God of Israel, afterwards as before, as he had just a moment before stated to the Council. If he was a Pharisee before, he still remained a Pharisee ; and so he now declared to the Council. In the words of Goethe's motto, *What he wished in youth, he had in age*, but in a way he had not dreamed of.

But what are we to understand when he calls himself a Pharisee? What meaning did this carry to him? In estimating this, we must remember what was the circle of ideas within which the trial necessarily moved. It turned on questions of the world and of life, not on philosophical theories.

The difference between Pharisee and Sadducee may be looked at from several different points of view, religious, philosophic, moral ; but in the practical facts of politics and society, within which the trial moved, the relation to Rome was the critical question. The Sadducees were in favour of compromise and agreement ; the Pharisees were the national party, who stubbornly resisted Roman encroachment, both in politics and in life. The Sadducees would sacrifice all those facts and elements in their religion and national life that tended to prevent the agreement with Rome and to impede their career in the Roman Empire, whose sway they accepted. The Pharisees would not sacrifice one jot or one tittle of the law.

Considering Paul's attitude towards the Empire, it was inevitable that he should seem to the Pharisees to be as much a Sadducee as a Christian. He accepted, as Jesus accepted, the practical fact of Roman rule. The common Pharisee could not see that both Jesus and Paul accepted the Roman government because, spiritually, it had no reality and no importance. Paul would concentrate the mind upon spiritual facts, and accept the merely outward and evanescent facts of the world, of politics, of society. The Sadducees saw nothing more real than the Roman government; Paul saw that among the realities of life the outward form of conquering rule had no place. The present form of government was an unreal and passing phenomenon, which never touched the truth and reality of life. Both the Sadducees and Paul recognised that they should accommodate themselves in the circumstances of life to the Roman rule. But the Sadducees would make their existence in the Roman Empire : they knew no higher life : they recognised nothing but the facts of worldly and material prosperity. Paul would live a life above the level of the Roman Empire.

So it was with everything that was distinctive in Judaism. The Sadducees would level down to the Roman standard. Paul would level up to the Jewish standard. The Sadducees would sacrifice everything that was inconvenient for the Roman career. Paul would not sacrifice one jot of the truth of the Law, or of its spiritual value. The Sadducees recognised no spiritual value in anything.

But these differences, infinitely great as they are, were not visible to the multitude; and to the multitude Paul necessarily seemed a mere Sadducee, and worse than a Sadducee, for he was said to despise and abolish even the externals of Judaic ritual, which the Sadducees regarded.

Our contention then is that, amid the reports and the inaccurate ideas current in Jerusalem about Paul's conduct and opinions, the statement which he made in that great scene was the best way of placing before a Jewish audience in a single introductory sentence his position and views of life. It is, of course, impossible to put one's entire philosophy and ideal of life into a score of words, or explain in a short sentence the whole of a complex problem; but Paul took the best way to destroy a most critical and fundamental misconception among his hearers. If the Sadducees condemned him as a Christian, the Pharisees condemned him quite as much for being a Sadducee.

The crux of the situation lay in this. Paul stood before the more patriotic members of the Council as the worst of Sadducees, the denier of principles dear to the Pharisees, the corrupter of the purity of the Law, the breaker-down of the proud Jewish isolation from the hateful world. His action had that character in his enemies' eyes. He denies that accusation in a word by declaring himself a Pharisee. The accusation is nowhere recorded in that precise form, for we are very inadequately instructed about the form which popular indignation and accusation against him took. But the assertion here sufficiently proves the form of a common and specially dangerous accusation. So also he assured Agrippa that he had lived a Pharisee, and in a passage addressed to the Philippians (which has most obviously the form of a reply to stinging accusations) he declares that he was "as touching the Law, a Pharisee". When we see in his writings such a repeated assertion, we recognise in it the answer to an accusation.

But, it is urged, "the Pharisaic spirit was in its very essence the antithesis of the Christian," and Paul was "in reality at variance with the Pharisees in every fundamental particular of their system".

Those statements are, to a certain degree, true. But it was rather the faults of the Pharisees, than the essence of the Pharisaic ideals, that were the antithesis of the Christian spirit. It is too easy to see only the faults of the Pharisees, and to forget that they were the patriotic, the earnest, the puritan party among the Jews. Much divided the Christian Paul from the ordinary Pharisees. But from another point of view it is true that he was still a Pharisee. In certain great questions, he could not better define in brief his position than by denying that he was a Sadducee and asserting that he was a Pharisee. Like the Pharisees he would not concede anything of Jewish truth to the Gentiles ; he would keep the entire Law. But, unlike the Pharisees, he would impose on the Gentiles only the spiritual facts and not the outward and unessential ceremonies of the Law. So, too, much divided the Christian Paul from the ordinary

Jews. But Paul claimed to be the true Jew and the true Pharisee.

Again, the Sadducees recognised no spiritual side to the Law, no spiritual and eternal side to human life. Here Paul was entirely the Pharisee. Belief in the resurrection of the dead was the briefest declaration of his position in this question.

Nor did his declaration before the Council draw attention away from the real fact that Paul was on trial as a Christian. To Paul the fact that Jesus was living was the guarantee of the resurrection of the dead, and to him, as to all Jews, the recognition that Jesus was living implied that Jesus was the Christ.[1]

Thus Paul's declaration to the Sanhedrin is found to be the briefest possible way of bringing home to the patriotic party among his judges that, though his acts had been directed towards establishing an agreement between the Jews and the Roman State and breaking down the isolation of the Jews, still he was resolute not to sacrifice one jot of the spiritual law, or sink in the smallest degree below the loftiest level of Judaism. What further explanations would have been made in the course of his speech we know not, for the speech was interrupted at that point.

IX

It is true that Luke's account of the scene is so expressed as to lend itself readily to the commonly accepted view. It may be allowed that possibly he interpreted the scene in that way; but that is far from certain. It is quite in accordance with the spirit of our theory to say, in the words

[1] On this see §§ IV., V.

of Luke, that "when Paul perceived that the one part were Sadducees and the other Pharisees, he cried out in the Council, Brethren, I am a Pharisee," etc. Let us conceive clearly how the action proceeded.

Paul opened his defence before the Council by declaring that he had lived in all good conscience before God until that day : he began by maintaining that his life had been spent in one continuous uninterrupted strain of zealous obedience to the God of Israel. That, as we have seen, is really the same essential truth which he afterwards expressed in another way.

The beginning was unfortunate. It offended his audience, instead of conciliating it—a serious fault in a speech for the defence, and one that Paul was seldom guilty of. The high-priest rebuked him brutally, and roused a very sharp and bitter retort. Paul had not known the high-priest, who was not presiding at the meeting, but was merely one of the general body of the Council. The Roman tribune had summoned the meeting, and necessarily was its president. As president, he brought Paul before the meeting (as Luke mentions), which was one of the recognised forms in the Roman theory of the chairmanship : Paul could not speak at such a meeting, unless the president introduced him.[1] In such circumstances, the high-priest would appear to have avoided wearing his official dress ; he was present, as it were, only unofficially. Probably, it was a matter of usage that the high-priest should not officially occupy a subordinate place in the assembly : when a Roman presided, the high-priest appeared without his official dress, and sat as an ordinary member. His action in interrupting Paul's defence was, therefore, all the more out of order ; and Paul,

[1] *Producere* was the technical term for this action of the chairman.

who did not recognise him, retorted sharply on his conduct as a juror, but apologised as soon as he learned that it was the high-priest who had spoken.

The meeting, however, was evidently disturbed through the violent feelings aroused by this unfortunate incident. Some discussion took place before Paul was again allowed to speak ; and in the course of the discussion Paul observed, as Luke says, "that the one part were Sadducees and the other Pharisees". The differences between the two parties were so strongly accentuated that a very little debate would reveal the facts to him. He immediately recognised that he might gain the sympathy of the Pharisees, if he put the plea, which he had previously pitched in a different tone, in a way that would appeal to them. In all probability we should find, if any information had come down to us on the subject, that the minority favourable to Paul among the Jews, which (as we have seen) existed in most of their towns and colonies, usually consisted of Pharisees ; and thus he knew at once where lay his chance of making an impression. But he did not alter his predetermined line of defence ; he merely changed the expression.

Luke's narrative suits this interpretation perfectly ; and in Paul's next defence—before Felix—Luke represents him as skilfully introducing the same plea in a double form : first, declaring that his life had been one of continuous conscientious obedience to the God of Israel, in conformity with the Law, from the beginning onwards, and afterwards actually quoting part of the controverted expression which he had given to the same fundamental truth.

But we are not concerned to maintain that Luke fully understood Paul's intention in giving this turn to his defence. Luke disliked the Jews, and gives us a prejudiced picture of

them, though his description is so true that we can always
see the real facts shining through his account, even where
we find it prejudiced.   Much as we must admire his historical genius, we must also recognise the limitations imposed
on him by his birth and training.   He was a Greek, and
could not always comprehend, or wish to comprehend,
Jewish nature.   The racial dislike between Greek and Jew
has always been, and still is, deep and ineradicable.

It is clear in Luke's account of the scene in the Council
that he was filled with contempt for the clamour and dissen-
sion that arose in the court as the result of Paul's brief defence.   He evidently regards the members of the court as a
set of howling fanatics, and mentally contrasts the scene with
the superior order and propriety that would prevail in the
Senate of a Greek or Roman city.   Perhaps he was not able
to be quite fair or sympathetic in his estimate of the Jewish
Council.

We are here tempted to draw a comparison between
Luke and Renan in this respect.   No one has been more
sympathetic in the interpretation of Luke than the great
French scholar.   No one has been more generously ap-
preciative of the charm of Luke's work.   His sympathy
has led Renan first to the right conclusion as to several of
the incidents in which Luke was concerned.   The sympathy
is founded on real similarity of nature.   Nowhere is the
similarity more conspicuous than in the inability of both
to understand the nature of the Jews.   We take as an
example the impression which Jerusalem and its surroundings left on their minds.

Luke could not forget his first view of Cyprus rising
out of the sea ; but the first view of Jerusalem, the most
marvellously interesting of scenes to one who has true

7

sympathy for Jewish history and Jewish religion, has left
no impression on his book. Again, he describes vividly
how he came to Rome, crossing first the distant bounds of
the Roman land, the boundary of Rome as a State, far in
the south of Latium, then traversing the parts of this great
Rome by the Appian Road, then entering the limits of the
city Rome in a narrower sense. But, though he tells how
he made the journey with horses from Cæsarea to Jerusalem, and stayed a night by the way in the house of Mnason,
one of the earliest Christians, he has nothing to say more
than that, "when we were come to Jerusalem, the brethren
received us gladly."

And now see what sort of impression the view of
Jerusalem made on Renan.

"The parched appearance of nature in the neighbourhood of Jerusalem must have added to the dislike Jesus
had for the place. The valleys are without water ; the soil
arid and stony. Looking into the valley of the Dead Sea,
the view is somewhat striking ; elsewhere it is monotonous.
The hill of Mizpeh, around which cluster the most ancient
historical remembrances of Israel, alone relieves the eye."

The allusion to the Dead Sea shows that Renan is
describing the view from the Mount of Olives, the most
entrancing in the world to the student of history. But
the most dull and ignorant of tourists could not have seen
less in it than the great French scholar saw. His words
are a perfect proof of his essential lack of sympathy with
the Hebrew mind. The man who could feel and speak
thus about that wonderful scene had not the soul—with all
his genius—to understand Judaism.

X

History is the supreme judge of all ideas. What verdict has it pronounced on Paul's idea? We do not ask what verdict it has pronounced on his religion—the question is impertinent, or premature—but on the new idea that he threw into the political movements of his time. Has history declared that his idea was vital and real? The reply to that question the writer has already attempted to give in a study of *The Church in the Roman Empire ;* and here we may sum it up in a sentence and a paragraph. The age was ripe for Paul's idea : the fulness of time was come.

In the mind of the ancients no union of men, small or great, good or bad, humble or honourable, was conceivable without a religious bond to hold it together. The Roman Empire, if it was to become an organic unity, must derive its vitality and its hold on men's minds from some religious bond. Patriotism, to the ancients, was adherence to a common religion, just as the family tie was, not common blood, but communion in the family religion (for the adopted son was as real a member as the son by nature). Accordingly, when Augustus essayed the great task of consolidating the loosely aggregated parts of the vast Empire, he had to find a religion to consecrate the unity by a common idea and sentiment. The existing religions were all national, while the Empire (as we saw) was striving to extirpate the national divisions and create a supra-national unity. A new religion was needed. Partly with conscious intention, partly borne unconsciously on the tide of events, the young Empire created the Imperial religion, the worship of an idea—the cult of the Majesty of Rome as represented

by the incarnate deity present on earth in the person of
the reigning Emperor, and by the dead gods, his deified
predecessors on the throne. Except for the slavish adula-
tion of the living Emperor, the idea was not devoid of
nobility ; but it was incapable of life, for it degraded human
nature, and was founded on a lie. But Paul gave the
Empire a more serviceable idea. He made possible that
unity at which the Imperial policy was aiming. The true
path of development for the Empire lay in allowing free
play to the idea which Paul offered, and strengthening
itself through this unifying religion. That principle of
perfect religious freedom (which we regard as Seneca's)
directed for a time the Imperial policy, and caused the
acquittal of Paul on his first trial in Rome. But freedom
was soon exchanged for the policy of fire and sword. The
Imperial gods would not give place to a more real religion,
and fought for two and a half centuries to maintain their
sham worship against it. When at last the idea of Paul
was, even reluctantly and imperfectly, accepted by the
Emperors, no longer claiming to be gods, it gave new life
to the rapidly perishing organisation of the Empire, and
conquered the triumphant barbarian enemy. Had it not
been for Paul—if one may guess at what might have been
—no man would now remember Roman and Greek civilisation. Barbarism proved too powerful for the Græco-Roman
civilisation unaided by the new religious bond ; and every
channel through which that civilisation was preserved, or
interest in it maintained, either is now or has been in some
essential part of its course Christian after the Pauline form.

IV

PAGAN REVIVALISM AND THE PER-
SECUTIONS OF THE EARLY CHURCH

IV

PAGAN REVIVALISM AND THE PERSECU-
TIONS OF THE EARLY CHURCH

THE opinion was stated by Mommsen in his epoch-making
study in the *Historische Zeitschrift*, 1890, pp. 389-429, that
the Roman Imperial Government during the first two
centuries was usually unwilling to carry into effect by active
measures of repression the deep-seated and unavoidable
opposition between itself and the Christians, but that isolated outbreaks of repressive activity occurred when it
was forced to act by the pressure of the general hatred
which was felt by the pagan population for the Christians.
That there is an element of truth in this view is acknowledged. That it is not complete and sufficient, but one-
sided, the present writer has always maintained. The
relation between the popular dislike and the Imperial disapproval is not so simple as Mommsen's view would make
it. It was not simply a case in which the one pushed and
the other was unwillingly impelled.

It is acknowledged by every one that in the two last
great persecutions the relation changed. The Imperial
Government was then intensely active, and probably went
far beyond public sentiment. At the beginning of the period
of persecution, also, Tacitus expressly declares that Nero's
action, while it began by using the public dislike for Imperial purposes, soon went far beyond, and was felt as an

outrage by, popular judgment. In the account which is given
in the Apocalypse of Domitian's persecution the same impression is conveyed. The Imperial Government, the Beast
that appears from the sea, is described as the active and
directing power, the great implacable, unwearied enemy.
Thus alike at the beginning and the end the Imperial policy
is seen to be actively stimulating, instead of being simply
pushed on by, popular feeling.

None of these facts are denied. All are admitted universally, except that the historical value and meaning of the
evidence contained in the Apocalypse might be contested
by some. The difference of opinion is with regard to the
intermediate period. It is admitted on all hands that there
was a middle time, lasting at least from Trajan to the
accession of Decius, in which persecution was intermittent
and fitful. During this period popular feeling was more
effective, and the Imperial Government was in general more
inert; but the fits of activity were probably very much of
the same general character as in the first and last stages.

The difference, then, between these views is chiefly a
matter of degree, and not of essential opposition. In such
a case it is always desirable to get away from generalities
and come to individual definite facts. Much of the long
controversy about the nature of the persecutions has been
due to the want of clear facts, and the restriction of the
discussion to generalities. The narratives of martyrdoms
furnished the whole store of facts, and these provoked
almost more controversy than the persecutions; they were
necessarily one-sided and strongly prejudiced against the
Government; the last thought of the writers was to give a
fair statement of the views entertained by the Empire.
Moreover, their date and credibility was often very doubt-

ful, and very few were universally admitted to be documents contemporary with the events or founded on contemporary documents.

In this uncertainty it would be valuable to have some evidence giving the views and ideas of the other side, the Government and the common people. A little evidence of this kind has gradually been accumulating during the last twenty years, and it is well to bring together some specimens of it.

If the question be asked how the relation between the Imperial Government and popular opinion was made operative practically, the first answer that suggested itself would probably be the one which is suggested by the most familiar and universally accepted of all the Acts of Martyrs, the story of Polycarp—that the clamour of the people forced their opinion and wish on the attention of persons in authority. Attention has been concentrated on this almost exclusively, and the restricted view has inevitably suggested that, while popular opinion by its clamour influenced the Emperors, no influence was exercised by the Emperors on popular opinion.

The method of clamour and even riot was certainly used, but it could never be so effective in an Empire that extended round the whole Mediterranean as in a great city or a small compact country. It was not the only method, and it was not the telling method. There was a way in which the Imperial Government could learn almost directly the wishes of the provinces and communicate its views to them. This was through the Assembly or Commune of the Province, a body composed of representatives of the cities and districts meeting for purposes chiefly religious; but religion was not so separate from social and political life then as it is now.

The Commune united the whole province in the State religion, and was the concrete expression of its patriotism
and its sense of the Imperial unity.[1]   The Emperor, as the
incarnate god in whose worship and service the Commune
met, was the head of the religion from every point of view :
he was the present god, and he was the supreme priest.
The ancient mind was familiar with the idea that the god
was the first and original priest of his own religion, for the
god revealed the ritual to men and showed them how to
approach him.

Thus the Provincial organisation of the State religion was
the natural medium of communication between the Emperor
and the popular feeling.   The feeling found expression in
and through the Commune.   In proportion as loyalty (according to the accepted idea of loyalty) was strong among
the people the Commune was active and powerful, because
it was expressing in the State ritual a strong popular feeling.
In proportion as the Emperor was in harmony with the
popular feeling was the sense of loyalty intensified in the
popular mind.

The present writer has tried to describe [2] how the Commune of Asia worked in the persecution of Domitian, as
that persecution is described in detail in our solitary authority, the Apocalypse, and the agreement of the picture
set before us in that book with the procedure of the last persecution, A.D. 303-311, was regarded as furnishing a complete proof of the truth and trustworthiness of the picture.

The writer's view is that a pagan revival accompanied
almost every persecution, partly arising spontaneously from
popular feeling, but partly engineered and guided by Imperial encouragement.   The Empire allied itself with the old

[1] *Letters to the Seven Churches*, p. 96.   [2] *Ibid.*, 97 ff., 105 f.

religion, and especially the Asiatic superstitions, which had a strong hold on their devotees, against the new Faith. In the last persecution "the Christian sacraments and institutions were imitated; heathen hierarchy established of men of high rank. For the mob there was a clever winking Jove; for the devout a daily heathen service."[1] Divine names were commonly taken by the leaders and priests: Theoteknos, God's Child, a Neo-Platonist philosopher, was the guiding spirit of the pagan revival.

Some examples will now be quoted of these pagan revivals, not with any intention either of exhausting the subject or of drawing any inferences, but merely to direct attention to the importance of collecting and studying the facts with a view to guiding the reasoning and opinion of all scholars on this subject.

1. The following was published in 1877 by MM. Radet and Paris in the *Bulletin de Correspondance Hellénique*, xi., p. 63, Isauria, but its real character was not recognised:—

> Ma, daughter of Pappas,[2] virgin, and by family right priestess of the goddess and the saints, restored and roofed with tiles the temple at her own expense.

The criteria of the reactionary movement are all evident here. The names are those of deities: Ma was the great Cappadocian goddess, Pappas (or Papas) was a widely spread name of the supreme god as the "Father" of his worshippers. The institutions and terminology of the Church are adopted, the Virgins and the Saints (as designation of the congregation of believers). So marked is the Christian tone that for

---

[1] Rev. H. B. Workman, *Persecution in the Early Church*, p. 280. I received this book through the author's courtesy, after my article was nearly finished, and extract the above as illustrating the subject clearly.

[2] The first editors read M. A. Pappa as a woman's name.

long I regarded the inscription as Christian, originating from
some heretic sect, Ma, priestess of the Mother of God ($\theta\epsilon o\hat{v}$,
abbreviation of $\theta\epsilon(o\tau\acute{o}\kappa)ov$), having renovated the local
church. But on that theory the paganisation of the Church
is so strongly marked that the document could not be placed
earlier than the fifth century, whereas it is almost certainly
not later than the third century or the beginning of the
fourth. Moreover, the pagan revival is now being recognised much more widely in the records of Asia Minor, and
many documents, which were formerly difficult to understand, fall readily into their proper place in the reaction and
revival.

The term " Parthenos " was indeed used in the Anatolian
religion to designate the female slaves of the sanctuary, and
it implies only unwedded. But I do not know that it was
ever used by pagans in this bare and simple fashion almost
like a title of hieratic rank: when it occurs in pagan documents there is something in the context to explain the
scope and sphere of the allusion, as, *e.g.*, in the inscription
quoted in my *Historical Commentary on Galatians*, p. 201.
Hence it seems practically certain that the term as applied
to Ma here proves that in the temple which she restored
there existed an order of " Virgins " similar to the Christian.

Still more clearly of Christian origin is the phrase
" priestess of the Saints ". In a fourth century inscription of
Ancyra, the phrase " presbyter of the Saints " occurs (*C. I. G.*,
9258). Generally the term " Saints " applied to the congregation of Christians belongs to the early time, but the
Ancyran inscription is a clear proof that the use lasted into
the fourth century. In that century "presbyter of the Holy
Church " took its place; as appears in many inscriptions
(examples quoted in the *Expositor*, Dec., 1905, p. 444).

It is highly probable that the inscription belongs to the time of Decius. This country was very thoroughly Christianised before that time. The old pagan temples had sunk into decay in Isauria—just as Pliny found that they had in Bithynia in A.D. 112, when he interfered to stop the Christian propaganda, and soon succeeded in having the temples restored and the worship reorganised.

2. A little epitaph found on an Imperial estate in North Galatia probably belongs to this class :—

> Anna was set up in honour by her children Am(m)on and Apollo and Manes and Matar, in remembrance.[1]

The designation of four children by four Divine names is quite distinctive of the pagan revival. The old Phrygian form Matar for the Mother-Goddess is a peculiarly interesting revivication of an ancient name. Manes is known only in this period of revival, and seems likewise to be an old name reintroduced (see below, No. 4).

3. Another example, engraved on two sides of a small altar, bearing pagan reliefs more or less defaced, belongs to Akmonia in Phrygia[2] :—

> (*a*) Good Fortune. Aurelius Epitynchanos and Aurelius Epinikos, along with their mother Tertulla, consecrated their father Telesphoros, (*b*) in the year 334 (A.D. 249-250), along with the religious society of which he was Hierophant.

The Fortunate and the Conquering were the sons of Telesphoros, who bore the name of the little god of Pergamum, the Consummator. The Divine nomenclature is

---

[1] Published by Mr. J. G. C. Anderson, in the *Journal of Hellenic Studies*, 1899, p. 84.

[2] It was published by the writer in the *Revue des Études Anciennes*, 1901, p. 275; the date was corrected by reading Δ for A, *ibid.*, 1902, pp. 84, 269.

evidently carefully selected. The word Epitynchanos is
never found in Greek literature, but occasionally in late
inscriptions: it is a false formation from the verb, and was
probably an invention of this late period. Telesphoros was
the Hierophant, the displayer of the sacred objects in the
mysteries celebrated by the religious society which had
been formed in Akmonia.

The date, which is fortunately stated in this inscription,
is peculiarly important, and gives the positive certainty that
this revival of paganism was coincident with the persecution of Decius. The society was apparently a private
association; and there is no direct proof that it had been
encouraged by the Imperial Government or the Commune.
But the same family is known from later documents, which
show that it enjoyed Imperial favour later.

4. Found near Akmonia in 1883: the stone is now in
Brussels, as Professor F. Cumont informs me. There are
many difficulties in the language; and the construction and
meaning are in some places very obscure.

(*a*) In the year 398 (A.D. 313-314), and waiting the commands of the immortals, and I that speak everything
am Athanatos Epitynchanos (Immortal Fortunate), initiated by an honourable priestess of the people bearing an honourable name Spatale, whom the immortal
gods glorified both within and beyond the bounds (of
the city-state Akmonia), for she redeemed many from
evil torments. The high-priest Epitynchanos, glorified
by the immortal gods, was consecrated by Diogas
Epitynchanos and his bride Tation, and their children
Onesimos and Alexander and Asklas and Epitynchanos.

(*b*) Athanatos Epitynchanos, son of Pius, glorified by
Hekate first, secondly by Manes Daos Heliodromos

Zeus, thirdly Phœbus Leader and Prophetic, truly I received the gift prophetic of truth in my own city . . . to the first high-priest Athanatos Pius, father of honourable sons, and to my mother Tatis, who bore honourable children, an honourable name. . . .

(c) The Athanatoi first high-priests, brothers, Diogas and Epitynchanos, saviours of their city, lawgivers.[1]

This inscription belongs to the last stage of the struggle against Christianity, under Maximin, and entirely confirms the account given by Eusebius and Lactantius of that Emperor's action. The imitation of Christian language (John iv. 6) and Christian zeal for conversion, the profusion of Divine names and epithets, the revival of old cults, the respect for prophecy, and the confidence in Divine favour and guidance—all are characteristic of the pagan revival. The use of the term high-priest implies Imperial approval: it cannot be doubted that in the pagan hierarchy the consent of the Pontifex Maximus and the Commune was a necessary condition in the bestowal of this title. Moreover, it is recorded that Maximin sought to create a hierarchy opposed to the Christian.

5. Epitynchanos is also mentioned in an inscription, which belongs either to the Phrygian city Meiros ("beyond the bounds of Akmonia") or to the Imperial estate Tembrion, as an astrologer, astronomer and diviner, honoured with the citizenship of many cities, and leaving sons who were equally skilled in his arts. This Epitynchanos must belong to the family mentioned in Nos. 3, 4. Now it was pointed out when this inscription was published[2] that Epitynchanos belonged to Akmonia, and flourished about A.D. 260 to 310.

[1] *Cities and Bishoprics of Phrygia*, ii., pp. 566-568.
[2] *Ibid.*, ii., p. 790: A. Souter, in the *Classical Review*, 1897.

He may therefore be probably regarded either as the son of, or as identical with, Epitynchanos son of Telesphoros, and we may suppose that he disused the commonplace name Aurelius (which was almost universally used about 250, and was much less fashionable about 313). This description of the character of Epitynchanos as astrologer and diviner completes the picture given in 3 and agrees exactly with that given in 4.

6. The most important evidence bearing on this question comes from the fragmentary Acta of a society called the Tekmoreian Guest-Friends on the Imperial estates near Pisidian Antioch. The constitution of this religious association is uncertain; but it seems in practice to have consisted of the population resident on the Imperial estates as organised for religious purposes (*plebs collegii*) together with various strangers, mainly visitors from other Imperial estates, but also to some extent persons from the Hellenic cities, who were falling away from Hellenism and relapsing into the older Orientalism of the country and deserting the Hellenic cities to settle in the villages on the Imperial estates. Numerous questions of history and sociology are roused by this unique series of documents; these questions are indicated, though space and time forbade full treatment, in the first complete publication of the documents, *Studies in the History and Art of the Eastern Roman Provinces*, written for the Aberdeen Quatercentenary and now published by Messrs. Hodder & Stoughton, 1906, pp. 305-377; but at present we only touch on the one subject of immediate interest.

The most important documents found in this locality are (1) lists of subscribers with the amount of their subscriptions; when the inscriptions are complete at the top there is a preamble describing the character of the subscribers and the purpose of the donations ; (2) dedications to the Goddess Artemis or to the God Emperor (once the Gods Emperors) ; (3) a village act, dated by a priest (of Artemis), who seems to be an Imperial procurator, and expressed in the name of the village people and a slave (of the Emperor), who resided on the estate as manager and member of the village Assembly (Gerousia) ; (4) the epitaph of a Roman, apparently freedman and procurator of the Emperor Claudius, holding the priesthood of Artemis.

The subscribers and dedicators are repeatedly called the Tekmoreian Guest-Friends.

That the Guest-Friends were a sort of secret society, so called because they recognised one another by a sign or Tekmor, was suggested in my *Historical Geography of Asia Minor*, p. 411, and *Cities and Bishoprics of Phrygia*, i., p. 97 ; ii., pp. 359, 630 ; but the alternative explanation that the epithet was local and derived from a place called Tekmoreion, was preferred by the only American and German scholars who have expressed an opinion. The connection with the old epic Greek word Tekmor was confirmed in 1905 by the discovery of a list in which the verb τεκμορεύειν is used. The name given to the members of the society was derived from the performance of some action designated by this verb. In one case it is mentioned that the act is performed for the second time.

Inasmuch as new words had to be invented for the occasion the act must have been a novel one. But the society was religious, uniting the old Anatolian ritual with the worship of the Emperor ; acts of the old ritual had old names ; therefore, the act which required a newly invented name must have been part of the new element in the combined religion, *i.e.*, it was connected with some sign of loyalty and devotion to the Imperial religion. What this sign was cannot as yet be determined from the extant evidence ; but every one must involuntarily think of "them that had received the mark of the Beast and them that worshipped his image". The large subscriptions of money recorded in the Tekmoreian lists were applied to the making of statues of the Lord Emperor and the Good Fortune of the Emperors and the great Goddess Artemis, together with various implements of the ritual: the purpose was always religious. The society was the expression of an alliance between the Imperial power and the old Anatolian religious authority ; that old authority seems to have been exercised by the Imperial procurator, who represented the Emperor and managed his interests. The only two priests of the great Goddess mentioned in the documents hitherto discovered were apparently procurators and Imperial freedmen (though owing to the circumstances the procuratorship is not mentioned). The character of the Imperial system was to maintain as far as possible the old system of government on the estates, and this could be most conveniently done by making the procurator hold the old priesthood with all the power that accompanied the office.

It is true that the anti-Christian purpose is never mentioned in the inscriptions. Even if we possessed much fuller and more elaborate copies of the Tekmoreian records, that purpose would probably not be alluded to. "It was apparently a fashion and an affectation among a certain class of Greek men of letters about A.D. 160-240 to ignore the existence of the Christians, and to pretend to confuse them with the Jews. Those high-souled philosophic Greeks would not even know the name, for it was a solecism to use such a vulgar and barbarous word."[1]   So I wrote in 1892; and now it is apparent that the affectation was widely spread over society generally, and not confined to Greek men of letters.   The educated Greeks were not unwilling to ally themselves with the uneducated Orientals against their common enemy; they failed to see that in doing so they were working out the ruin of Greek education.   In allying themselves with the uneducated they must gradually sink to the lower level; and one of the many remarkable and interesting features of the Tekmoreian lists is that they show the way in which individuals were leaving the Greek city life and going back to the lower educational level of Oriental peasant life.[2]   Christianity was the religion of an educated people, and the last and worst evil of the long struggle was that in Diocletian's persecution the more cultured section of the Church was to a large extent killed out, so that on both sides education deteriorated and the quality of society in general was depreciated.[3]

Nor is any allusion ever made in the Tekmoreian documents to Imperial suggestion or approval.   On the contrary, it is apparent that an intentional silence is preserved with regard to the action of Imperial officials.   In the Tekmoreian lists, only village officers as a rule are mentioned.   Even the priest does not appear in them, because the priesthood was held by the procurator.   As is pointed out in the publication of the documents,[4] there is no other explanation possible of this peculiar fact except

[1] *The Church in the Roman Empire*, p. 264.
[2] *Studies in the History and Art of the Eastern Provinces*, p. 357.
[3] *Cities and Bishoprics of Phrygia*, ii., p. 509.
[4] *Studies*, etc., p. 313.

that "the intention was to show the spontaneous nature of the movement". The procurator and managers (*actores*) took no direct part; and the *acta* emanate directly from the populace. Yet this semblance conceals what must have been the real facts. It must be remembered that the population on the Imperial estates were in a different position from the rest of the population of the provinces. The Emperor was their lord; they were his immediate subjects. He was the heir to the personal authority over them, which had once belonged to the deity, whose servants they were; and his procurator was the priest of the deity, and exercised that authority on the Emperor's behalf. Although there is no proof that the constitution of this society was approved by the Emperor, I do not see how this can be doubted. The society aimed only at pleasing the Emperor; it acted in loyal and eager devotion; it lived for the Emperor and the great Goddess Artemis. That it had reason to believe that its action was approved by the Emperor is beyond doubt; it is a fundamental and inevitable part of the situation.

Here then we have clear proof of a considerable organisation, emanating from the Antiochian Imperial estates, and embracing members from many Asian Imperial estates, working for the revival of the old Anatolian religion in association with the Imperial worship. What is the date of formation? It is pointed out in the already quoted publication, p. 350 ff., that the Tekmoreian lists fall into two groups separated by an interval of about a generation (somewhere about twenty to forty years). The later group mentions a single Emperor and cannot therefore have been composed under Diocletian (except in the first year of his reign). While certainty is not attainable until further documents are found, the probability is that the earlier group belongs to the time about A.D. 215-225 and the later about 245-255. Thus, perhaps as early as the first quarter of the third century, certainly not later than about the middle, we have proof of the existence of this great religious association springing from a pagan revival, lasting for at least about thirty years, and countenanced by the Imperial authority. "We can hardly be mistaken in connecting this institution with the greatest political fact of the third century, the war between the State and the Christian faith. The critical and determining question about each successive Emperor at that time turns on his attitude to the Christians; and the test of the real import of every event then is its bearing on the relation between the Christians and the State. The history of the Empire requires to be rewritten from a more statesmanlike point of view, *viz.*, how the great struggle of religions and the social systems which they implied was fought out on the field of the Roman world." [1]

This dating would well explain the origin of the movement. The alliance of philosophy with a revived paganism (studiously ignoring Christianity) is the guiding and originating thought in Philostratus' *Life of Apollonius of Tyana*, an imaginative work which was suggested in court circles and composed in Rome about A.D. 210-220. Philosophy is in this work the criterion of the good and virtuous man; and the good man is he who worships the gods within the earth, the wicked man he who despises them.[2] The Tekmoreian society shows the same idea, spreading in humbler circles from a court origin.

[1] *Studies in the History and Art of the Eastern Provinces*, p. 347.
[2] See, *e.g.*, ii., 39.

A conjecture about the Tekmor may be added here. From the words of Basil, *Epist.* 191,[1] it appears that there was an old custom (apparently no longer practised in his time), "which was once the boast of the Church. Brothers from each church, travelling from one end of the world to the other, were provided with little tokens (*Symbola*), and found all men fathers and brothers."

In *Epist.* 203 he again alludes to the same ancient Christian custom, now quite obsolete: "We, the sons of fathers who made the law that by brief notes the proofs of communion (σύμβολα ἐπιμιξίας) should be carried about from one end of the earth to the other, and that all should be citizens and familiars with all, now sever ourselves from the whole world".

These two letters were written about A.D. 374-375; and the custom to which they allude evidently belongs to the pre-Constantine period : it was one of the devices for maintaining the unity of the early Church.

The Tekmoreian society may have been formed on the analogy of the Church, separated in its parts but united by constant intercourse and hospitality. Members of the society, on this view, would come from many parts of Phrygia and Pisidia to share in the worship of Artemis of the Lakes (just as the Christians still come to the Panegyris of the Virgin-Mother of the Lakes from great distances) ; and displayed in the celebration of the Mysteries their Symbolon, as a proof of their participation in the resistance to the common enemy.

7. At Temenenothyrae (Ushak) occurs a very brief epitaph (*C. I. G.*, 3865 ; *Studies in the History, etc., of the Eastern Provinces*, p. 25):—

---

[1] Quoted more fully in this volume, Art. XV.

(the tomb) of Marcus, citizen,[1] philosopher, friend of all.

In these five words is summed up the Hellenic reaction. The citizenship is emphasised, because the unwillingness of Christians to perform the duties of citizenship was always an offence to the Hellenes. Philosophy is the religion and the guiding principle of Marcus's life. The last phrase is peculiarly characteristic. The Christians had made charity and kindness to others a prime duty ; and the phrase "friend of all" ($\pi\acute{a}\nu\tau\omega\nu$ $\phi\acute{i}\lambda o\varsigma$) in an epitaph was almost a proof of Christianity. At Nova Isaura the epitaph of the Blessed Papas applies this phrase to him in the third century.[2] At Ancyra in the fourth century, we find the epitaph already quoted from *C. I. G.*, 9258 :—

> Here lies the slave of God Theodore, presbyter of the saints and silver-worker,[3] the friend of all. He was perfected on November 15, Ind. 5.

While it is difficult to judge about such a short document, the epitaph of Marcus seems to be earlier than Diocletian ; and some may consider it to prove that pagans used the formula "friend of all," and that the Christians adopted this, as they did many other pagan customs and expressions. But, while not disposed to maintain that the Christians invented the formula and quite ready to admit that they took it from pagan usage, I feel convinced that Marcus of Temenenothyrae belonged to the popular philosophic reaction against the new religion, and that his epitaph

---

[1] The word $\pi o\lambda\iota\acute{\eta}\tau ov$ is better taken as a common noun in Ionic form ; but some may prefer to render " Marcus Poliêtês ". Poetic and Epic forms are not rare in the Greek of Central Asia Minor about A.D. 200-400.

[2] *Studies in the History of the Eastern Provinces*, p. 22.

[3] See Art. XV. of this volume.

emphasised the points in which he (or his friends for him [1]) gloried in surpassing the Christians.

8. Mr. J. G. C. Anderson considers (in all probability justly) that the few markedly and obtrusively pagan inscriptions found on the Imperial estate of Tembrion are connected with this "awakening of pagan devotion towards the end of the third century".[2] One of these is inscribed on an altar.[3]

> Erected by Symmachos, son of Antyllos, and his sons Antyllos, Alexander and Symmachos, to Apollo of Klaros in accordance with an oracle.
> Stablish me in this land an altar of fragrant incense [4] looking towards the rays of the far-seeing sun ; and holy sacrifices offer thereon every month, so that I be your helper and make your fruits grow in their season.   For I am he that provideth the fruits for mortal men, whom I wish to preserve and whom I know how to glorify.

The proper names are commonplace and not divine, so that one sign of the pagan revival is missing. But we have here the establishment of a new cult in a district where Christian inscriptions abound. It is quite probable that the new cult and the oracle originated from Epitynchanos, whose influence in this neighbourhood we saw to have been active in the second half of the third century. The persons mentioned are the ordinary people of the district, the devotees and perhaps the dupes of the astrologer. Hence they do not bear divine names : it was the leaders that took such names.

---

[1] He probably prepared his own grave, a common Phrygian custom. The possibility, however, remains that his friends composed his epitaph after his death ; but, if so, they certainly composed it in his spirit and tone.

[2] *Studies in the History and Art of the Eastern Roman Provinces*, ed. by W. M. Ramsay (Hodder & Stoughton, 1906, p. 128), p. 200.

[3] *Ibid.*, p. 128.

[4] The word is πανθηέα (otherwise unknown) whose meaning is doubtful : perhaps " conspicuous ".

In general, when one finds late inscriptions showing strong pagan sentiment in a district where Christian inscriptions of early period abound, one is justified in suspecting that they belong to the pagan reaction ; but all or most of the criteria described in Nos. 1-5 must be united before the suspicion can be strengthened into certainty.

It is worthy of note that so many of the inscriptions bearing on this subject are connected with Imperial estates. Besides the whole group of Tekmoreian lists, Nos. 2 and 5 and 8 come from Imperial estates, and 3 and 4 refer either to the same person as 5 or to his family, and were found on the fringe of the same estate. It is not impossible that even 4 may originally have been actually erected on that estate ; and in fact it was found within the limits (as I have placed them) of the estate ; but the term high-priest seems more favourable to the origin from a city such as Akmonia, and 3 was found in the territory of that city, which was conterminous with the estate. A wider survey of the documents of this class would probably confirm the principle that the Imperial estates were the centres of the anti-Christian movement and of the pagan revivals; but further exploration is needed and the discovery of more documents may be confidently expected. What is certain is that the connection between the Emperor and the population of his estates was close and direct, that the cultivators of his soil were under his almost direct superintendence through his procurator, and that personal loyalty to him was peculiarly strong among them. Nowhere in Asia, and especially Phrygia, should we expect that the Imperial institutions and religion would be so strong as on the Imperial estates in Asia and in Galatic Phrygia ; and the inscriptions found on the enormous Ormelian and Antiochian estates confirm this expectation. On the other hand, on the estate of Tembrion Christianity was remarkably strong in the third century, though far from universally triumphant. But such are the anomalies that mark the spread of the new faith. It is well known that "the household of Cæsar" was one of the earliest strongholds of Christianity in Rome; and the Tembrian estates of Cæsar form an exception to the rule that the Imperial estates were the strongholds of paganism in Asia Minor.[1]

NOTE.—As my wife reminds me, the use of *symbola* to rouse religious feeling against an enemy (in the way supposed on p. 118) is well known in Asiatic history. As an example she quotes the cakes (chupatties) which were passed round as a preliminary to the Indian Mutiny, and were sometimes carried long distances; and this example recalls the suggestion which I have made about the nature of the Tekmor in *Studies in the History and Art of the Eastern Provinces*, p. 349.

[1] *Studies in the History of the Eastern Provinces*, pp. 312 f., 348 ff., 358.

V

THE WORSHIP OF THE VIRGIN MARY
AT EPHESUS

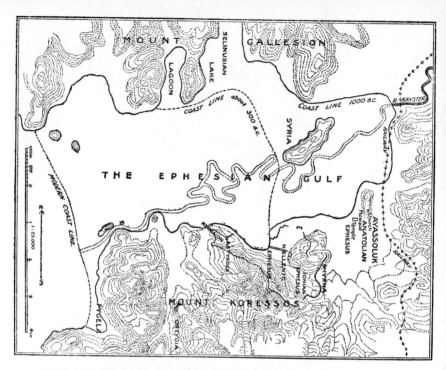

THE PANAGIA KAPULU.

The Panagia Kapulu and the Plain of Ephesus.

V

THE WORSHIP OF THE VIRGIN MARY AT EPHESUS

I. THE HOUSE OF THE VIRGIN

THE recent discovery of the so-called House of the Virgin at Ephesus, where the mother of the Saviour spent the latter part of her life, and where she died and was buried, forms a curious and interesting episode in the history of religion—not indeed the history of the Christian religion, for it hardly touches even the fringe thereof, but certainly the history of Anatolian religion or religiosity. Briefly put, the story is that an uneducated woman in a German convent saw in a vision the place in the hills south of Ephesus where the Virgin Mary had lived, and described it in detail, immediately after she had the vision; that her vision was printed and published in Germany; that after the lapse of fifty years the book came in 1890 into the hands of some Roman Catholics in Smyrna, by whom the trustworthiness of the vision was keenly discussed; that a priest in Smyrna, who took a leading part in controverting the authority of the vision, made a journey into the mountains in order to prove by actual exploration that no such House existed; that on the third day of continuous search in the rugged unknown mountains, on Wednesday, 29th July, 1891 (the Feast of St. Martha), he found the House exactly as it was described in the published account of the vision, some miles south of Ephesus, amid surroundings which were also accurately described therein ; and that he returned to Smyrna convinced of the truth against his previous judgment. A Roman Catholic festival has since the discovery been arranged and celebrated annually at the holy spot. Though the justifiability of this festival is warmly disputed by other Catholics outside of the neighbourhood of Smyrna and Ephesus, it may perhaps gradually make its way to general recognition and ultimately receive official authorisation.

What seems to be the most real point of interest in this story is that through this strange and roundabout method the permanence of Anatolian religion has asserted itself. Those Catholics who maintain that this is the House of the Virgin have really restored the sanctity of a locality where the Virgin Mother was worshipped thousands of years before the Christian era, and have worked out in perfection a chapter in the localisation of Anatolian religion. We do not mean by this that there has been any deception in the gradual evolution of the " discovery ". When the story was first told to the present writer at Smyrna in 1901, the highest character was attributed by quite trustworthy and unprejudiced informants to the Catholic priest who finally made the discovery of the House. He was described as an engineer, a man of science and education, who had entered the priesthood in mature years after a life of activity and experience, and also as a man of honour and unimpeachable veracity; and his original attitude of scepticism and strong disapproval in face of the statements narrated in the vision, at the time when the book first became known in Smyrna, was said to have been a public and well-authenticated fact. There seems to be no reason (apart from the fixed resolve to disbelieve) for doubting his good faith and his change of opinion when he went and saw for himself.

Equally improbable is it to suppose that there can be any bad faith or deception in the earliest stages of the evolution of this modern legend. The earliest publication of the visions of the German nun, Anne Catharine Emmerich, is not accessible to the present writer, and Professor A. Souter finds that it is not in the Bodleian Library; but a translation in English was published long before the actual discovery took place; and any person may with a little trouble satisfy himself of the existence of the printed record of this and other visions in the first half of the nineteenth century.[1]

Nor is it a reasonable supposition that Anne Catharine Emmerich had access to any careful description of the localities south of Ephesus. Those hills have been unexplored and unknown. Although the sacred place is not far from the site of the ancient city, yet the scanty population of the modern village Ayassoluk (Hagios Theológos, St. John) have no interest or knowledge in such matters; and western explorers had never penetrated into the hill

[1] The fundamental authority seems to be the publication of C. Brentano on the *Life of the Blessed Virgin founded on the Visions of A. C. Emmerich* (Cotta, Stuttgart, 1841). See also the *Life of A. C. E.* by Helen Ram (London, Burns & Oates, 1874); and also various works published after the "discovery," *Panaghia-Capouli, ou Maison de la Sainte Vierge près d'Éphèse* (Oudin, Paris and Poitiers, 1896); *Éphèse ou Jérusalem Tombeau de la Sainte Vierge (id., ib., 1897); The Death of the Blessed Virgin Mary and her Assumption into Heaven*, from the Meditations of A. C. E.: translated from the French by Geo. Richardson (Duffy & Co., Dublin, 1897). I have seen only the third and fourth of these five books; also a Greek counterblast by Archdeacon Chrysostomos, printed at Athens and published at Smyrna in 1896, under the title of Καπουλῆ-Παναγία. I have visited Ephesus with a French translation of the first in my hands.

country, which was extremely dangerous as a resort of brigands until a quite recent date. Moreover, the nun is described as having had little education: she was the daughter of poor peasants of Westphalia, who is said to have had an aversion to reading, and rarely to have touched a book. Her visions, so far as we know them, confirm this account. They are the imaginings of a simple mind, trained in the popular Roman Catholic ideas and traditions about the Saints, Anna, Joachim, and the rest, and weaving slightly elaborated forms of the ordinary tales. There are also some evident traces of information gained from reading or hearing descriptions of Ephesus (as distinguished from the hills south of Ephesus), and this information is not always accurately worked up in the details.

One who was bent on finding deception in the incidents would seize on the circumstances in which the visions were committed to writing. The nun's fame came to the knowledge of the world when there appeared marks on her body like those on the body of the Saviour; and medical and ecclesiastical examination vindicated her personal character. Count Stolberg's letter to a friend, describing his visit to her, was printed, and attracted the attention of the poet Brentano. The latter went to see her for the first time on 24th September, 1818; and in subsequent visits he wrote down her visions, which he afterwards published. Probably the literary power of the amanuensis improved the literary quality of the visions; but we may justifiably refuse to think that Brentano invented anything, or made pure additions to the words of Anne. It is, however, true that a considerable interval elapsed between his hearing the visions from Anne and his publication of them. Anne died in 1824, and Brentano's book appeared only in

1841. But even those who would maintain that the visions are the highly idealised memory or the invention of Brentano, and not the imaginings of Anne, only put the difficulty one step away. They explain nothing. There is no reason to think that Brentano could have had access to any peculiar source of knowledge of Ephesian localities and mountains, from which he could learn anything important about the history of that nook among the hills during the Middle Ages.

The remarkable fact, quite inexplicable by the hypothesis of fraud or deliberate invention, remains that there is a sacred place where the House was discovered : it has been a sacred place, to which the Orthodox Greek peasants went on pilgrimage, throughout later Christian times : in the present article an attempt will be made to prove that it was a sacred place in the remote pre-Christian times. It seems a more credible thing that the vision of a secluded and imaginative maiden should have suggested the search and the discovery of this obscure locality than that the fanciful invention of a German poet should do so.

But it is really an unimportant detail whether the nun saw in her ecstatic meditation the House among the Ephesian hills (as it seems to us most probable that she did), or the poet invented the description by reconstructing into a poetic picture with happy power the elements which he had gained from reading and study. Either of these theories is almost equally remote from the one practical fact, *viz.*, the process whereby the unity of Ephesian religion worked itself out, turning to its own purposes certain Christian names and forms, and trampling under foot all the spirit of Christianity.

The brief reference to this subject in the present writer's

Letters to the Seven Churches of Asia, p. 218, has caused some inquiries, and this episode in the history of religion seems worthy of more careful and detailed study.

II. The Survival of Pagan Cults

The fundamental fact, *viz.*, the continuity of religious history in Asia Minor, is one which there is no need to prove. Yet it forms so remarkable a chapter in the history of religious ideas, that we may profitably give a sketch of the prominent facts.

The introduction of Christianity into the country broke the continuity for the moment. But the old religious feeling was not extirpated: it soon revived, and took up the struggle once more against its new rival. Step by step it conquered, and gradually destroyed the real quality of Christianity. The old local cults took on new and outwardly Christianised forms; names were changed, and outward appearance; a show of Christian character was assumed. The Iconoclasts resisted the revival for a time, but the new paganism was too strong for them. The deep-seated passion for art and beauty was entirely on the side of that Christianised paganism, into which the so-called Orthodox Church had degenerated; and architecture together with the painting of images (though not sculpture) was its chosen servant. Whereas the rhetorician Aristides in the second century had invoked in his sickness the guidance and healing power of Asklepios of Smyrna, the emperor John Vatatzes, in the thirteenth century, when he was afflicted by disease, went to invoke the Christ of Smyrna.[1]

[1] Ὅπως τῷ ἐκεῖσε προσκυνήσῃ Χριστῷ, *Acrop.*, p. 91. See *Histor. Geogr. of Asia Minor*, p. 116, *Church in R. Emp.*, p. 466. I know no other case in which the person of Christ is degraded into a mere local deity. As a general

The old Greek sailors and Roman merchants, when voyaging or about to voyage in the changeable weather of the Black Sea (where dangerous and sudden storms might occur at almost any season of the year and where there was no sure season of fair weather, such as could be calculated on with confidence in the Aegean or the Mediterranean), had appealed to Achilles Pontarches, the Lord of the Sea (Pontus), to protect and guide them. The sailors of the Christian period appealed to St. Phocas of Sinope for aid. Similarly the sailors of the Levant, who had formerly prayed to the Poseidon of Myra, afterwards invoked St. Nicholas of Myra.[1] There is little essential difference in religious feeling between the older practice and the new : paganism is only slightly disguised in these outwardly Christianised cults.

Examples might be multiplied. They occur in all parts of the country, as exploration enables us to gather some idea of the religious history of the different districts. Local variety is inevitably hostile to the Christian spirit, because Christianity is unity, and its essence lies in the common brotherly feeling of the scattered parts of a great single whole. In the centre of Cappadocia one of the greatest sanctuaries of the land was that of Zeus of Venasa (where the name Zeus is the Hellenisation of a native

rule, some saint takes the place of the old local impersonation of Divine power, and the figure of the Saviour stands apart on a higher plane; but here (and perhaps in other cases unobserved by me) the analogy of Asklepios the Saviour has been seductive. Zeus the Saviour would also be a tempting analogy.

[1] *St. Paul the Traveller* (1895), p. 298. Add to the remarks there given a reference to *Mélanges Perrot* (1902), p. 25, where M. Bourguet remarks that the existence of a Church of St. Nicholas at Castri, the ancient Delphi, would alone have been a sufficient proof that Poseidon had a worship there in old time, but that now epigraphic proof has been discovered of the existence of a shrine of Poseidon called Poteidanion.

Cappadocian divine idea); his annual progress through his own country was one of the greatest festivals of the year; and it may be taken for granted that in the usual Anatolian style the chief priest wore the dress and even bore the name of the god. In the fourth century, when we find that a Christian deacon at Venasa takes the leading part in a festival of somewhat orgiastic character accompanied by a dancing chorus of women celebrants, and that this leader does not appear in his own character, but wears the dress and plays the part of the Patriarch, we recognise the old pagan elements in a slightly varied garb. This particular manifestation of the reviving paganism was put down by the strict puritan spirit of Basil the Great; but it was rare that such tendencies, which broke out broadcast over the land, found a champion of Christian purity to resist them. The feeling of the mass of the Cappadocian Christians seems rather to have been against Basil in this case, though his energy and intense fervour of belief, combined with his authority as supreme bishop of the province, swept away all opposition, and converted lukewarm friends or even opponents into his agents and servants in resisting the new paganism.[1]

On the frontier of Pisidia and Phrygia there is a fine fountain of cold water beside the village of Yassi-Euren. The village is purely Mohammedan; but the Christians once a year come on pilgrimage to it as a sacred fountain, or Ayasma, and this Christian name is applied to it even by the Mohammedan villagers. Finding there a Latin inscription dedicated to Hercules Restitutor, we cannot doubt that Hercules (who is often known as the god of

---

[1] On the whole episode see *The Church in the Roman Empire*, chap. xviii., p. 443 ff.

medicinal, and especially of hot, springs) was regarded as the Divine power who restored health to the sick by means of this healing spring, Hercules being, of course, merely a Latinised expression for the native Anatolian god of the healing power. Article VI. gives other cases.

Frequently the same saint is, through some natural and obvious association, selected in widely different localities to be the Christian embodiment of a pagan deity. The choice of St. Nicholas at Delphi, already quoted, may be a case of transference and imitation. But the choice of St. Demetrios in place of the goddess Demeter in various parts of Greece was probably suggested separately and independently in several different places; and the cause must have been pure resemblance of name, since the sex differs and there is no other apparent correspondence. Moreover, in Anatolia, the Great Mother, the Meter, experiences the same transformation, and, beyond all doubt, the same reason caused the selection of this particular Christian substitute; thus, for example, the holy Phrygian city, Metropolis,[1] the city of the Mother goddess, was transformed into the Christian Demetrioupolis.

For a totally different reason the correspondence of the goddess Artemis to the Virgin Mary was equally striking and widely recognised. In both cases the virgin nature was a fundamental principle in the cult, and yet in both cases motherhood was an equally, if not more, deep-seated element of the worship on its mystic side. For reasons

[1] The proof seems now fairly complete and convincing that the site of this Metropolis was a few miles farther north than I formerly placed it. It was the city centre of the territory in which were the great monuments of early Phrygia, the tombs of Midas and the other kings of the archaic dynasty, the true metropolis of early Phrygia.

that have been fully explained often elsewhere[1] the Virgin Artemis was the divine mother and teacher and guide of her people. It will not be difficult to show that there was a similar thought underlying the worship of the Virgin in Anatolia.

The best authority for the early stage of the worship of the Virgin Mother of God at Ephesus is the Acts of the Council held there in A.D. 431 (on which see below, § iii.). A sermon delivered in A.D. 429 by Proclus, Bishop of Cyzicus, apparently at Constantinople, forms a sort of introduction to the Acts of the Council. The occasion and sacred ceremony at which the sermon was delivered is there formally entitled "The Panegyris of the Virgin" (παρθενικὴ πανήγυρις).

The subject of the sermon is "celebrating the glorification of the race of women"; it is "the glory of the Female,"[2] due to her "who was in due time Mother and Virgin". "Earth and Sea[3] do honour to the Virgin." "Let Nature skip in exultation: women are honoured. Let Humanity dance in chorus: virgins are glorified. The sacred Mother of God, Mary, has brought us here together." She is called, in terms hardly distinguishable from the language of paganism, "the fleece very pure, moist from the rain of heaven, through whose agency the Shepherd put on Him (the form and nature of) the sheep,[4] she who is slave and mother, virgin and heaven, the sole bridge by which God passes to men."

---

[1] E.g., Hastings' Dictionary, art. "Diana," and "Religion of Greece and Asia Minor".

[2] Τοῦ γένους τῶν γυναικῶν καύχημα τὸ τελούμενον and δόξα τοῦ θήλεος.

[3] Capitals are needed here to express the strong personification, which approximates to the pagan conception of Gaia and Thalassa as deities.

[4] Ὁ τοῦ ἐξ οὐρανῶν ὑετοῦ καθαρώτατος πόκος, ἐξ οὗ ὁ Ποιμὴν τὸ πρόβατον ἐνεδύσατο.

It seems impossible to mistake or to deny the meaning implied in this language. The Anatolian religious feeling desiderated some more clear and definite expression of an idea dear to it, beyond the expression which was otherwise contained in the rites and language of Christianity. That idea was the honour, the influence, the inevitableness in the world, of the female element in its double aspect of purity and motherhood. "Purity is the material,"[1] but purity that is perfected in maternity. The Virgin, the Mother, the purity of motherhood, was to the popular Anatolian religious sentiment the indispensable crown of the religious idea. This beautiful and remarkable sentiment shows on what a real and strong foundation the worship of the Virgin in Anatolia rested, and how the Iconoclast movement was weakened by its opposition to a deep-seated Anatolian sentiment. Perhaps in the West the worship of the Virgin rests on a different basis. So far as I am aware her character has been regarded in the West rather as a mere adjunct or preparation for the Divine nature of her Son, while in the Anatolian cult (if I am right) it has been looked at and glorified for its own sake and as an end in itself, as the Divine prototype of the nature and duty of womanhood in its most etherealised form.

It would be an interesting and useful task to investigate how far the view which was taken in the West can be traced as guiding the writings of the great writers and theologians who championed the worship of the Virgin in the Eastern Church. There was, certainly, a marked diversity in the East between the popular view and what may be called the sacerdotal view, held by the educated

[1] Ἔχει γὰρ ἀγνείας ὑπόθεσιν.

theologians. The former was much more frankly pagan.
The latter took on a superficial adaptation to Christian
doctrine, and for this purpose the person of Christ had to
be made the central, governing thought and the Mother
must be regarded only as subsidiary. But this subject lies
outside the scope of this article, and beyond the powers and
knowledge of the present writer. It may be added, however, that the divergence can probably be traced down to
the present day in the cult of the Virgin Mother at Ephesus.
The Greek sacerdotal view seems never to have been that
the Virgin Mary lived or died at Ephesus, though it recognised the holiness of the sacred place and regarded it as
specially devoted to the person of the Virgin and as a
special abode of her power. The popular view desired her
personal presence there during her life, and maintained in a
half-articulate fashion the idea that she came to Ephesus
and lived there and died there. The sacerdotal expression
seems in some cases to have shrunk from a frank and
pointed contradiction of the popular view, while it could
not formally declare it in its thoroughgoing form. In the
Acts of the Council of Ephesus this intermediate form of
expression seems to rule. As we shall see in § iii. there is
nothing said there which can be taken as proving that the
belief in the real living presence of the Virgin Mary at
Ephesus was held. But the champions of Mariolatry relied
on the popular support; and, in the Council which was
called to judge and condemn the views of Nestorius, the
opponent of Mariolatry, they were unwilling to say anything
that could be seized on by him and his followers as telling
against the worship of Mary, or that might tend to alienate
popular feeling.

    It is equally impossible to overlook the fact that something approximating to that idea of the sanctity and Divine authority of the maternal and the feminine element was peculiarly characteristic of Anatolian religion and society in all ages and variations of the common general type. The idea was not so beautifully expressed in the older religion; the ritual form was frequently allied to much that was ugly and repulsive; it was often perverted into a mere distortion of its original self. But in many cases these perversions allow the originally beautiful idea to shine through the ugliness that has enveloped it, and we can detect with considerable probability that the ugliness is due, at least in part, to degradation and degeneration. The article "Diana of the Ephesians," in Hastings' *Dictionary of the Bible*, suffers from the failure to distinguish between earlier and later elements in the Anatolian ritual; the writer attained to a clearer conception of the subject in preparing the article in the same work on the "Religion of Greece and Asia Minor," though even there it is not expressed with sufficient precision and definiteness.

Closely connected with this fundamental characteristic in Anatolian religion is the remarkable prominence of the female in the political and social life of the country. Many of the best attested cases of *Mutter-recht* in ancient history belong to Asia Minor. Even under the Roman rule (when Western ideas, springing from war, conquest, and the reign of violence and brute strength were dominant), the large number of women mentioned as magistrates and officials, even in the most Hellenised and Romanised cities of the whole country, strikes every student of the ancient monuments as an unusual feature. It can hardly be explained except through the power of that old native belief and respect for the mother and the teacher. The Mother-

Goddess was merely the religious prototype and guarantee and enforcement of the social custom.[1]

An indubitable example of the Virgin Artemis transformed into the Christian Mother of God is found at the northern end of the great double lake, called Limnai in ancient times, and now known by two names for the two parts, Hoiran-Göl and Egerdir-Göl. Near the north-eastern corner of the lakes there is still said to be a sacred place of the Christians, to which they come on pilgrimage from a distance, though there is no Christian settled population nearer than Olu-Borlu (the ancient Apollonia). A large body of inscriptions has been collected from the neighbourhood, showing that there was here a peculiar worship of the goddess Artemis, which preserved the native Anatolian character unimpaired through the Greek and Roman periods, and to which strangers came from great distances.

Our view is that the similar Virgin Artemis of Ephesus, who in the mystic ritual was set before her worshippers as the mother, nurse, governor and leader of her swarming people, the great Queen-Bee, was transformed into the Ephesian Mother of God ; and that the same change was made independently all over the Anatolian land. She is shown in Greek and Anatolian ideals on and facing p. 160.

But the question may be asked whether the view advocated in this article is not prejudiced and one-sided. Are we not advocating too strongly the Anatolian element and neglecting the possibility of development within the bounds

---

[1] A young French scholar, who collected with much diligence from inscriptions examples of the custom surviving in the Roman time, advanced the theory as an explanation that these magistrates were rich women whom the people wanted to wheedle out of their money ; P. Paris *Quatenus feminae in Asia Minore r. p. attigerint:*

of Christianity? The dogmatic side may safely be left to others. There are plenty of able advocates always ready to discuss matters of dogma and systematic theology, and the present writer never has presumed to state an opinion on such lofty matters. But there are some historical points which may be briefly noticed in the following § iii.

As I sit writing these lines and looking out over the site of the Temple of the Ephesian goddess, I have before me a small terra-cotta image which was found in the excavations now going on amid the ruins of that famous Temple. This statuette, which is given below, p. 160, represents the goddess sitting and holding an infant in her arms. This rather rudely formed expression of popular belief was taken at the first moment of discovery by some of those who saw it as a mediæval image of the Madonna and Child, though more careful contemplation showed that it must have been made several centuries before the time of Christ. It is a complete proof, in its startling resemblance to the later Christian representation, of the perfect continuity of Anatolian religious sentiment amid outward differences.

There is, therefore, in this popular tendency a real cause, continuously and effectively operative, in many, doubtless in all, parts of the Anatolian country. It was strenuously opposed by a party in the Church. The conflict between the two opinions lasted for many centuries; but finally the popular opinion was victorious and established itself as the "Orthodox" principle, while the more purely Christian opinion became the "heretical" view and its supporters were proscribed and persecuted; and the division seriously weakened the Christian Empire in its struggle against Mohammedanism.

The view which this paper is intended to support is that

the establishment of the cult of the Virgin Mother of God at Ephesus is a critical, epoch-making date in the development of Byzantine government and religion. The whole process by which it was established is an important page in the history of the Empire. Ephesus, which had long been the champion of a purer faith [1] and the touchstone of error, as both John and Ignatius emphatically declare, was now made the stronghold of an Anatolian development, a recrudescence of the old religion of the Divine Mother.

III. EARLY WORSHIP OF THE MOTHER OF GOD IN EPHESUS [2]

The Ephesian tradition has all the appearance of being a popular growth, frowned on at first by the Church, and never fully and cordially accepted, but only permitted as a concession to popular feeling. The Orthodox Church gained the general support of the populace in the fifth century by tacitly (or even sometimes openly) permitting the reinvigoration of the old paganism under outwardly Christianised forms, freed from the most debasing elements and accretions which were formerly attached to it. The views of the people about the world and the life of man and the constitution of society were dominated by certain ideas and principles, which had been wrought into form by the experience of many generations and thus had sunk deep into, and almost constituted the fabric of, their minds. In the old pagan religion those ideas were envisaged and ex-

---

[1] *Letters to the Seven Churches*, pp. 239-242.

[2] I am indebted to my friend and old pupil, Professor A. Souter of Mansfield College, for much help and all the quotations which are here printed. The article had to be written far from books during the journey, in the course of which I visited Ephesus at the beginning of May, 1905.

pressed to them as gods and guides of their life; and the Christianised people began to long once more for Divine figures which might impersonate to them those ideas. The Divine Mother, the God-Son, were ideas that came close to the popular nature and lay deep in the popular heart, and the purely Christian theology and ethics were too remote and incomprehensible to insufficiently educated minds. The old paganism, amid much that was ugly and hateful, had contained in its hieratic forms much of the gradually elaborated wisdom of the race. The rules of worship and ritual were the rules of useful practical life and conduct in the family and society. The ugliest part was due to degeneration and degradation.[1] The earlier steps in this recrudescence of pagan ideas in the Christian Church of Asia (a growth which was vainly, and not always wisely, resisted by the various Iconoclastic[2] sects) cannot now be traced. In the fifth century the traces become clear and evident: in the fourth century they can be guessed.

The oldest allusion to the worship of the Virgin Mary at Ephesus as already a popular cult (perhaps the earliest[3] in the whole of Anatolia) is contained in the Acts of the Council or Synod which met at Ephesus in A.D. 431.[4] The sermon, which had been preached by Proclus, Bishop of

---

[1] This is a brief, and therefore too dogmatic and harsh, *résumé* of the thesis which was gradually worked out in the process of writing the article on " Religion of Greece and Asia Minor " in Hastings' *Dictionary*, vol. v.

[2] The term " Iconoclastic " is used here generically.

[3] The allusion in the epitaph of Avircius Marcellus (St. Abercius), *c.* A.D. 192, shows great respect for her, and places her relation to Jesus among the most sacred and fundamental articles of the Christian faith, without the slightest trace of worship; but that stage is already clearly marked in the letters of Ignatius.

[4] Several extracts from the exordium of this sermon have been quoted on page 134 f.; for the complete sermon, see Migne, *P. G.*, lxv., p. 680 ff.

Cyzicus, in 429, is incorporated in the record of the Council ;
and this fact seems to show that the proceedings and the
sermon must be read in the light which each throws on the
other. The sermon was considered to be a fair statement
of the view which the Council regarded as right ; and thus
we must interpret the formal business of the Synod, which
was really a protest by the "Orthodox" party against the
depreciation of the worship of the Virgin Mother of God by
Nestorius and his followers. The circumstances in which
the Synod was called are as follows :—

Theodosius II. had summoned Nestorius from Syrian
Antioch to be patriarch of Constantinople; and he brought
with him Anastasius, a presbyter of Antioch. The latter
in a sermon had declared that the title "Mother of God"
ought not to be applied to Mary, inasmuch as God cannot
be born of woman; Mary was the mother only of the man
Jesus, while the Divine Jesus was the Son of God alone.
Mary, as he said, was only the mother of Christ, not Mother
of God (Christotokos, not Theotokos). The orthodox majority of the Church rose in horror against this duplication
of the person of Christ, and condemned the authors at the
Council of Ephesus. Along with this condemnation it was
inevitable that the actual worship of the Virgin Mother of
God (as she was henceforward officially called) received new
strength in the popular mind, as if it had been now formally
sanctioned.

The Council assembled at Ephesus "in the most holy
church which is called Maria". The very existence of a
church bearing such a name is in itself proof that a strong
idea of the divinity of the Virgin Mother of the Saviour
had already fixed itself in the popular mind at Ephesus.

The name applied to the church called "Maria" was

apparently popular rather than official. The expression used strongly indicates this;[1] and no other origin for the name seems possible. The church was in A.D. 431 not "the church of Maria," or "the church dedicated to Maria"; it was "the church called Maria". Probably the full expression of the meaning of the Greek would be "the most holy church (of God), which bears the name Maria". Popular feeling gave the name, and attached its own character to the worship; but the official or sacerdotal view did not formally approve this, though it went a long way in making concession to it, and in practice apparently gave almost full freedom to it. Where a strong popular feeling is concerned, the Council which condemned the one great opponent of that feeling, and formally authorised, as binding on all Christians, one expression of that feeling (*viz.*, the expression "Mother of God") must be regarded as tacitly permitting those other expressions, public at the time, which it did not condemn. It is of course certain that afterwards the dedication to the Virgin Mary of this and other churches was fully accepted by the priesthood and by most of the Church leaders.

The opinion has been expressed by the present writer in an article on Ephesus (Hastings' *Dictionary of the Bible*, vol. i.) that the "church called Maria" was the double church whose remains must be familiar to all visitors to the ruins, as they form one of the loftiest and most imposing buildings on the site. The recent Austrian excavations have confirmed this opinion. The eastern church in this connected pair, which is the later of the two, has been found to be of the age of Justinian; the older western half was almost certainly in existence before 431, and was dedicated to

[1] ἐν τῇ ἁγιωτάτῃ ἐκκλησίᾳ τῇ καλουμένῃ Μαρίᾳ.

the Virgin, and Mr. Heberdey, the distinguished director of the Austrian enterprise, considers it to be the church in which the Council was held. It remains uncertain as yet whether the eastern church also was dedicated to her.

It was only during the fourth century that the leaders or the great writers of the Christian Church seem to have begun to interest themselves in the story of the life of the Virgin Mary for her own sake. Epiphanius about A.D. 375 remarks that the Scriptures say nothing about the death of the Virgin, whether she died or not, whether she was buried or not, and that in the Scriptures there is no authority for the opinion that when John went away into (the Province) Asia, he took her with him.[1]

But from these words of Epiphanius it seems clear and certain that popular tradition had already before his time been busy with her later life. Starting from the one recorded fact that she remained until her death under the care and keeping of St. John, it had woven into this something in the way of an account of her death, and the circumstances connected with it and with the burial. Doubtless it had interwoven some marvellous incidents in the story; and it would be possible to guess how these originated and were gradually elaborated. But the one thing that concerns our purpose is that Epiphanius must have known of the story that the Virgin had gone with St. John to Ephesus; otherwise he would not have taken the trouble to deny that it rested on any Scriptural foundation.

---

[1] Epiph. *adv. Haer.* III., 1, haer. 78, § 11 (Migne, *P. G.*, xlii., 716B): 'Αλλὰ καὶ εἰ δοκοῦσί τινες ἐσφάλθαι, ζητήσωσι τὰ ἴχνη τῶν γραφῶν, καὶ εὕρωσιν ἂν οὔτε θάνατον Μαρίας, οὔτε εἰ τέθνηκεν, οὔτε εἰ μὴ τέθνηκεν, οὔτε εἰ τέθαπται, οὔτε εἰ μὴ τέθαπται. Καίτοι γε τοῦ Ἰωάννου περὶ τὴν Ἀσίαν ἐνστειλαμένου τὴν πορείαν, καὶ οὐδαμοῦ λέγει ὅτι ἐπηγάγετο μεθ' ἑαυτοῦ τὴν ἁγίαν παρθένον κ.τ.λ.

The popular tradition in Asia is therefore as old at least as the middle of the fourth century. And, whereas in the fifth century the Church leaders (as we have already seen) in the time of the Council of Ephesus, A.D. 431, refrained from either contradicting or confirming expressly the popular Ephesian belief, Epiphanius in the fourth century points out that this and all other stories about her death and burial were devoid of authoritative foundation. We are in presence of a popular belief, disclaimed and set aside as valueless in the fourth century, but treated with more careful respect, though not confirmed, in the fifth century. The sacerdotal teaching could not admit the popular belief as authoritative, but it tacitly permitted the belief to reign in the popular mind, and to govern popular action and religion, in the same way as it gradually came to acquiesce, without either affirmation or denial, in most of the popular local cults of saints.

This Ephesian tradition has continued in effective operation to the present day. When the Roman Catholic discoverers of the " House " of the Virgin began to inquire into the situation, they found that the Greeks of Kirkindje, a village among the hills south-east of Ephesus, to which the remnants of the Christian population are said to have retired in the middle ages, regarded the place as sacred, called it Panagia Kapulu,[1] " the All Holy (Virgin) of the Door," and held certain annual ceremonies there. Since the Catholics made the discovery, they have bought a large tract of ground round the ruin; and the Greeks have in some degree lost their devotion to the spot. An English lady, however, who speaks Greek as fluently as she does English, told me that she asked the Greek servant who guided her to the Panagia Kapulu whether the Orthodox

[1] Kapulu is a Turkish word, "possessed of or connected with a door ".

IV. THE VISION OF ANNE CATHARINE EMMERICH

Now arises the question how far any value as evidence can be set on the vision of the German nun, Anne Catharine Emmerich. In the first place, I should repeat what was already stated in Section I. of this article, that it seems unjustifiable to throw doubt on the honest intentions both of the seer and of the reporter, the poet Brentano. After fully weighing all the evidence, I do not entertain the smallest doubt that she saw those visions or dreams, and that they have been faithfully reported to us. The visions are exactly what a nun in such surroundings as Anne Catharine's would think, and ought to think. But they lie almost wholly within the narrowest circle of commonplace mediæval pseudo-legend, hardly worthy to be called legendary, because it is all so artificial.

The experience of a foreign friend, whose name (if I were free to mention it) would be a certificate of wide reading and literary power, illustrates the probable bent of Anne Catharine's mind. His family travelled for some time in the company of a lady educated in a convent : her conversation generally showed quite remarkable lack of knowledge or interest, but in picture-galleries she displayed an equally remarkable familiarity with lives of the saints, identifying at a glance every picture relating to them, telling the story connected with each sacred picture in the fullest detail, and explaining numerous little points about the symbolism, which might escape even fairly well-informed observers.

In hurriedly reading over the visions about the life of the Virgin in a French translation, while I was visiting Ephesus in the beginning of May, 1905, I have observed only two points which seem to lie outside of this narrow circle.

One of these is the date of the birth of Christ. It is not fixed at Christmas, but on the 24th November. I do not know how far this divergence may be connected with any stories or legends likely to be within the ordinary circle of knowledge of a German nun, of humble origin and without any special education, at the beginning of the nineteenth century. But it seems not at all impossible or improbable that she may have come in contact with educated persons, or may have learned in other ways so much of the results of historical investigation as to hear that there is no substantial foundation for the common ceremonial practice of celebrating the birth of Christ at the end of December.

The other and by far the most interesting passage in the whole book is the minutely detailed account of the home of the Virgin and the small Christian settlement in the neighbourhood of Ephesus. It is worth quotation in full.

"After the Ascension of our Lord Jesus Christ, Mary lived three years on Sion, three years at Bethany, and nine years at Ephesus, to which place John had conducted her shortly after the Jews had exposed Lazarus and his sisters on the sea.

"Mary did not live exactly at Ephesus, but in the environs, where were settled already many women who were her friends. Her dwelling was situated three leagues and a half from Ephesus, on a mountain which was seen to the left in coming from Jerusalem, and which rapidly descended towards Ephesus—coming from the south-east the city was seen as if altogether at the foot of a mountain, but it is seen to extend all round as you continue to advance. Near Ephesus there are grand avenues of trees, under which the yellow fruits are lying on the ground. A little to the south, narrow paths lead to an eminence covered with wild plants. There is seen an undulating plain covered with vegetation, which has a circuit of half a league ; it is there that this settlement was made. It is a solitary country, with many small, agreeable and fertile elevations, and some grottoes hollowed in the rock, in the midst of little sandy places. The country is rough without being barren ; there are here and there a number of trees of pyramidal form with smooth trunks, whose branches overshadow a large space.

"When St. John conducted to this spot the Blessed Virgin, for whom he had already erected a house, some Christian families and many holy women were already residing in this country. They were living, some under tents, others in caves, which they had rendered habitable by the aid of carpentry and wainscoting. They had come here before the persecution had burst forth with full force. As they took advantage of the caves which they found there, and of the facilities which the nature of the places offered, their dwellings were real hermitages, often separated a quarter of a league from each other; and this kind of colony presented the appearance of a village with its houses scattered at a considerable distance from each other. Mary's house stood by itself, and was constructed of stone. At some distance behind the house the land rises and proceeds across the rocks to the highest point of the mountain, from the top of which, over the small elevations and trees, the city of Ephesus is visible, [and the sea] with its numerous islands. The place is nearer the sea than Ephesus itself, which lies at some distance. The country is solitary and little frequented. In the neighbourhood was a castle, occupied, if I mistake not, by a deposed king. St. John visited him frequently, and converted him. This place became, later on, a bishopric. Between this dwelling of the Blessed Virgin and Ephesus a river flowed, winding in and out with innumerable turnings."[1]

What value can be set upon this extremely interesting passage?

It is unnecessary to do more than mention the impossibility of the assumption made in the vision that St. John, going to Ephesus in the sixth year after the Crucifixion, could have found there already a Christian community. This is as absurd as the statement (made at a later point in the book) that before the Virgin's death, less than fifteen years after the Crucifixion, Thomas had already evangelised India and Bactria, Philip Egypt, James Spain, etc. But it might quite fairly and reasonably be argued by any defender of the general trustworthiness of the nun's visions, that, in regard to numbers and estimates of time and distance, her evidence stands on a less satisfactory basis than in other more important respects. Her statements of distance would be regarded by such a champion as only conjectural estimates according to the appearance presented in her vision, and therefore standing, so to say, outside the vision, as her own opinion about what she saw. The lapse of years was expressed as part of the visions: she saw the numbers

---

[1] *The Death of the Blessed Mary, and Her Assumption into Heaven, containing a Description of Her House at Ephesus, recently discovered. From the Meditations of Anne Catharine Emmerich. Translated from the French.* By George Richardson (Dublin: Duffy & Co., 1897), pp. 1-4. When I read over this extract from the English translation, as it was inserted in the proof sheets by the care of Mr. Souter, I feel that it gives a different impression from the French translation, which I read at Ephesus. I have not the opportunity of comparing the two; but the English (published after the discovery of the House) strikes me as perhaps more in accordance with the localities than the French (published before) seemed to be when I was reading it at Ephesus; but I may be wronging the translator.

of years presented to her eyes in Roman figures,[1] and in relating what she had seen she stated that she saw a V with a I beside it which she understood to mean six, *viz.*, the number of years that the Virgin remained in (or near) Jerusalem after the Crucifixion. Such a defender might point out that the Virgin is described as being in extreme old age, and yet the years of her life are stated as sixty-four; and he might fairly argue that a healthy Jewess of sixty has not the appearance or feebleness of extreme age, and that the numbers must therefore be regarded on a secondary plane, so that St. John's journey to Ephesus with her can be placed at a reasonable and possible date, later than the formation of a Christian Church in Ephesus, and probably even later than the death of St. Paul, when the Virgin Mary was a very old woman, over ninety years of age.

That seems a quite fair method of interpretation; but though it avoids chronological difficulties, it leaves others untouched. The idyllic picture of the Christians living in a little community of their own away from the city, apart from the ways of men, separate from their pagan fellow-townsmen, is the dream that springs from a mind moulded by monastic habits and ideas, but is as unlike as can be to the historic facts. Had Christianity begun by retiring out of the world, it would never have conquered the world. Every inquirer into history knows that the Christians of that first period were involved in the most strenuous and crowded struggle of life. The nun's vision is a picture of

---

[1] The editor of the French translation mentions this in a footnote, and explains the discrepancy between two statements about the time of the Virgin's residence at Jerusalem (which is given as four years in one passage, and six in another) as due to Anne Catharine's unfamiliarity with Roman symbols, which caused her to confuse between iv. and vi.

quiet seclusion and peace. This alone is sufficient to show that the vision has a purely subjective origin.

Still more evident is the nature of the vision, when we consider the localities described. The minuteness of detail with which the description is given stands in remarkable contrast to the rest of the book. There is a clear conception of the approach from Jerusalem (through the Mæander valley and) across the mountains, so as to approach Ephesus from the south-east. The view of the city, as one comes near it, is very beautiful; and the description given in the vision, though rather general in its character, is quite good, except in three important respects.[1]

In the first place, at a distance of three leagues and a half no view of the city can possibly be got; the road at that point is still entirely secluded among the mountains : only when one comes within about two or three miles of the south-eastern gate of Ephesus, the Magnesian Gate, does the city come into view.

In the second place, there is not at any point on the road, or near it on the left, this complete view of the city as a whole. From any such point considerable part of the city is hidden behind Mount Pion. This complete view can be obtained only by approaching from the north, as modern travellers and tourists do in almost every case.

In the third place, a winding river is described as running between the approaching travellers and the city. This winding river is the Cayster, now called the Menderez (*i.e.,* Mæander). Its course is quite as circuitous and tortuous as the vision represents it; but it is hardly visible from the south-eastern road, or from a point on the left hand of that

---

[1] The plan of Ephesus in the writer's *Letters to the Seven Churches* is compared with a map of Kapulu Panagia on p. 124.

PLATE I.

FIG. 1.—Ephesus, looking from the Top of the Theatre (in West Side of Mount Pion) looking down the Street to the City Harbour and Hill of St. Paul. On the left is Mount Coressus, behind which lies the Panagia Kapulu (Mr. D. G. Hogarth).

To face p. 152.

road. It is only as one comes from the north that this river and its wanderings form so striking a part of the scene; and further, one must come over the higher ground in order to get the view perfectly. Moreover, this mæandering river runs on the north side of the city; so that only to the traveller coming from the north does it flow between him and the city.

In the fourth place there are not at the present day numerous islands[1] visible from the peak above Kapulu Panagia. Samos shuts out the view of those beyond it. But in ancient times there were several islets in the gulf of Ephesus (which is now silted up and converted into solid land or marsh), so that the ancient state of things was less unfavourable to the nun's description than the modern state is. It is however uncertain whether the islets in the gulf would be visible from the peak: this point has never been investigated.

It seemed beyond doubt or question to me, as I sat in the Ephesian plain and read the description, that the whole has taken its origin from a description given by some traveller or tourist of his approach to Ephesus. How this came to Anne Catharine's knowledge is uncertain; but there seems no difficulty in supposing that some traveller or some reader of a printed description had talked to her (she is said not to have been a reader); and the narrative had sunk into her mind and moulded quite unconsciously the vision that she saw. Only the appearance from a rising-ground on the north is inaccurately represented as seen by the traveller coming from the south-east. There is, thus, a curious mixture of accuracy and inaccuracy. St. John approaches, as he would in fact do, from the south-

[1] The expression in the French translation, I think, is *innombrables*.

east; but he sees the view that would be presented to a traveller coming from the north, if he diverged a little from the low road to a rising-ground, or if he approached by a short path across the hills.

Again, it is a detail which at first sight seems very impressive that the travellers approaching from the south-east diverged a little from the road towards the left and there found the small Christian community. In such a situation, some miles off to the left of that road, the so-called " House of the Virgin " was found by the Catholic explorers. This House lies among the mountains in a secluded glen, divided by the high ridge of Mount Coressus from the city; and beyond doubt no modern traveller had ever penetrated into those mountains away from the regular paths, until the Catholic explorers went to seek for the House and found it beside the spring.

It is also a striking point that there is a peak over the House, and that this peak is nearer the sea than Ephesus is, just as the vision has it; but from the peak one sees (as I am informed by several visitors) only the site of the temple of Diana outside the city, together with the Magnesian Gate and the walls on the highest ridge of Coressus, while the city as a whole is hidden behind Coressus.

In short, the view of the city which is described in the vision is plainly and certainly the view got from a ledge or shelf on the hills that bound the valley, where they slope down towards the city and the plain, and not from a point shut off from most of the plain by a lofty ridge of mountains. A continuous slope with an uninterrupted view down over the city is described in the vision; and one could almost look to identify the shelf that is described, were it not that such a feature can be found in almost any similar sloping hillside.

It is needless to touch on the supposed correspondence between the shape and interior arrangements of the " House " and those described in the vision. To the nun it seemed clear that the Virgin must have lived and died in a building of the nature and shape of a church, having an apse : she had acquired sufficient knowledge of the form of the Eastern churches. It is certain that the mind of the person who saw those visions was fixed steadily on those subjects ; and I cannot but think that she must have often conversed and asked about Eastern places and things, and that from the little knowledge she thus acquired, combined with her training in the mediæval Western legends of the saints and the Holy Family, the visions gradually took their form without conscious effort on her part. But she had heard two descriptions of Ephesus, one as the city first appears to the tourist (who always approaches it from the north, as Smyrna is the harbour from which Ephesus is easily accessible) beyond a winding river, the other stating its relation to the road that comes from Jerusalem ; and these two descriptions have unconsciously welded themselves together in her fancy into a single picture.

V. CONCLUSION

We have thus arrived at the result, first, that the Ephesian belief as to the residence of the Virgin Mary in their city, though existing at least as early as the fourth century, rests on no recorded authority, but was a purely popular growth, and is therefore possessed of no more credibility than belongs to the numberless popular legends, which everywhere grow up in similar circumstances ; and, secondly, that the nun's vision, interesting as it is, furnishes no real evidence.

The Roman Catholic writer[1] of a book already quoted, *Panaghia-Capouli*, p. 90, while fully admitting that the entire body of Greek clerical opinion has been against that Ephesian tradition, argues that a tradition which persists in the popular mind through the centuries, in spite of the contrary teaching of the clergy, is likely to rest on a real foundation.

We can only repeat what has been shown in detail in Section II., that numberless examples can be quoted of the growth of such popular beliefs without any historical foundation. They spring from the nature of the human mind; and they prove only the vitality of the old religious ideas. Take an example which came to my knowledge after the former part of this paper was printed. Three or four miles south of Pisidian Antioch we found in a village cemetery an altar dedicated to the god Hermes. On the top of the altar there is a shallow circular depression, which must probably have been intended to hold liquid offerings poured on the altar, and which was evidently made when the altar was constructed and dedicated. A native of the village, who was standing by as we copied the inscription, told us that the stone was possessed of power, and that if any one who was sick came to it and drank of the water that gathered in the cup, he was cured forthwith of his sickness. This belief has lasted through the centuries; it has withstood the teaching and denunciation of Christians and Mohammedans alike; but it is not therefore possessed of any real foundation. It springs from the superstitious nature of

[1] Though it has no bearing on the question of credibility, it is right to guard against the impression that general Roman Catholic opinion is in favour of the Ephesian tradition. The ruling opinion in Roman Catholic circles is against it; but as a rule the Catholics of the Smyrna district favour it.

the popular mind, and the stubborn persistence of the old
beliefs. You may in outward appearance convert a people
to a new and higher faith; but if they are not educated up
to the level of intellectual and moral power which that
higher faith requires, the old ideas will persist in the popular
mind, all the stronger in proportion to the ignorance of
each individual; and those ideas will seize on and move the
people especially in cases of trouble and sickness and the
presence or dread of death.

Such is the nature of the Ephesian tradition. The
Virgin Mother in Ephesus had been worshipped from time
immemorial; and the people could not permanently give her
up. They required a substitute for her, and the Christian
Mother of God took her place, and dwelt beside her in the
hearts of the people. This belief soon created a locality for
itself, for the Anatolian religion always found a local home.
The home was marked out at Ortygia in the mountains on
the south of the Ephesian valley, where the pagan Virgin
Artemis was born, and where probably her original home
had been, until she as the great Queen-bee led her mourning
people to their new home in the valley by the shore of the
sea [1] and became the "goddess and mother and queen" of
Ephesus. The Christian worship of the Virgin Mother
seems to have originated at so early a period that it could
not establish itself directly on the home of the older Virgin
Artemis. It could only seek a neighbouring home in the
same hilly country a little farther eastwards. When this
home was found for the new belief, a sacred legend inevit-

---

[1] *Letters to the Seven Churches*, p. 217. On the map there Ortygia, which
lies really outside of the limits of the map, is indicated wrongly. It was
necessary to put in the name, but the actual locality is a little south-east
of the place where the name stands.

ably grew up around it according to the usual process in the popular religion of antiquity. The legend had to be adapted to the Christian history. It could not imitate exactly the pagan legend that the Virgin was born at Ortygia; but the belief that the Mother of God had lived in old age and died there, grew up and could readily be adapted to the record.

It will always remain a question, as to which opinions will differ widely, how far it is right or permissible to make concessions to so deep-seated a feeling as that belief must have been. On the one hand, a concession which takes the form of an unhistorical legend and a ceremonial attached to a false locality will meet with general disapproval. On the other hand, it seems certain that injudicious proselytising combined with wholesale condemnation and uprooting of popular beliefs has often done much harm in the history of Christianity. The growing experience and wisdom of primitive races wrought out certain rules of life, of sanitation, purity, consideration for the community, and many other steps in civilisation; and these rules were placed under the Divine guardianship, because there was no other way of enforcing them on all. Practical household wisdom was expressed in the form of a system of household religious rites. It is true that these rules were often widened by false analogy, and applied in ways that were needless and useless; but there remained in them the residuum of wisdom and usefulness.[1] It has often been an unwise and almost fatal error of Christian missionaries (an error recognised and regretted by many of them in recent time) to treat all these rules as superstitious and try to eradicate them before any

---

[1] See " Religion of Greece and Asia Minor " in Dr. Hastings' *Dictionary of the Bible*, v., 133 and *passim*. The process of degradation constantly came in to make these rules deteriorate, as is shown in that article.

system of habitual good conduct in society and ordinary life had been settled and rooted in the minds of proselytes.

That the belief in the Mother, and especially the Virgin Mother, as the teacher, guide and nourisher of her people, was capable of infinite expansion as a purifying and elevating principle, has been shown in Section I. That it has been of immense influence on Asia Minor is patent in the history of the country; even Turkish Conquest, though it attained its purposes by general massacre, especially of the male population, has not wholly eradicated it. That it is a principle which belongs to a settled and peaceful age and state of society, and that it must be weakened in a state of war and disorder, is evident in itself, and has been shown in detail elsewhere.[1]

The vision of the nun in Westphalia and the rediscovery of the House of the Virgin form simply an episode in the history of that religious principle and a proof of its vitality.

[1] See the article quoted in the preceding footnote.

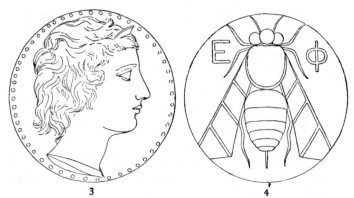

3   4

The Hellenic Virgin Goddess of Ephesus and the Anatolian Mother of
Ephesus, the Queen-Bee.

5   6

The Anatolian Mother of Ephesus, half anthropomorphized.

PLATE II.

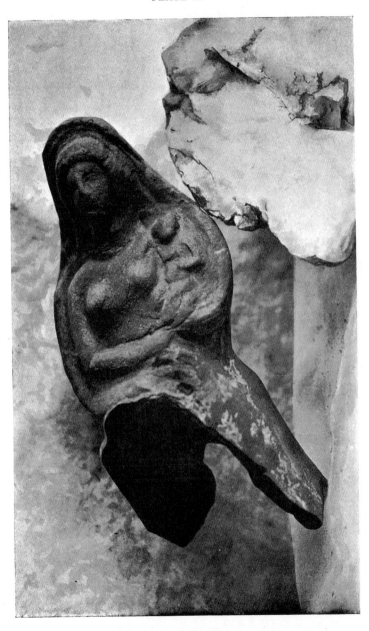

FIG. 2.—The Mother-Goddess of Ephesus Anthropomorphized
(Mr. A. E. Henderson).

To face p. 160.　　　　　　　　　　*See p.* 159.

VI

THE PERMANENCE OF RELIGION AT HOLY PLACES IN WESTERN ASIA

Tomb of a Christian Virgin of the Third Century (see p. 298).

VI

THE PERMANENCE OF RELIGION AT HOLY PLACES IN WESTERN ASIA

IN the preceding article in this volume, describing the origin of the Ephesian cult of the Mother of God, the permanent attachment of religious awe to special localities was briefly mentioned. In that cult we found a survival or revival of the old paganism of Ephesus, *viz.*, the worship of the Virgin Mother of Artemis. The persistence of those ancient beliefs and rites at the chief centres of paganism exercised so profound an influence on the history of Christianity in Asia Minor, that it is well to give a more detailed account of the facts, though even this account can only be a brief survey of a few examples selected almost by chance out of the innumerable cases which occur in all parts of the country. I shall take as the foundation of this article a paper read to the Oriental Congress held at London in autumn, 1902, and buried in the Transactions of the Congress, developing and improving the ideas expressed in that paper, and enlarging the number of examples.

The strength of the old pagan beliefs did not escape the attention of the Apostle Paul ; and his views on the subject affected his action as a missionary in the cities of Asia Minor, and can be traced in his letters. On the one hand, as the present writer has several times tried to prove, he regarded the Anatolian superstition as a more direct and

dangerous enemy than the Greek.   Amid the many enemies
against which he had to contend, some were less dangerous
than others.   Sophia, the Greek philosophy, seemed to Paul
much less dangerous than Greek religion ; it was rather, in
a way, a rival erring on false lines than an enemy ; and at
first the outer world regarded the doctrine of Paul as simply
one form of Græco-Oriental philosophy, and listened to it
with a certain degree of tolerance on that understanding.
Greek religion, in its turn, hateful as was its careless poly-
theism, was not nearly so dangerous as the Phrygian devotion and enthusiasm.

On the other hand, Paul saw also that there was, or
rather had originally been, an element of truth and real
perception of the Divine nature.   The view which he entertained, and states clearly in his letter to the Romans, is that
there existed originally in the world a certain degree of
knowledge about God and His character and His relation
to mankind ; but the deliberate action of man had vitiated
this fair beginning ; and the reason lay in idolatry.   This
cause obscures the first good ideas as to the nature of God ;
and thus the Divine Being is assimilated to and represented
by images in the shape of man who is mortal, and birds and
quadrupeds and reptiles.   In idolatrous worship a necessary
and invariable accompaniment was immorality, which goes
on increasing from bad to worse in physical passions, and
thus corrupts the whole nature and character of man
(Rom. i. 19 ff.).

But men are never so utterly corrupt that a return to
truth is impossible.   If they only wish it, they can choose
the good and refuse the evil (Rom. ii. 14 f.).   The Gentiles
have not the Law revealed to the Jews, but some of them
through their better nature act naturally according to the

Law, and are a Law unto themselves: the practical effect of the Law is seen in their life, because it has been by nature written in their hearts and they have a natural sense of the distinction between right and wrong, between good and evil; and their conscience works in harmony with this natural Law in their hearts, prompting them to choose the right action and making them conscious of wrong if they choose wrong action. This beginning of right never fails utterly in human nature, but it is made faint and obscure by wrong-doing, when men deliberately choose the evil and will not listen to the voice of God in their hearts.

Yet even at the worst there remains in the most corrupted man a sense that out of this evil good will come. We all are in some degree aware that evil is wrong, because it is painful, and the pain is the preparation for the birth of better things (Rom. viii. 19-22). The eager watching expectancy of the universe [man and nature alike, as of a runner with his eye fixed on the goal], waits for the revealing of the sons of God. For the creation was subjected to vanity, not of its own will, but by reason of man who subjected it, and in this subjection there arises a hope that the creation itself also shall be delivered from the bondage of corruption, so as to attain unto the liberty of the glory of the children of God. For we know that the whole creation in all its parts is groaning in the birth-pangs from which shall emerge a better condition, and we also who are Christians and have already within ourselves the first practical effects of the Spirit's action, are still in the pain and hope of the nascent redemption.

This remarkable philosophic theory of Paul's bursts the bonds of the narrower Judaism. It is not inconsistent with the best side of Hebrew thought and prophecy; but it was utterly and absolutely inconsistent with the practical facts of the narrower Judaism in his time. The man who thought thus could not remain in permanent harmony with the party in Jerusalem which was inexorably opposed to the early followers of Christ. It was only in maturer years that Paul became fully and clearly conscious of this truth; but as he became able to express it clearly to himself and to others, he also became conscious that it had been implicit from the beginning in his early thought. He had it in his nature from birth. It was fostered and kept alive by the circumstances of his childhood. He had come in contact with pagans, and knew that they were not monsters (as they seemed to the Palestinian zealots), but human beings. He had been in such relations with them, that he felt it a duty to go and tell them of the truth which had been revealed (Rom. i. 14). He had learned by experience of the promptings to good, of the preference for the right, of self-blame for wrong-doing, which were clearly manifest in their nature. Doubtless, he had also been aware of that deep and eager longing for the coming of something better, of a new era, of a Saviour, of God incarnate in human form on the earth, which was so remarkable a feature in Roman life before and after his birth.[1]

Before glancing at the effect of the old paganism on the development of the Christian Church, it is well to point out that the influence is still effective down to the present day. The spirit of Mohammedanism is quite as inconsistent with and hostile to the pagan localisation of the Divine nature at particular places as Christianity is; but still it has been in practice very strongly influenced by that idea, and the ignorant Moslem peasantry are full of awe and respect

[1] Virgil, *Eclogue* 4.

both for Christian and for ancient pagan superstitions. A brief outline of the most striking classes of facts observable at the present day will set in a clearer light the strong pressure which popular ideas were continually exerting on the early Christian Church. In giving such an outline I know that it is dangerous for one who is not an Orientalist to write on the subject. I can merely set down what I have seen and heard among the peasantry, and describe the impression made on me by their own statement of their vague ideas.

In regard to their religious ideas, we begin by setting aside all that belongs strictly to Mohammedanism, all that necessarily arises from the fact that a number of Mohammedans, who live together in a particular town or village, are bound to carry out in common the ritual of their religion, *i.e.*, to erect a proper building, and to perform certain acts and prayers at regular intervals. Anything that can be sufficiently accounted for on that ground has no bearing on the present purpose. All that is beyond this is, strictly speaking, a deviation from, and even a violation of, the Mohammedan religion ; and therein lies its interest for us. Mohammedanism admits only a very few sacred localities —Mecca, Medina, Jerusalem. Possibly even the Sunni Mohammedans may allow one or two others, as the Shiya do, but I do not remember to have heard of them. But the actual belief of the peasantry of Asia Minor attaches sanctity to a vast number of localities, and to these our attention is now directed. Without laying down any universal principle, it will appear easily that in many cases the attachment of religious veneration to particular localities in Asia Minor has continued through all changes in the dominant religion of the country.

In the cases where this permanence of religious awe is certain, the sanctity has, of course, taken at the present day some new form, or been transferred from its original bearer to some Mohammedan or Turkish personage. Four kinds of cases may be distinguished.

1. The sanctity and awe gather round the person of some real character of Mohammedan history earlier than the Turkish period. The typical example is Seidi Ghazi (the Arab general Abd-Allah al Sayyid al Battal al Ghazi, the Lord the Wicked the Conqueror[1]), who was slain in the battle of Acroenos in A.D. 739, the first great victory which cheered the Byzantine Emperors in their attempt to stem the tide of Arab conquest. How this defeated Arab should have become the Turkish hero of the conquest of Asia Minor, after the country had for two centuries been untrod by a Mohammedan foot, is not explained satisfactorily by any of the modern writers, French and German, who have translated or described the Turkish romance relating the adventures of this stolen hero.[2]

Seid became one of the chief heroes of the Bektash

[1] I give the spelling and translation as a distinguished Semitic scholar gave them to me many years ago; but my friend Mr. Crowfoot writes to me from Khartoum suggesting that the first epithet is not the word meaning "wicked," but a very similar cognate word which means "hero". Seid, of course, is strictly a generic word, but it has in Turkey become a personal name. I find in my notes that Robertson Smith wrote to me, "Battal in old Arabic denotes rather prowess than wickedness".

[2] See Hermann Ethé, *Fahrten des Sayyid Batthal*, Leipzig, Brockhaus, 1871, and the review of this translation by Mohl, in *Journal Asiatique*, 1874, p. 70 ff. In the Turkish romance it is said that no worship was paid to Seidi Ghazi till the reign of Sultan Ala-ed-din of Konia (1219-1236), when the place where he died was discovered by special revelation, and a tomb was built for him at the ancient city Nakoleia (which from that time has borne his name), far north of the fatal battle, and a great establishment of dervishes formed. The dervishes were scattered and the building going to decay when I was there in 1881 and 1883.

dervishes, that sect to which all the Janissaries belonged from the time when their beginning was blessed by Hadji Bektash near Amasia.[1] On Mount Argæus strange stories about him are told. He shares with others the awe attaching to this mountain, the loftiest in Asia Minor, and worshipped as divine by the ancient inhabitants. On the site of an old Hittite city, Ardistama, rediscovered in 1904 on the borders of Cappadocia and Lycaonia, he is known as Emir Ghazi, the Conqueror Emir. At Nakoleia, in Phrygia, once one of the greatest establishments of dervishes in Asia Minor, now passing rapidly into ruins, his tomb is shown, and that of the Christian princess, his supposed wife.

The mention of the Christian wife of the Moslem conqueror throws some light on the legend. The idea was not lost from the historical memory of the Mohammedans that they were interlopers, and that the legal right belonged to the Christians whom they had conquered. The representative hero of the Moslems must therefore make his possession legitimate by marrying the Princess, who carries with her the right of inheritance. This is a striking example of the persistence of the old Anatolian custom that inheritance passed in the female line. Greek law had superseded the old custom ; Roman law had confirmed the principle that inheritance passed in the male line ; Christian and Mohammedan custom agreed in that principle. Yet here in the Moslem legend we find the old custom of the land still effective. In Greek legend and Greek history the same tendency for the conquerors to seek some justification and legitimisation of their violent seizure is frequently observed ; so, *e.g.*, the Dorian conquest of the Peloponnesus is represented in legend as the Return of the Heracleidæ : the foreign

[1] See below under 2.

conquerors represent themselves as the supporters and champions of rightful heirs who had been dispossessed and expelled. In many of the old cities of the land (probably in all of them, if we only knew the Moslems better) there linger stories, beliefs and customs, showing that the Mohammedans recognise a certain priority and superiority of right as belonging to the Christian. In the Mosque of St. Sophia at Constantinople the closed door is pointed out through which the priest retired carrying the sacred elements when the capture of the city interrupted the celebration of the sacrament; and every one acknowledges that, when the door is opened again, the priest will come back to continue the interrupted ritual of the Christians. In front of the walls of Constantinople is the sacred spring with the fish which shall never be caught until the Christians recover the city: they were taken from the gridiron and thrown into the spring by the priest who was cooking them when the city was stormed, and there they swim until the Christians return. At Damascus, Jerusalem, Thyatira, etc., similar tales are told. At Iconium, on the summit of the hill above the Palace, is a transformed church, once dedicated (as the Greeks say) to St. Amphilochus, Bishop of Iconium about 372-400. It was made into a mosque, but every Mohammedan who entered it to pray died (the tale does not specify whether they died at the moment or later), and it ceased to be used as a mosque. Thereafter a wooden clock-tower was built upon it, and the building is at the present day called "the Clock". Inside this is said to be the spring of Plato, which is now dry. In this absurd story we trace the degraded remnants of ancient sanctity; and there is a mixture of old religious belief in a holy spring, and perhaps an Asylum, with the later Mohammedan idea that intrusion into a Christian shrine always was accompanied by a certain risk.

2. Some personage of Turkish history proper becomes the bearer of the religious awe attaching to certain spots, *e.g.*, Hadji Bektash, who, I am told, led the Janissaries at the capture of Mudania, and from whom the chief seat of the Bektash dervishes derives its name. At this place, now called Mudjur, in Cappadocia, Hadji Bektash has succeeded to the dignity and awe which once belonged to the patron saint of the bishopric of Doara.

Another such character is Karaja Ahmed, who has his religious home in several parts of the country, sometimes, at least, with tales of miraculous cures attaching to his grave.[1] I assume him to be a historical character, as he is found in several places, but I do not know whether any actual record survives. Many other names might be quoted, which I assume to have belonged of old to real persons, often probably tribal ancestors unknown to fame : *e.g.*, Sinan Pasha and Hadji Omar or Omar Baba : the latter two names I suppose to belong to one personage, though they are used at different places. Sinan Pasha was the name of several persons distinguished in Ottoman history, the eldest being a Persian mollah, scholar and mystic, under the early Ottoman chiefs in the fourteenth century.

3. The *dede* or nameless heroised ancestor is spoken of at various places. In many cases his name has been entirely lost, but in other cases inquiry elicits the fact that the *dede*

---

[1] I have observed the veneration of Karaja Ahmed at a village six hours S.S.W. from Ushak and about three hours N.W. from Geubek ; also at a village one hour from Liyen and two from Bey Keui (one of several spots which divide the religious inheritance of the ancient Metropolis). At the latter, sick persons sit in the Turbe all night with their feet in a sort of stocks, and thus are cured. The villages bear Ahmed's name.

belongs to Class 2, and that some of the villagers know his name, though the world in general is acquainted with him only as the nameless *dede*, father of the tribe or settlement.

4. The word *dede* is also used in a still less anthropomorphic sense to indicate the mere formless presence of Divine power on the spot. Many cases hang doubtfully between this class and the preceding: it is not certain whether the *dede* once had a name and a human reality which has afterwards been lost, or whether from the beginning he was merely the rude expression of the vague idea that Divine power dwelt on the spot.

As an example the following may be selected. In the corner beneath the vast wall of Taurus, where Lycaonia and Cappadocia meet, at the head of a narrow and picturesque glen, there flows forth from many outlets in the main mass of Taurus a river—for a river full grown it issues from the rock. Rushing down the steep glen, it meets at its foot a quieter stream flowing from the east through a rich soil, and long after the junction the clear water from the glen refuses to mix with the muddy water from the rich soil of the valley. The stream flows on for a few miles to the west, turning this corner of the dry Lycaonian plain into a great orchard, and there it falls into the Ak Göl (White Lake). The lake is one of those which vary greatly in extent in different years. In 1879[1] it reached close up to the rock-wall of Taurus, and flowed with a steady stream into a great hole in the side of the mountain. In 1882 and in 1890 it did not reach within a mile of the mountain side.

---

[1] This I learned from the late Sir Charles Wilson. Recently the scene has been carefully described by an Austrian traveller, Dr. Schaffer, in *Ergän-zunsheft* No. 141 to Petermann's *Geogr. Mittheilungen*.

PLATE IV.

FIG. 9.—The Peasant God at Ibriz.

To face p. 172.

This remarkable river has always been recognised by the inhabitants of the glen as the special gift of God, and about B.C. 800 they carved on a rock near the source one of the most remarkable, and even beautiful, monuments of ancient days, figuring the god presenting his gifts of corn and wine —whose cultivation the river makes possible—to the king of the country. The king is dressed in gorgeous embroidered robes, the god is represented in the dress of a peasant; he is the husbandman who, by patience and toil, subdues Nature for the benefit of man. This old conception evinces imagination, insight, poetic sympathy with Nature, and artistic power to embody its ideas in forms that appeal directly to the spectator's eye.

The modern peasantry recognise as fully as the ancients that the Divine power is manifested here ; they express their belief differently. The tree nearest the spring is hung with patches of rag, fastened to it by modern devotees. In the contrast between the ancient sculpture and the modern tree you have, in miniature, the difference between Asia Minor as it was 2,700 years ago, and Asia Minor as it is under the Turk. The peasants' language is as poor as their ritual. If you ask them why they hang their rags on the tree, the one explanation is " *dede var* " (there is a *dede*).

There can be little doubt that the idea of the sacred tree here is older than the sculpture. A sacred tree hung with little offerings of the peasantry was no doubt there before the sculpture was made, and has in all probability never been wanting in the religious equipment of the place. It has survived the sculpture, which has now no nearer relation to the life and thoughts of the people than the gods in the British Museum have to us, while the tree is probably a more awful object to the peasants than the village mosque.

The extreme simplicity of the peasants' way of expressing their religious idea is interesting; it is so contrasted
with the manifold mythopoetic power of the Greek or Celtic
races.   It throws some light on their religious attitude to
observe that in their topographical nomenclature there is
the same dearth of imaginative interpretation of Nature.
The nearest stream is commonly known as Irmak, the
river, Su, the water, Tchai, the watercourse; half the population of a village know no other name for it, while the
other half, more educated, know that it is distinguished from
other streams as Kizil Irmak (red river), or Ak Su (white
water), or Gediz Tchai (the stream that flows by the town
of Gediz).   The mountain beside the village is commonly
termed simply "*dagh*"; if you ask more particularly, you
learn that it is the "*dagh*" of such and such a village; if
you ask more particularly still, you find that some one
knows that it is Ala Dagh (the Spotted Mount), or Ak
Dagh, or Kara Dagh (White or Black Mount).   Very rarely
does one find such a name as Ai Doghmush, the Moon
Rising; a name that admirably paints the distant view of
a beautiful peak near Apamea-Celænæ, as it appears rising
over some intervening ridge.   The contrast between a name
like this and the common Turkish names might suggest
that it is a translation of an old pre-Turkish name; and the
same thought suggests itself in the case of Hadji-Baba,
"Pilgrim Father," a lofty and beautiful peak that overhangs
the old city of Derbe (see Art. XI.).

Wherever the sacred building is connected with or
directed by a regular body of dervishes, it is called a *teke;*
where it is little more than a mausoleum, it is called a *turbe*.
The most characteristic form of the *turbe* is a small round
building with a sloping roof rising to a point in the centre

and surmounted by the crescent; but it also occurs of various forms, degenerating into the meanest type of building. Often, however, there is no sacred building. The Divine power resides in a tree or in a grove (as at Satala, in Lydia, the modern Sandal), or in a rock, or in a hill. I cannot quote a specific case of a holy rock, though I have seen several; but of several holy hills the most remarkable occurs about two hours south-east from Kara Bunar, which probably is the modern representative of the ancient Hyde the Holy, Hiera Hyde. Here, within a deep circular depression, cup-shaped and about a quarter of a mile in diameter, there rises a pointed conical hill to the height of several hundred feet, having a well-marked crater in its summit. A small lake nearly surrounds the base of the hill. The ground all around is a mere mass of black cinders, without a blade of vegetation. I asked a native what this hill was called; he replied, "Mekke; Tuz-Mekkesi daiorlar" (Mecca; they call it the Salt-Mecca). Mecca is the only name by which the uneducated natives can signify the sacredness of a place.

In connection with the maintenance of *tekes* and *turbes*, we find an interesting case where the method of Roman law has survived through Byzantine times into Turkish usage. These religious institutions have been kept up by a rent charged on estates: the estates descended in private possession, according to the ordinary rules of inheritance, charged with the rent (*Vakuf*). The system is precisely the same as that whereby Pliny the younger provided a public school in his own city Novum Comum (Ep. vii., 18); he made over some of his property to the municipality, and took it back from them in permanent possession at a fixed rent (so far under its actual value as to provide for contingencies); and the possession remained with his heirs, and could be sold.[1]

Much difficulty has been caused in Turkey owing to the rents having become insufficient to maintain the religious establishments. Many of the establishments, as, *e.g.*, that of Seidi Ghazi at Nakoleia (now called Seidi Ghazi, after the hero), are rapidly going to ruin. The Government has made great efforts to cope with the difficulties of the case; but its efforts have only been partially successful; and many of the old establishments have fallen into ruins. It is only fair to remember and to estimate rightly the magnitude and difficulty of the task which the Government had to undertake, but the fact remains that the Evkaf Department is popularly believed to be very corrupt, and its administration has been far from good. It must, however, be acknowledged that in the last few years the traveller observes (at least in those districts where I have been wandering) a very marked improvement in this respect.

There appear to be cases in which the actual rites and forms, or at least the accompaniments, of a pre-Mohammedan, or even pre-Christian, worship are preserved and respected by Mohammedans. A few examples out of many may be given here in addition to those which have been mentioned in the preceding article, § 2.

1. The Ayasma (any holy spring to which the Christians resort) is also respected by the Mohammedans, who have sometimes a holy tree in the neighbourhood. In general a Christian place of pilgrimage is much respected by the

---

[1] This custom is the same as that which, according to Professor Mommsen, is called *avitum* in an inscription of Ferentinum (*C. I. L.*, x., No. 5853) and in one of the receipts found in the house of Cæcilius Jucundus at Pompeii, and which is termed *avitum et patritum* in another of Cæcilius Jucundus's receipts (*Hermes*, xii., p. 123).

PLATE V.

FIG. 10.—The Bridge over the Pyramos at Missis (Mrs. Christie of Tarsus).

See p. 273.

PLATE VI.

FIG. 11.—The Bridge over the Saros at Adana (Mrs. Christie of Tarsus).

To face p. 176. See p. 274.

Turkish peasantry. At Hassa Keui, the old Sasima, in Cappadocia, the feast of St. Makrina on 25th January attracts not merely Christians from Konia, Adana, Cæsarea, etc., but even Turks, who bring their sick animals to be cured.[1] Many great old Christian festivals are regarded with almost equal awe by the peasant Turks and by the Christians, as we saw above.

2. Iflatun Bunar; springs with strange virtues and having legends and religious awe attached to them, are in some cases called by the name of the Greek philosopher Plato, which seems to imply some current belief in a magician Plato (like the mediæval Virgil). One of these springs of Plato is in the acropolis of Iconium: the history of Iconium is not well enough known to enable us to assert that the spring was holy in former times, however probable this may be. Another is situated about fifty miles west of Iconium, and from the margin of the water rise the walls of a half-ruined little temple, built of very large stones and adorned with sculptures of a religious character, showing the sanctity that has attached to the spring from time immemorial. The sculptures belong to the primitive Anatolian period, generally called Hittite.

We may note in passing that Plato's Springs belong to the neighbourhood of Iconium, the capital of the Seljuk kingdom of Roum, where a high standard of art and civilisation was maintained until the rise of the Ottoman Turks. The name of Plato probably was attached to the springs in the Seljuk period, when Greek philosophy was studied and perhaps Plato was popularly known as a wise man or magician (just as Virgil was the great magician of European mediæval superstition and literature).

---

[1] Carnoy et Nicolaides, *Traditions populaires de l'Asie Mineure*, p. 204.

3. The Takhtaji, woodcutters and charcoal-burners, are not pure Mohammedans. Their strange customs have suggested to several independent observers the idea that they are aboriginal Anatolians, who retain traces of a religion older even than Christianity.[1] Nothing certain is known about their rites and the localities of their worship, except that cemeteries are their meeting-place and are by the credulous Turks believed to be the scene of hideous orgies.

The Takhtaji must be classed along with several other isolated peoples of the country, who retain old pre-Christian rites. They are all very obscure, poor and despised ; and it is extremely difficult to get any information about them. A friend who has been on friendly terms with some of them from infancy told me that, however intimate he might be with some of them, it was impossible to get them to talk about their religious beliefs or rites. Two things, however, he had learned—one of which is, I think, unrecorded by other inquirers.[2] In the first place, there is a head or chief-priest of their religion, who resides somewhere in the Adana district, but makes visits occasionally to the outlying settlements—even as far as the neighbourhood of Smyrna (where my informant lives). This high-priest enters any house and takes up his abode in it as he pleases, while the owner concedes to him during his stay all rights over property, children and wives. This priest is evidently the old priest-king of

---

[1] See Humann and Puchstein, *Reisen in Kleinasien und Nordsyrien.* Mr. Hyde Clarke has long had this idea, which is, he says, fully proved by what he has seen and heard among the people. On their ethnological character see Von Luschan in Benndorf-Niemann, *Lykia*, vol. ii. My ideas have been gained originally from Sir C. Wilson.

[2] *E.g.*, Von Luschan in *Lykia* (Benndorf-Niemann, etc.), ii., p. 186 ; Crowfoot, *Journ. Anthr. Inst.*, 1900, *Man*, 1901.

the primitive Anatolian religion, who exercises in a vulgar-
ised form the absolute authority of the god over all his
people. In the second place, my informant corroborated
the usual statement about them, that their holy place—
where they meet to celebrate the ritual of their cult—is the
cemetery. He had not been able to learn anything about
the rites practised there. This again is a part of the primitive religion of the land. It is a probable theory [1] that the
early custom was "to bury the dead, not along the roads
leading out from the city (as in Greece, and beside the
great Hellenised cities of Anatolia), but in cemeteries beside
or around the central Hieron ". " It may be doubted whether
in old Phrygian custom there was any sacred place without
a grave. Every place which was put under Divine protection for the benefit of society was (as I believe) consecrated
by a grave." " The dead was merged in the deity, and
the gravestone was in itself a dedication to the god." In
death the people of the Great Goddess returned to her,
their mother and the mother of all life, and lay close to her
holy place and home. " The old custom remains strong
throughout Christian and Moslem time." The grave of a
martyr, real or supposed, gave Christian consecration to
some of the old holy places. " Wherever a Moslem Turbe
is built to express in Mohammedan form the religious awe
with which the Moslem population still regards all the old
holy places, there is always in or under it the grave of some
old supposed Moslem hero, and a Moslem legend grows up,
and Divine power is manifested there with miraculous cures."

4. The music and dancing of the Mevlevi dervishes have
much of the character of the old ritual of Cybele, toned

[1] The following sentences are quoted from my *Studies in the Eastern
Roman Provinces* (Hodder & Stoughton, 1906), p. 273.

down and regulated by the calmer spirit of the Mohammedan religion and the Turkish character.

5. In the Hermus Valley, in the neighbourhood of Sardis, are several villages, in which dwell a strange people, who practise a mixed sort of religion.[1]   In outward appearance they are Mohammedans.   But the women do not veil their faces in the presence of men, and the two sexes associate freely together.   This freedom is, of course, usual among many Anatolian tribes of a nomadic character, Turkmen, Avshahr, Yuruk, etc., and is the perpetuation of primitive Turkish custom before the Turks came in contact with Semitic people and adopted the religion of Islam.   But in the villages of the Hermus Valley the freedom probably has a different origin, as the other characteristics of the people show.   While the men bear only Mohammedan names, the women are said often to have such Christian names as Sophia, Anna, Miriam, etc.   They do not observe the Moslem feast of Ramazan, but celebrate a fast of twelve days in spring.   They drink wine, which is absolutely forbidden by the law of Mohammed ; yet we were told that drunkenness is unknown among them and that they are singularly free from vice.   They practise strict monogamy, and divorce is absolutely forbidden among them, which stands in the strongest contrast with the almost perfect freedom and ease of divorce among the Mohammedans. In the usual Turkish villages there is always a mosque of some sort, even if it be only a tumble-down mud hovel, between which and the ordinary houses of the villagers the difference is hardly perceptible to the eye of the casual

---

[1] The following sentences are quoted nearly *verbatim* from an account published by Mrs. Ramsay in the *British Monthly*, March, 1902, shortly after we had visited the place.

traveller ; but in those villages of the Hermus Valley there is no mosque of any description. There is, however, a kind of religious official, called popularly " Kara-Bash," one who wears a black head-dress, who visits the people of the different villages at intervals, when they assemble in one of the houses. How these assemblies are conducted, our brief stay did not enable us to discover. Our informant, a Christian resident of Albanian origin, was quite convinced that these villagers were Christians with a thin veneer of Mohammedanism, and declared that, if there were no Sultan, missionaries could make them by the hundred come over to profess Christianity openly. He himself was in the habit of reading the New Testament to them privately, to their great satisfaction.

Some few of these details we were able to verify personally ; but most of them rest on the authority of our informant, who is a perfectly trustworthy person.

The same situation for great religious centres has in many cases continued from a pre-Mohammedan, and even from a pre-Christian, period. In some cases, as in great cities like Iconium, the mere continuity of historical importance might account for the continuity of religious importance ; but in other cases only the local sanctity can explain it, for the political prominence has disappeared from many places which retain their religious eminence.

The fact which is most widely and clearly observable in connection with the localities of modern religious feeling is that they are in so very many cases identical with the scenes of ancient life, and often of ancient worship. Every place which shows obvious traces of human skill and human handiwork is impressive to the ruder modern inhabitants. The commonest term to express the awe that such places

rouse is *kara*.   In actual usage *kara* (literally, *black*) is
not much used to indicate mere colour.   A black object is
siakh ; but *Kara Mehmet* means, not Mehmet with black
complexion, but big, or powerful, or strong, or dangerous
Mehmet.   Ancient sites are frequently called *kara :* thus
we have Sanduklu, the modern town, and Kara Sanduklu,
five miles distant, the site of the ancient Phrygian city
Brouzos.

No village names are commoner in modern Turkey in
Asia than Kara Euren, or Karadja Euren, and Kizil Euren.
I have never known a case in which Kizil Euren marks an
ancient site ; [1] whereas a Kara or Karaja Euren always, in
my experience, contains remains of antiquity, and often is
the site of an ancient city.

The awe that attaches to ancient places is almost invari-
ably marked by the presence of a *dede* and his *turbe*, if not
by some more imposing religious building ; and a religious
map of Asia Minor would be by far the best guide to the
earlier history of the country.   Even a junction of two
important ancient roads has its *dede :* for example, the
point where the road leading north from the Cilician Gates
forks from the road that leads west is still marked by a
little *turbe*, but by no habitation.   [It must, however, be
added, as I have since discovered, that the village Halala
was probably situated there : see Art. XI.]

The exceptions to this law are so rare, that in each case
some remarkable fact of history will probably be found
underlying and causing it, and these exceptions ought
always to be carefully observed and scrutinised ; some apparent exceptions turn out to be really strong old examples

[1] The name usually marks some obvious feature of the modern village,
e.g., reddish stones.

of the rule, as when some very insignificant mark of religious awe is absolutely the sole mark of modern life and interest existing upon an otherwise quite deserted site. Two ancient cities I have seen, and yet cannot actually testify to the existence of an unbroken religious history on their sites— Laodicea on the Lycus, and Comana in Cappadocia—but in the latter case the construction of a modern Armenian village on a site where fifty years ago no human being lived has made such a break in its history, that very close examination would be needed to discover the proof of continuity. Both these cases are, perhaps, not real exceptions, but I have never examined them with care for this special purpose, for it is only in very recent times that I have come to recognise this principle, and to make it a guide in discovery.

If we go back to an earlier point in history, no doubt can remain that the Christian religion in Asia Minor was in a similar way strongly affected in its forms by earlier religious facts, though the unity of the Universal Church did for a time contend strenuously and with a certain degree of success against local variations and local attachment.

1. The native Phrygian element in Montanism has been frequently alluded to, and need not be described in detail. The prophets and prophetesses, the intensity and enthusiasm of that most interesting phase of religion, are native to the soil, not merely springing from the character of the race, but bred in the race by the air and soil in which it was nurtured.

2. A woman, who prophesied, preached, baptised, walked in the snow with bare feet without feeling the cold, and wrought many wonders of the established type in Cappadocia in the beginning of the third century, is described by

Firmilian, Bishop of Cæsarea.[1] The local connection did not interest Firmilian, and is lost to us.

3. Glycerius the deacon, who personated the patriarch at the festival of Venasa, in Cappadocia, in the fourth century, was only maintaining the old ritual of Zeus of Venasa, as celebrated by the high-priest who represented the god on earth. The heathen god made his annual progress through his country at the same festival in which Glycerius led a ceremonial essentially similar in type to the older ritual. See my *Church in the Roman Empire*, ch. xviii.

4. The Virgin Mother at the Lakes replaced the Virgin Artemis of the Lakes, in whose honour a strange and enigmatic association (known to us by a group of long inscriptions and subscription lists) met at the north-eastern corner of the Lakes.[2]

5. The Archangel of Colossæ, who clove the remarkable gorge by which the Lycus passes out of the city, no doubt was the Christian substitute for the Zeus of Colossæ, who had done the same in primitive time : Herodotus alludes to the cleft through which the Lycus flows, but does not mention the religious beliefs associated with it (*The Church in the Roman Empire*, ch. xix.).

6. The Ayasma at Tymandos, to which the Christians of Apollonia still go on an annual festival, was previously the wonder-working fountain of Hercules Restitutor, as we learn from an inscription.

7. In numerous instances the legends of the local heathen deities were transferred to the local saints, to whose prayers were ascribed the production of hot springs, lakes and

---

[1] See Cyprian, Epist. 75, § 10.

[2] See Articles IV. and V. of this volume. Other examples are quoted in Article IV., § 2.

other natural phenomena. The examples are too numerous to mention. Sometimes they enable us to restore with confidence part of the hieratic pagan legends of a district, as, for example, we find that a familiar Greek legend has been attached to Avircius Marcellus, a Phrygian historical figure of the second century, and he is said to have submitted to the jeers of the mob as he sat on a stone. We may feel confident that the legend of Demeter, sitting on the rock called ἀγέλαστος πέτρα and mocked by the pitiless mob, which was localised by the Greeks at Eleusis, had its home also in this district of Phrygia. See also p. 188.

We can then trace many examples of the unbroken continuance of religious awe attached to special localities from the dawn of historical memory to the present day. What reason can be detected for this attachment? In studying this aspect of the human spirit in its attitude towards the Divine nature that surrounds it, the first requisite is a religious map of Asia Minor. This remains to be made, and it would clear up by actual facts, not darken by rather hazardous theories (as some modern discussions do), a very interesting phase of history.[1]

The extraordinary variety of races which have passed across Asia Minor, and which have all probably without exception left representatives of their stock in the country, makes Asia Minor a specially instructive region to study in reference to the connection of religion with geographical facts. Where a homogeneous race is concerned, a doubt always exists whether the facts are due to national character —to use a question-begging phrase—or to geographical

---

[1] The observation and recording of all *turbes* may be urged on every traveller in Asia Minor, especially on the French students of the *Ecole d'Athènes*, from whom there is so much to hope.

environment.   But where a great number of heterogene-
ous races are concerned, we can eliminate all independent
action of the human spirit, and attain a certainty that,
since races of most diverse character are similarly affected
in this country, the cause lies in the natural character of
the land.

One fact, however, is too obvious and prominent to be a
matter of theory.   In a considerable number of cases the
sacred spot has been chosen by the Divine power, and
made manifest to mankind by easily recognised signs.   An
entrance from the upper-world to the world of death and of
God and of the riches and wonders of the under-world, is
there seen.   The entrance is marked by its appearance, by
the character of the soil, by hot springs, by mephitic odours,
or (as at Tyana) by the cold spring which seems always
boiling, in which the water is always bubbling up from
beneath, yet never overflows.   The god has here manifested
his power so plainly that all men must recognise it.

One fact, however, I may refer to in conclusion, on a
subject on which more knowledge may be hoped for.
Throughout ancient history in Asia Minor a remarkable
prominence in religion, in politics, in society characterises
the position of women.   Most of the best attested and
least dubious cases of *Mutterrecht* in ancient history belong
to Asia Minor; and it has always appeared to me that the
sporadic examples which can be detected among the Greek
races are alien to the Aryan type, and are due to inter-
mixture of custom, and perhaps of blood, from a non-Aryan
stock whose centre seems to be in Asia Minor; others, who
to me are friends and φίλοι ἄνδρες, differ on this point, and
regard as a universal stage in human development what I
look on as a special characteristic of certain races.

Herodotus speaks of the Lycian custom of reckoning descent through the mother, but the influence of Greek civilisation destroyed this character, which was barbarian and not Greek, and hardly a trace of it can be detected surviving in the later period. Lycia had become Greek in the time of Cicero, as that orator mentions. When, however, we go to regions remoter from Greek influence, we have more hope of discovering traces of the pre-Greek character, *e.g.*, the inscriptions of a little Isaurian town, Dalisandos, explored two years ago by my friend Mr. Hogarth, seem to prove that it was not unusual there to trace descent through the mother even in the third or the fourth century after Christ.

Even under the Roman government, and in the most advanced of civilised cities of the country, one fact persisted, which can hardly be explained except through the influence of the old native custom of assigning an unusually high rank to the female sex. The number of women magistrates in Asia Minor is a fact that strikes one on an even superficial glance into the later inscriptions.

In the Christian period we find that every heresy in which the Anatolian character diverged from the standard of the Universal Church was marked by the prominent position assigned to women. Even the Jews were so far affected by the general character of the land, that the unique example of a woman ruler of the synagogue occurs in an inscription found at Smyrna.[1]

We would gladly find some other facts bearing on and illustrating this remarkable social phenomenon. My own theory is that it is the result of the superiority in type, pro-

---

[1] See my *Church in the Roman Empire*, pp. 161, 345, 360, 375, 438, 452-459, 480.

duced to a noticeable degree by the character of the country in the character of the women at least of the Greek race, for the poorer Turkish women are so overworked from childhood that their physical and mental growth is stunted.[1]

[1] *Impressions of Turkey*, pp. 43, 49, 168, 258, 270 f.

Note to p. 176 f.—The Turks' reverence for a Christian holy place (certainly pre-Christian also), is shown at the monastery of St. Chariton, five miles W.N.W. of Iconium, in a narrow rocky glen.   The monastery is deserted, but the buildings are complete and in good order, and the Greeks celebrate an annual Panegyris there on 28th September, staying several days at the holy place.   Inside the monastery is a small Turkish mosque, to which the Moslems resort ; and the story goes that the son of a Seljuk sultan fell over the precipice under which the buildings are, and was saved by St. Chariton. Inside are shrines also of the Panagia, Saba, and Amphilochius.   Chariton founded monasteries in Palestine.   His biography, written after 372, says he was born at Iconium (Prov. Lycaoniae), and was arrested and liberated under Aurelian (quite unhistorical).

In a similar glen, a mile north, is a village Tsille, full of holy places, St. George, Ayios Panteleêmon, Panagia, Prophet Elias, Archangel Michael (whose church was built by Constantine and Helena), and above all the hole in the rock into which St. Thekla was received, and St. Marina on a hill opposite her (proving the craving for a female representative of the Great Goddess (see p. 134 f.).   Near St. Marina is a place Ayanni, *i.e.*, St. John.

These lie round the base of St. Philip (see p. 296), and attest the holiness of this mountain region, within which, further north, dwells the Zizimene Mother at her quicksilver mines.

THE ACTS OF THE APOSTLES

VII

THE ACTS OF THE APOSTLES

THE question with regard to the historical trustworthiness
and the date of composition of the Acts of the Apostles is
at present in a somewhat delicate and wavering position.
A marked change has taken place during the last ten years
in the attitude of the school which we must call by the
misleading epithet of the "critical" party toward the question. Twenty or fifteen years ago there was a large body
of learned opinion in Europe which regarded the question
as practically decided and ended, with the result that the
Acts was a work composed somewhere toward the middle
of the second century after Christ, by an author who held
strong views about the disputes taking place in his own
time, and who wrote a biased and coloured history of the
early stages in Christian history with the intention of in-
fluencing contemporary controversies. The opinion was
widely held in Europe that no scholar who possessed both
honesty and freedom of mind could possibly dispute this
result.

Such extreme opinions are now held chiefly by the less
educated enthusiasts, who catch up the views of the great
scholars and exaggerate them with intense but ill-informed
fervour, seeing only one side of the case and both careless
and ignorant of the opposite side. Setting aside a small
school in Holland, it would be difficult to find in Europe

any scholar of acknowledged standing who would not at once admit that criticism has failed to establish that extreme view, and that an earlier date and greater trustworthiness can reasonably be claimed for the book. But when we go beyond this general admission, we find that critical and scholarly opinion is now wavering and far from self-consistent; it has not attained complete and thorough consciousness of its own position, and it tries to unite prejudices and feelings of the earlier narrow and confident critical period with the freer and less dogmatically positive attitude of the most recent scholarship.

While we are glad at the decisive defeat of the hard-and-fast confidence expressed by the older criticism, we desire to acknowledge fully the service that its bold and acute spirit has rendered to New Testament study. We believe that, while its results are to a very great degree mistaken, and its books may safely be relegated to the remotest shelves of libraries, its spirit was in many respects admirable, and it formed a necessary stage in the slow progress towards truth. We honour many of those whose views we treat as so mistaken more highly than we do some whose opinions seem to us to approximate practically much more closely to the truth, but whose spirit showed little of the enthusiastic devotion to historical method which characterised the great critical scholars.

But if their spirit was so admirable and their learning so great, why were their results so far from the truth? That question must rise to the lips of every reader. Apart from psychological reasons, such as the too strong reaction and revolt from the tyranny of an assumed and unverified standard of orthodox opinion, the great cause of error lay in misapprehension as to Roman Imperial history. The history

PLATE VII.

FIG. 12.—The Bridge over the Cydnus on the East of Tarsus
(Mrs. Christie of Tarsus).

To face p. 192.   *See p.* 274.

of the Empire has been recreated in the last quarter of a century. The main facts indeed remain unmodified, but the spirit, the tone, the point of view are entirely changed. The Roman Empire has now become known to us in an entirely different way. The ancient historians recorded striking events and the biographies of leading personages. They were almost wholly silent as to the way in which the Empire was organised and administered, the relation of the parts to each other, the development of the provinces, and, in short, almost everything which the modern historian regards as really important. The mad freaks of Caligula, the vices of Nero, were recorded in minute detail ; but we look vainly in the old historians for any account of the method whereby the first six years of Nero's reign were made one of the best and happiest periods in the history of the world.

The truth is that the machinery of government was so ably put together that it was to a considerable degree independent of the personal character of the Emperor, whose vices and crimes might run riot in the capital and keep his immediate surroundings in a state of continuous panic without doing much harm to the general administration of the Empire. The city of Rome was no longer the heart and brain and seat of life for the Empire. The provinces were growing every year in importance ; and the pre-eminence of Rome was becoming in some degree a superstition and an antiquarian survival. But the old historians did not see the truth ; they still thought that it was beneath the dignity of Rome to regard the provinces as more than ornamental appendages and embellishments of her dignity.

In recent years the continuous study of the details of administration has resulted in bringing them together in

13

such numbers that some conception can be gained of the real character of Roman Imperial history. Mommsen has been the organiser of the study. He has had many coadjutors. Scholars of many nations have worked under his direction, formally or informally; but it is he that has mapped out the work and indicated the proper method; and he beyond all others has been able to take a comprehensive survey of the whole field. But, unfortunately, he has never written the history of the Empire. He has published a survey of the provinces of the Empire, lucid and able, but so brief in its treatment of each separate country that it is more valuable as teaching general principles than as a record of the actual facts in each province.

Thus the results of the new methods of Imperial history have not been fully applied to the study of early Christian history. They have been little known to the theologians, and have certainly never been thoroughly appreciated by them. Now Christianity was the fullest expression of the new spirit in the Roman Empire, the refusal of the provinces to accept tamely the tone of Rome. In Christianity the provinces conquered Rome and recreated the Empire. To study Christianity from the proper historical point of view, it is therefore peculiarly necessary to stand on the level of the new Roman history. There lies the defect in the theological criticism of the New Testament on its historical side; it has missed the vital factor in the history, and with many wise and able suggestions it has erred seriously in the general view. On the whole, German criticism of early Christian history has been, and still is, in the pre-Mommsenian stage as regards its historical spirit.

Let us take an example. For many years critic after critic discussed the question of Imperial persecution of the

Christians, examined the documents, rejected many indubitably genuine documents as spurious, and misinterpreted
others, with the result that with quite extraordinary un-
animity the first idea of State persecution of Christians was
found in Trajan's famous " Rescript," written about A.D.
112 in answer to a report by the younger Pliny. Now
observe the result. If there never was any idea of State
persecution before that year, then all documents which
allude to or imply the existence of State persecution must
belong to a period later than 112. At a stroke the whole
traditional chronology of the early Christian books is de-
molished, for even those which are not directly touched by
that inference are indirectly affected by it. The tradition
lost all value, and had to be set aside as hopelessly vitiated.

   But now it is universally admitted, as the fundamental
fact in the case, that Pliny and Trajan treat State persecution of the Christians as the standing procedure. Pliny
suggests, in a respectful, hesitating, tentative way, reasons
why the procedure should be reconsidered. Trajan recon-
siders it and affirms again the general principle; but in its
practical application he introduces a very decided ameliora-
tion. The only marvel is that any one could read the two
documents and not see how obvious the meaning is. Yet
a long series of critics misunderstood the documents, and
rested their theory of early Christian history on this extraordinary blunder. Beginning with this false theory of dating
and character, they worked it out with magnificent and in-
exorable logic to conclusions which twenty years ago the
present writer, like many others, regarded as unimpeachable,
but which are now seen to be a tissue of groundless fancies.

   This change of view as regards the attitude of the Roman
state toward the Christian Church, while it affects the whole

New Testament, has been the turning-point in the tide of
opinion regarding the Acts.   That book is the history of early
Christianity in the Roman Empire; there were indubitably
some attempts to propagate Christianity toward the east
and south, beyond the limits of the Empire, but the author
of the Acts regarded these efforts as unimportant and omits
them entirely from his view.   The idea that Acts was composed about the middle of the second century was based on
the false conception of the relation between Christianity and
the state, and the new views have driven the current of
educated opinion toward a first-century date.   There is a
widespread consensus that, so far as the time of composition is concerned, there is no reason why the Acts might
not have been written by the friend and companion of Paul,
the beloved physician Luke.

But that conclusion as to authorship is vehemently denied
by most of the European "critical" scholars (to use again
that most objectionable and misleading epithet, which has
become so fixed in the language that it can hardly be
avoided).   They find other reasons which seem to them to
prove that this book, written during the probable lifetime
of Luke, could not possibly be the work of an associate of
Paul.   It seems to them too full of inaccuracies and even of
blunders as to facts.   Two causes, especially, conspire to
produce this opinion (which we think erroneous).

In the first place, the minute dissection and scrutiny of
details made by the older critics still exercise a great influence even on those who unhesitatingly reject the general
result.   Forgetful that a scrutiny made under a false prepossession and with a false method cannot be trustworthy,
they approach each detail with the stern "critical" judgment still ringing in their ears and biasing their minds

unconsciously. Thus there is manifest in their work much wavering and uncertainty of view. At one moment they condemn the old judgment; but on another page the earlier criticism rises as fresh and strong as ever, and opinions and principles are assumed which have no defence except in the older critical view, and which are mere assumptions unjustifiable on the more modern view. Accordingly, what is urgently required at the present time in early Christian history is a completely new start, free from all assumptions whether on the "critical" or on the "traditional" side. We have to begin by stripping ourselves of all our inherited views and all the views put into us by teachers (often justly revered and almost idolised teachers), and test every suggestion and every opinion before we begin to utilise them in rebuilding the fabric of our knowledge. Such is the method in which the Acts of the Apostles should now be studied.

In the second place, while part of the old misconception as to the relation between the Empire and the Christians has been cleared away, much misapprehension still remains. It is not recognised clearly enough that Paul, from a very early stage in his career, must have had a clear idea of a Christian Roman Empire. The new religion was to conquer the whole world, to recognise no bounds of nationality, and to include the barbarian and the Scythian as well as the Jew, the Greek, and the Roman. But his method of conquering the world was to begin with the Empire of which he was a citizen. Starting with the great cities of Southern Galatia, he was eager next to go to Ephesus; and though diverted from it for a time by the Divine revelation, which led him first to Macedonia and to Corinth, yet he returned to it again. There is a remarkable passage in the late Dr. Hort's *Lectures on Colossians and Ephesians*, p. 82, pointing out how

Macedonia, of Galatia. The first three names indicate Roman provinces; no one questions that. The fourth also must equally indicate a Roman province. But there lies the difficulty and controversy, which must be settled before any further progress is possible. That Galatia in Paul's epistles must be regarded as the province is now very widely admitted in Britain, and, as I am told, also in America; in Germany a growing number of distinguished scholars also hold that view, *e.g.*, Zahn, Clemen, and many others, but there the majority is distinctly on the opposite side. It is unnecessary to mention here the many serious questions of early Christian history that depend on this controversy, trivial as it seems in itself; the present writer and many much abler and more learned scholars have discussed them in a series of works. This is the next point which must be agreed upon in the study of the Acts, before any serious progress can be made.

The present writer, starting with the confident assumption that the book was fabricated in the middle of the second century, and studying it to see what light it could throw on the state of society in Asia Minor, was gradually driven to the conclusion that it must have been written in the first century and with admirable knowledge. It plunges one into the atmosphere and the circumstances of the first century; it is out of harmony with the circumstances and spirit of the second century. In the first century the chief fact of Roman Imperial policy in the centre and east of Asia Minor was the gradual building up of the vast and complex province of Galatia (as the Romans, including the Roman Paul, called it), or the Galatic Territory (as the Greeks, including the Greek Luke, who composed the Acts of the Apostles, called it). That was no longer the case in the second century; that state of things had then ceased to exist, and it was not a conception that could be restored by historical investigation; it had been a matter of spirit and tone and atmosphere, which when it ceased was never again appreciated or understood till the latest development of Roman historical study had recreated the process which we may call the Romanisation of Asia Minor.

Starting with the belief that Galatia in the New Testament was not the province, the writer found that Acts and the Epistles plunged him into the movements and forces acting in Asia Minor during the first century, when the Roman sphere of duty called Galatia was the great political fact. As he gradually and by slow steps threw off the misconceptions in which he had been trained, and realised that Paul thought as the Romans thought and spoke about the provinces of Rome, he found that, one by one, the difficulties which had been seen in the Acts disappeared, because they had their origin in misconceptions as to the period and circumstances of history. This view, that Paul wrote from the Roman standpoint, was only partially grasped in the present writer's earlier works, and has probably not yet been fully utilised by him. But already it has enabled him to appreciate the close relations and perfect harmony of view between the apostle and his disciple, the author of the Acts, and to set forth, in however imperfect fashion, the conception which both of them entertained of the growth of the early Church, as the subjugation of the Empire by the new provincial power of life and truth, the vitalising influence first for the Roman state and later for the world.

VIII

THE LAWFUL ASSEMBLY

VIII

THE LAWFUL ASSEMBLY

(ACTS XIX. 39)

WHILE it is a very important thing to study the books of the New Testament in connection with the actual life and circumstances of the countries and cities in which the events occurred, it is doubly important that the circumstances by which it is sought to illustrate the books should be correctly conceived, as otherwise the light that is cast may be misleading. If I venture in these pages to bring forward some examples to show the necessity of carefulness in this useful work of illustrating the New Testament writers, it is not that I have any claim to be immaculate myself. I welcome any criticism which aids me to find out the errors which I know must exist in my poor attempts; but the criticism that is useful to a writer in this respect must begin by really trying to understand what end he is striving to attain, and what are the steps by which he proposes to attain it, and must not condemn him off-hand for differing from what the critic has accepted beforehand as the recognised view.

The example I shall here select is in *Acts* xix. 39, which is rendered in the Authorised Version, " but if ye inquire any thing concerning other matters, it shall be determined in a lawful assembly," while the Revised Version has it, " but

(203)

if ye seek anything about other matters,[1] it shall be settled
in the regular assembly ".   I propose only to consider the
last phrase and the discrepancy between the two versions.
Two questions suggest themselves : why did the Revisers
alter " a lawful Assembly " into " the regular Assembly," [2] and
is the alteration an improvement ?

The answer is by no means easy.   In seeking the solution we shall see that hasty comparison of a phrase in an
author with a usage in an inscription may be misleading, if
it is not guided by consideration of the general sense of the
whole passage.   In doing so we shall incidentally observe
that a scholar who is simply studying the evolution of constitutional history, in the Græco-Asian cities, so far from
finding any reason to distrust the accuracy of the picture of
Ephesian government in this episode, discovers in it (as did,
e.g., Bishop Lightfoot and Canon Hicks) valuable evidence
which is nowhere else accessible.   The practical man, and
the scholar who studies antiquities for their own sake, will
always find *Acts* a first-hand and luminous authority.   It is
only the theorist (eager to find or to make support for his
pet theory about the steps by which Church history developed, and annoyed that *Acts* is against him) that distrusts
the author of *Acts*, and finds him inadequate, incomplete, or
inaccurate.   And, as Luke is so logical, complete and
" photographic " in his narrative, the only useful way of
studying him is to bring practical knowledge and sense of the
connection and fitness of things to bear on him.   There is

---

[1] περὶ ἑτέρων as in the vast majority of MSS.   There can, however,
hardly be any hesitation in preferring περαιτέρω with B, confirmed by the
Latin *ulterius* in Codex Bezæ (where the Greek has περὶ ἑτέρων), and in the
Stockholm old-Latin version (Gig.).

[2] The Greek is ἐν τῇ ἐννόμῳ ἐκκλησίᾳ : we shall use the rendering, " the
duly constituted Assembly ".

no author who has suffered so much from the old method of study practised by the scholar, who sits in his library and cuts himself off from practical life and the interest in reality, and in the things of reality.

Romans and Greeks were alike familiar with the distinction between a properly and legally convened Assembly of the people—in exercise of the supreme powers that belonged to the people and could be exercised only through a lawful Assembly called together according to certain rules— and a mere assemblage of the people to hear a statement by a magistrate or give vent to some great popular feeling in a crisis. An assemblage of the latter class was liable to pass into disorder, and was certainly disliked and discouraged by the Imperial administration. In the Republican period of Rome magistrates often hastily convened such an assemblage of the people, when they wanted to impart some important news; but the assemblage, which was known as a *contio*, could exercise no authority and pass no resolution, but merely listen to the statement of the magistrate who convened it and of any one whom the magistrate invited to speak (*produxit in contionem*). Such assemblages often became disorderly in the later Republican period, and under the Empire were almost wholly disused in Rome, and discouraged in the provincial cities.

It happens that the text of the latter part of the speech, delivered by the Secretary of the State of Ephesus[1] to the noisy assembly in the theatre, is very doubtful; but, fortunately, the general run of the meaning and argument is quite

---

[1] The rendering "Town-clerk," or "Clerk," suggests an inadequate idea of the rank and importance of this official. Lightfoot, in the paper which we shall quote in this article (*Contemporary Review*, March, 1878, reprinted in appendix to *Essays on Supernatural Religion*), was the first properly to appreciate and emphasise this,

clear. The Secretary pointed out (v. 38) that, if Demetrius and the associated guild had any ground of complaint, they had a legal means of redress before the proper court, *viz.*, the Roman "Assizes" (*conventus*), at which the proconsul presided;[1] (v. 39) if they sought anything further, *i.e.*, if they desired to get any resolution passed with regard to the future conduct of the citizens and of resident non-citizens[2] in reference to this matter,[3] the business would be carried through in the duly constituted Assembly, *i.e.*, in the public Assembly meeting with powers to transact business (whereas the present meeting had no power to transact business); (v. 40) and in fact there was a serious risk that the present utterly unjustified and unjustifiable meeting should be regarded by the Imperial government (*i.e.*, the proconsul, in the first instance) as a case of riot, and should lead to stern treatment of the whole city and curtailment of its liberties and powers.

What then is the exact sense of the term "duly constituted Assembly" in v. 39? Apparently the argument is this: "the present Assembly is not duly constituted, and you cannot serve your own purpose by persisting in it, for it is not qualified to pass any measure or transact any business; and therefore you should go away and take the recognised necessary steps for having your business brought before a properly constituted Assembly. But, further, the present meeting may lead to very serious consequences and to punishment which will fall heavily on the whole city,

[1] We note that the Secretary assumes at once that the ground of complaint is something serious. In a city like Ephesus trifling actions were disposed of by the city magistrates; their limit of power in this respect is uncertain, but was certainly very humble.

[2] οἱ ξένοι οἱ κατοικοῦντες, or ἐπιδημοῦντες, Acts xvii. 21.

[3] I follow Mr. Page's sensible note on εἰ δέ τι περαιτέρω ζητεῖτε.

including your own selves." Consequently the whole force of the argument compels us to treat the Greek term as meaning "the people duly assembled in the exercise of its powers". In the constitution of Ephesus, as a free Greek City-State (πόλις), all power ultimately resided in the Assembly of the citizens; and in the Greek period the Assembly had held in its own hands the reins of power, and exercised the final control over all departments of government. In the Roman period the Assembly gradually lost the reality of its power, for the Imperial Roman administration, which had abolished the powers of the popular Assembly in Rome, was naturally not disposed to regard with a favourable eye the popular Assemblies of cities in the provinces. Hence meetings of the popular Assembly in Ephesus and other Asian cities tended to become mere formalities, at which the bills sent to it by the Senate of the city were approved. But, at the period in question, the Assembly of the people was still, at least in name, the supreme and final authority; and with it lay the ultimate decision on all public questions. Not merely did it continue to be mentioned along with the Senate in the preamble to all decrees passed by the City-State under the Roman Empire, as giving validity and authority ;[1] it still probably retained the right to reject the decrees sent before it by the Senate.[2]

The term "lawful Assembly" therefore embraces all meetings of the Assembly qualified to set in motion the

---

[1] That form of preamble "it was resolved by the Senate and the popular Assembly" (ἔδοξε τῇ βουλῇ καὶ τῷ δήμῳ) continued for more than two centuries later, after it had become a mere form corresponding to no real expression of the popular will.

[2] At a later date it certainly lost this right, and met merely to accept the decrees.

powers resident in the People. These meetings were of two
kinds: (1) stated, regular meetings held on certain regular,
customary days (called νόμιμοι ἐκκλησίαι in an inscription
of Ephesus,[1] and κυρίαι ἐκκλησίαι at Athens); (2) extraordinary meetings held for special or pressing business
(called σύγκλητοι ἐκκλησίαι at Athens, while the Ephesian
technical term is unknown). One seems driven to the
conclusion that the intention of the Secretary was to select a
term that included both regular and extraordinary meetings.
What he said amounted to this, " Bring your business before
a meeting that is qualified to deal with it, either taking the
proper steps to have a special meeting called to discuss your
business, or, if it is not so immediately urgent and you
prefer the other course for any reason, bringing it after due
intimation before the next ordinary, regular meeting of the
People".

On this interpretation it would seem that the rendering
in the Authorised Version "lawful" is correct, and that the
Revisers were not well advised in substituting the term
"regular". The term "regular" suggests only νόμιμοι
ἐκκλησίαι and shuts out specially summoned meetings of
the People, whereas the Secretary desired to use a term
that should include every legal class of meetings.

Further, the Secretary seems distinctly to use the term
"Lawful Assembly" in contrast to the present illegal meeting, which he styled "riot" and which the historian calls
a confused Assembly,[2] inasmuch as the majority did not
know what was the business before the meeting (v. 32).
This also would suggest that "lawful" is the antithesis
required, and would defend the Authorised Version.

[1] Hicks, *Greek Inscriptions of the British Museum*, No. 481, l. 340.
[2] ἐκκλησία συνκεχυμένη (v. 40).

PLATE VIII.

FIG. 13.—St. Paul's Gate on the West of Tarsus (Mrs. Christie of Tarsus).
To face p. 208. *See p.* 275.

On the other hand, however, the evidence [1] seems to be strong that in Greece ἔννομος was an equivalent but less common term for the regular ordinary Assembly (νόμιμος being far commoner); and the evidence has convinced most scholars—Wetstein, Lightfoot, Wendt, Blass, and many others (including *Stephani Thesaurus*). In that case, apparently, we are bound to prefer the translation "regular" in v. 39, and the Revisers would appear to be right in altering the Authorised Version. Thus two different lines of investigation lead to opposite conclusions.

But we must bear in mind that the reasoning in the last paragraph is founded on a distinction that belongs to purely Greek constitutional conditions. Ephesus was no longer a Greek city. It retained indeed the external appearance of Greek city government; but the real character of the old Greek constitution was already seriously altered, and even the outward form was in some respects changed. We cannot therefore attach very great importance to an analogy with a fact of the old Greek constitutional practice until it is clearly proved, or at least made probable, that that practice remained unaffected by the Roman spirit. It is certain, indeed, that a distinction of ordinary (νομίμους καὶ συνηθεῖς) and extraordinary meetings was Roman as much as Greek ; but the question must be settled how the Roman administration affected the Greek Assembly (ἐκκλησία) in Ephesus.

I think that the true solution is furnished by some remarks of M. Lévy in an instructive and admirable study of the constitution of the Græco-Asian cities, which he has recently published in the *Revue des Etudes Grecques*, 1895,

---

[1] It may be found in any good lexicon and in the commentators.

pp. 203-255.[1] If he is right, and he seems to me to be so, we must look at the incident recorded in Acts as an episode in the gradual process, by which the central Roman administration interfered in the municipal government of these cities. As he says on p. 216, the Roman officials exercised the right themselves to summon a meeting of the Assembly whenever they pleased, and he also considers that distinct authorisation by the Roman officials was required before an Assembly could be legally summoned. Now, as we have already seen, the Imperial government was very jealous of the right of popular Assemblies. We may therefore conclude with confidence that the Roman officials were unlikely to give leave for any Assembly beyond that certain regular number which was agreed upon and fixed beforehand.[2] Thus the "regular" Assemblies had come to be practically equivalent to the "lawful" Assemblies; the extraordinary Assemblies called by the officers of the city, which in the Greek period had been legal, were now disallowed and illegal; and extraordinary

---

[1] While the paper, which is only the first of a promised series, enables me already to add much to the slight general sketch of the constitution of these cities given in chap. ii. of my *Cities and Bishoprics of Phrygia*, it seems to me not to necessitate any change of importance in what I have said (though I should of course like now to rewrite in better form not merely that chapter, but every chapter I have ever written). [In Lévy, p. 216, *n.* (2), read " II., 236 ".]

[2] Dion Chrysostom's Oration XLVIII. was delivered at Prusa in an extraordinary meeting of the Assembly (ἐκκλησία) held by permission of the proconsul Varenus Rufus ; but we observe that (1) the elaborate compliment to the proconsul for his kindness in permitting the Assembly suggests that it was an unusual favour, (2) the business seems to have been merely complimentary and ornamental, to judge from Dion's speech ; (3) the administration of Bithynia fell at the period in question into a state of great laxity (even the law against *collegia* was suffered to be violated), so that Trajan had to send Pliny on a special mission to reform the government of the province (see Hardy's *Introduction* to his edition of Pliny, pp. 24, 48).

Assemblies were now only summoned by Roman officials. It was therefore necessary for Demetrius to wait until the next regular Assembly, before he could have any opportunity of legally bringing any business before the People.

We conclude, then, that neither the rendering of the Authorised nor that of the Revised Version is in itself actually incorrect in point of Greek; but the former alone is correct in the actual circumstances of this case. It is indeed true that the Greek term used by Luke generally bears the meaning which the Revised Version attributes to it. But it was not the technical term ordinarily used in Ephesus in that sense; and, as a matter of fact, special Assemblies had ceased to be convened before this time, and the Secretary could not have been thinking of such Assemblies.

Accordingly we fail to find any sufficient reason for altering a rendering which was quite good and had become familiar; and we cannot acquit the Revisers of having made the change under the influence of an inadequate conception of the constitutional facts involved.[1] They are in no wise to be blamed for their incomplete understanding of the facts, for the materials were not accessible to them; and until M. Lévy's masterly exposition of them, the difficulty was apparently insoluble. But none the less is it regrettable that they altered the text, for the idea of a lawfully constituted Assembly qualified to exercise the powers resident in the People is demanded here by the logic of the passage as a whole, and is better expressed by the word "lawful". In fact, it would appear that the Secretary was not at the moment thinking of the technical distinction between regular and extraordinary meetings. Had he been thinking

---

[1] We may understand that they would not have made a change, unless they had considered that "lawful" was distinctly incorrect.

of that distinction, he would have used the technical term
νόμιμος, which seems naturally to have risen to the lips of
an Ephesian when that distinction was prominent in his
thought.   Thus in the inscription already quoted,[1] it is provided that a statue of Athena, as patroness of education and
all arts, dedicated to Artemis and to the rising generations
of Ephesus in future times, should be brought into every
regular meeting of the People (*κατὰ πᾶσαν νόμιμον ἐκ-
κλησίαν*).   The extraordinary meetings are here excepted
from the provision recorded in this inscription, either because they were hastily summoned and time did not permit
of the necessary preparations for bringing the statue, or
because they were only summoned by Roman officials, and
were not in the same strict sense voluntary meetings of the
Ephesian People exercising its own powers.

APPENDIX : THE TEXT OF ACTS XIX. 40

We naturally proceed to inquire whether the new light
thrown by M. Lévy on the circumstances of this Ephesian
meeting help to solve the difficulty of the reading in v. 40,
in which Westcott and Hort consider " some primitive
error probable ".   In that sentence the Secretary proceeds
to forecast the possible future, with a view to intimidate
the disorderly assemblage and induce them to disperse
quietly.   In forming an opinion as to the text, therefore,
we must, in the first place, try to forecast the possible
sequence of events.   As M. Lévy says, the Roman administration had the power to prohibit indefinitely the right of
holding meetings of the People; and it depended solely on
their goodwill when they should allow a city to resume the

[1] Hicks, No. 481, l. 340.

right, after it had once been prohibited. The occurrence of this large meeting in the theatre might be looked into by the Roman officials. It had not been authorised by them ; and the city would have some difficulty in explaining satisfactorily its origin. The only explanation that could be accepted would consist in showing that some serious cause had existed for the unusual occurrence. It is then natural that the Secretary, when representing to the assemblage the danger which they were incurring, should point out that when the Roman administration investigated the case, it would not be possible to assign any cause which could justify the concourse. His oration, as actually delivered, undoubtedly emphasised this point at some length, and pressed home the danger of the situation; for this is the climax and peroration of the speech, which was so efficacious as to calm the excited crowd, and induce them to retire peaceably ; and nothing but fear was likely to calm the rage of an Ionian city. But in the brief report that has come down to us the peroration has been compressed into one single sentence (v. 40) ; and the sentence, which describes the probable investigation and the want of any sufficient plea in defence, has become obscure through the attempt to say a great deal in a few words. The stages of the future are thus sketched out : there is likely to be an investigation and charge of riotous conduct (κινδυνεύομεν ἐγκαλεῖσθαι στάσεως) arising out of to-day's Assembly (περὶ τῆς σήμερον);[1] we shall be required to furnish an explana-

---

[1] Blass understands περὶ τῆς σήμερον (ἐκκλησίας). Page and Meyer-Wendt understand περὶ τῆς σήμερον (ἡμέρας), and Page compares xx. 26. The ultimate sense is not affected by the difference. Personally, I should follow Blass, whose understanding of the words gives a much more effective and Lukan turn to the thought; but the Bezan Reviser evidently agreed with Page. See below, under (3).

tion of the concourse to the Romans, whose maxim is " *divide to command* " and who are always jealous of meetings that bear in any way on politics or government (λόγον ἀποδοῦναι περὶ τῆς συστροφῆς ταύτης) ; no sufficient reason exists by mentioning which [1] we shall be able to explain satisfactorily the origin of the meeting (μηδενὸς αἰτίου ὑπάρχοντος περὶ οὗ δυνησόμεθα λόγον ἀποδοῦναι).

Here we have, in the text of the inferior MSS., a logical and complete summary of the future, stated in a form that can be construed easily, even though brevity has made the expression a little harsh.[2] On the other hand, the great MSS. give a reading [3] which cannot be accepted for the following reasons: (1) We observe that those warm defenders of the great MSS., Westcott and Hort, with their great knowledge of Lukan style, consider it to involve a corruption; and most people will come to the same conclusion.

(2) The only possible construction of this text connects μηδενὸς αἰτίου ὑπάρχοντος with the preceding clause κινδυνεύομεν . . . σήμερον; but, as we have seen, the logic of the speech connects the thought involved in these words with the following clause.

(3) It is clear that the Bezan Reviser (whom we believe to have been at work in the second century of our era)

---

[1] This use of περί approximates closely to the common sense "as regards," or "with reference to " (*quod attinet ad*), as in some of the examples quoted in the lexicons. Compare *ad* in Tertullian, *Apol.*, 25. Blass seems to hold that the sense is, " since there exists no charge, concerning which we shall be able to frame a defence " (which conveys no clear idea to me).

[2] The harshness arises chiefly from the sense of περὶ οὗ, (*with reference to which cause* we may render an explanation of the concourse), immediately before περὶ τῆς συστροφῆς, where the preposition has a different sense. The Bezan Reviser felt the awkwardness, and modified the sentence to avoid the second occurrence of περί. See below, under (3).

[3] περὶ οὗ οὐ δυνησόμεθα, κ.τ.λ.

had before him the text of the inferior MSS., and in his usual style he modified it to avoid some of the harshness of the original, κινδυνεύομεν σήμερον ἐγκαλεῖσθαι στάσεως, μηδενὸς αἰτίου ὄντος περὶ οὗ δυνησόμεθα ἀποδοῦναι λόγον τῆς συστροφῆς ταύτης.

(4) The corruption in the great MSS. is easily explained : there was a natural temptation to get the form " we shall not be able to explain this concourse," and this was readily attained by doubling two letters, reading περὶ οὗ οὐ δυνησόμεθα. We find that the same fault occurs in two other places in this scene : one letter η is doubled in vv. 28 and 34 so as to produce the reading μεγάλη ἡ Ἄρτεμις, where, as I have elsewhere [1] argued, the Bezan reading μεγάλη Ἄρτεμις coincides with a characteristic formula of invocation, and deserves preference.

(5) If we follow the authority of the great MSS., and read περὶ οὗ οὐ, Meyer-Wendt's former suggestion,[2] that μηδενὸς αἰτίου ὑπάρχοντος was placed by the author after συστροφῆς ταύτης and got transposed to its present position, would give a sense and logical connection such as we desire ; but it involves the confession that all MSS. are wrong. Moreover, the text of the inferior MSS. and the Bezan reading cannot be derived from it by any natural process.

Thus we find ourselves obliged to prefer the reading of the inferior MSS. to that of the great MSS.

[1] *Church in Rom. Emp.*, p. 135 f.; *St. Paul the Traveller*, p. 279.

[2] In the latest edition they coincide with Page's construction, which gives sense, but which (as above implied) we must, with Westcott and Hort, reject as not of Lukan style, and as illogical. It would, however, give much the same ultimate meaning as that which we get from the inferior MSS.

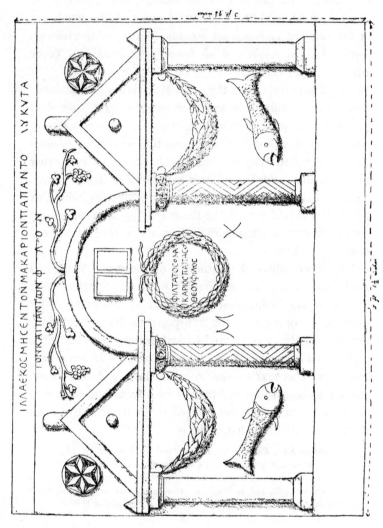

Tomb of a Bishop of the Third Century (see p. 298).

IX

THE OLIVE-TREE AND THE WILD-OLIVE

PLATE IX.

Fig. 15.—The American College in Tarsus and the Snowy Taurus (Mrs. Christie of Tarsus).

See p. 278.

To face p. 218.

IX

THE OLIVE-TREE AND THE WILD-OLIVE[1]

I

But if some of the branches were broken off, and thou, being a wild olive, wast grafted in among them, and didst become partaker with them of the root of the fatness of the olive tree ; glory not over the branches : but if thou gloriest, it is not thou that bearest the root, but the root thee. Thou wilt say then, Branches were broken off, that I might be grafted in. Well ; by their unbelief they were broken off, and thou standest by thy faith. Be not highminded, but fear : for if God spared not the natural branches, neither will He spare thee. Behold then the goodness and severity of God : toward them that fell, severity ; but toward thee, God's goodness, if thou continue in His goodness : otherwise thou also shalt be cut off. And they also, if they continue not in their unbelief, shall be grafted in : for God is able to graft them in again. For if thou wast cut out of that which is by nature a wild olive tree, and wast grafted contrary to nature into a good olive tree : how much more shall these, which are the natural branches, be grafted into their own olive tree ?—Romans xi. 17-24.

FEW passages in St. Paul's writings have given rise to so much erroneous comment as the above ; and the widespread idea that he was unobservant and ignorant of nature and blind to the ordinary processes of the world around him seems to be mainly founded on the false views that have

---

[1] I have consulted my colleague Professor J. W. H. Trail, Professor of Botany, on the subject of this paper ; and he has cleared up several points for me ; but I refrain from quoting his opinion on any special point, lest I should be mixing my own with his more scientific ideas.

been taken of his allusion to the process of grafting.   The
misunderstanding of this passage has caused such far-reaching misapprehension that a careful discussion of it seems to
be urgently called for.   It is advisable to treat the subject
in a wider view than may at first sight seem necessary ; but
the wider treatment is forced on the writer by the necessities
of the case and the demands of clearness, though his first
intention was only to write a short statement on the subject.
The unfortunate omission in Dr. Hastings' *Dictionary of the
Bible*, iii., 616, of any description of the cultivation of the
Olive, closely though the subject bears on the understanding
of many passages in the Bible, at once compels and excuses
the length of the treatment here.   Dr. Post, who wrote
the article "Olive" in the *Dictionary*, would have been an
excellent authority on this subject, on account of his long
residence in Syria ; but by some oversight he has omitted
it entirely.   A fuller account of the tree is given by Dr.
Macalister under "Food" (ii., 31) and "Oil" (iii., 591) ; but
the culture of the tree could not well be treated under those
headings, and is therefore wholly omitted in the *Dictionary*.
Under "Grafting" Dr. Hastings himself refers forward to
"Olive," anticipating the account which after all is not there
given.   Moreover Dr. Post's article "Oil-Tree" (iii., 592) states
views which are in some respects so diametrically opposed
to ordinary opinions and supported by arguments which are
in some respects so questionable, that the subject requires
further treatment.[1]

The expression "questionable," which has been applied
in the preceding paragraph to a statement made by so good

---

[1] Mr. McLean's articles "Olive" and "Oil-Tree" in *Encyc. Bibl.* are good
but very brief.   He is bold enough to hint that there is no proof of the recently invented British view that the Oleaster is *Eleagnus angustifolia*.

an authority as Dr. Post, needs justification. He says (iii., 591) that, when Nehemiah viii. 15, in a list of five kinds of foliage brought from the mountains " to make booths," mentions both Wild-Olive and Olive, " the difference between the latter and the Wild-Olive is so small, that it is quite unlikely that it would have been mentioned by a separate name in so brief a list of trees used for the same purpose ". Accordingly he infers that the Hebrew word, which is there translated " Wild-Olive," is the name of a different tree, and that Wild-Olive is a mistranslation.[1] It is difficult to justify this inference. Pausanias (ii., 32) mentions Olive and Wild-Olive in a list of three trees; Artemidorus (iv., 52) mentions them as two different kinds of foliage used for garlands. The Olive crown was considered by the ancients essentially different from the Wild-Olive crown, sacred to a different deity and used for a different purpose. Many modern botanists (as Professor Fischer mentions in his treatise[2] *Der Oelbaum*, p. 4 f.) consider that Olive and Wild-Olive are two distinct species, wholly unconnected with one another. It seems natural and probable that the order should be issued, as Nehemiah says, to bring both Olive and Wild-Olive branches : had either name been omitted the order would have excluded one of the most abundant and suitable kinds of foliage.

I do not pretend to be able satisfactorily to give the required treatment of the subject ; but I may at least be able to call attention to it, point out defects in the recognised English authorities and in the statements which are repeated by writer after writer as if they were true, and provoke a

---

[1] It will be necessary to discuss the nature of the Wild-Olive more fully in the second part of this article.

[2] This work is more fully described below.

more thorough treatment by some better scholar. Even, if
I should in turn make some mistakes in a subject in which I
am only an outsider, devoid of scientific knowledge, these will
be corrected in some fuller discussion which may hereafter
be given. The present article is written by a geographer
and historian, not by a botanist ; but the modern conception
of geography, and especially of historical geography, compels
the writer in that subject to touch often on historical botany,
the diffusion of trees, and the discovery and spread of the
art of domesticating and cultivating and improving fruit-trees.

Clearness will probably be best attained by stating first
of all the interpretation which is suggested by the actual
facts of Olive-culture, and thereafter it will be easier to see
how mistaken are many of the inferences that have been
drawn from misinterpretation of the passage. I had long
been puzzled by it, feeling that there was something in it
which was not allowed for by the modern scholars who discussed it, and yet being unable to specify what the omitted
factor was. The perusal of an elaborate study of the Olive-
tree and the Olive-culture of the Mediterranean lands by
Professor Theobald Fischer, who has devoted thirty years
to the study of the Mediterranean fruit-trees, revealed the
secret. Professor Fischer has discovered a fact of Olive-
culture which had escaped all mere tourists and ordinary
travellers, and even such a careful observer as Rev. W. M.
Thomson in that excellent old work *The Land and the Book*
(which deserves a higher rank than many much more imposing and famous studies published by more recent
scholars and observers, who had not seen nearly so much
as Mr. Thomson did during his thirty years' residence, and
who in respect of accuracy about facts and details of
Palestine sometimes leave something to be desired).

No better authority than Professor Fischer could be desired or obtained. He knows the subject in all its breadth better probably than any other living man : an experienced practical Olive-cultivator might surpass him in certain points of knowledge as regards one country, but Professor Fischer has studied it for all countries and all times. He has created a method and a sphere of research, and gathered around him a school to carry out his system of observation and study. As regards Palestine, but no other Mediterranean country, he points out that the process which St. Paul had in view is still in use in exceptional circumstances at the present day. He mentions that it is customary to reinvigorate an Olive-tree which is ceasing to bear fruit, by grafting it with a shoot of the Wild-Olive, so that the sap of the tree ennobles this wild shoot and the tree now again begins to bear fruit.[1]

It is a well-established fact that, as a result of grafting, both the new shoot and the old stock are affected. The grafted shoot affects the stock below the graft, and in its turn is affected by the character of the stock from which it derives its nourishment. Hence, although the old stock had lost vigour and ceased to produce fruit, it might recover strength and productive power from the influence of the vigorous wild shoot which is grafted upon it, while the fruit that is grown on the new shoot will be more fleshy and richer in oil than the natural fruit of the Wild-Olive. Such is the inevitable process ; and it is evident from the passage

[1] " An das noch heute in Palästina geübte Verfahren, einen Ölbaum, der Früchte zu tragen authört, zu verjüngen, indem man ihn mit einem der wilden Wurzeltriebe pfropft, so dass der Saft des Baumes diesen wilden Trieb veredelt und der Baum nun wieder Früchte trägt, spielt der Apostel Paulus an Römer ii. 17 " (*Der Oelbaum*—Petermanns Mitteil., Ergänzungsheft, No. 147, p. 9).

in Romans, even without any other authority, that the ancients had observed this fact and availed themselves of it for improving weak and unproductive trees. The words of Romans xi. 17 show the whole process employed in such cases ; the tree was pruned, and after the old branches had been cut away the graft was made. The cutting away of the old branches was required to admit air and light to the graft, as well as to prevent the vitality of the tree from being too widely diffused over a large number of branches.

This single authority would be sufficient proof to one who brings to the account a right estimate of St. Paul's character as a writer; but further independent ancient authority corroborates him, though set aside by modern writers. Columella (v., 9) says that when an Olive-tree produces badly, a slip of a Wild-Olive is grafted on it, and this gives new vigour to the tree. This passage suggests that the tree was not thoroughly cut down, for the intention is not to direct the growth entirely to the graft alone, but to invigorate the whole tree by the introduction of the fresh wild life. Columella does not say whether the engrafted shoot was affected by the character of the root; but St. Paul's statement that it was so affected is confirmed by the modern views as to the effect of grafting, *viz.*, that the old and the new parts are affected by one another. The fully grown tree is presumably able to affect more thoroughly the engrafted wild shoot, whereas in the first grafting the young tree was thoroughly cut down, and the whole was more affected by the character of the engrafted shoot, which constitutes the whole tree. See p. 227 f.

A frequently quoted passage of Palladius, who, though he wrote in verse about grafting, was also a recognised authority on agriculture and horticulture, confirms Columella and St.

Paul that the Wild-Olive graft invigorated the tree on which
it was set, though he adds, apparently, that the wild graft
did not itself bear the olives which the rest of the tree bore :
this last statement is probably a rhetorical flourish, and he
means only that the Wild-Olive had never borne olives such
as it caused the reinvigorated tree to bear. The fruit of
the Wild-Olive was poor and contained little oil; but the
oil which it produces is not bad in quality though poor in
quantity.

The comparison which St. Paul makes is sustained
through a series of details. The chosen people of God, the
Jews, are compared to the Olive-tree, which was for a long
time fertilised and productive. The cause of their growth
and productiveness, the sap which came up from the root
and gave life to the tree, was their faith. But this chosen
people ceased to be good and fertile ; the people lacked
faith ; the tree became dry, sapless and unproductive.
Surgical treatment was then necessary for the tree; the
more vigorous stock of the Wild-Olive must be grafted on
it, while the sapless and barren branches are cut off. In
the same way many of the chosen people have been cut
off because of their lack of faith ; and in the vacant place
has been introduced a scion of the Gentiles, not cultivated
by ages of education, but possessing some of the vigour
of faith. The new stock makes the tree and the congregation once more fertile. But the new stock is helpless in
itself, unproductive and useless, a mere Wild-Olive ; only in
its new position, grafted into the old stock, made a member
of the ancient congregation of God, is it good and fertile ;
it depends on and is supported by the old root. Faith, or
the want of faith, determines the lot of all; if the Gentiles,
who have been introduced into the old congregation of God,

15

lose their faith, they too shall be cut off in their turn; as every unproductive branch of the tree is rigorously eliminated by the pruner. If the Jews recover their faith, and do not continue in their unbelief, they shall be restored by being regrafted on the tree. They are naturally of noble stock, and the regular natural process of grafting the Olive with noble stock shall be carried out afresh for them. They have far greater right, for they are the chosen people, and the noble scion is the ordinary graft; and if God can, contrary to the ordinary process, graft the Wild-Olive scion into the Olive-tree in certain exceptional circumstances, much more will He give a place in the congregation to all true Israelites and graft the noble scion into the tree.

This complicated allegory, carried out in so great detail, suits well and closely; and the spiritual process is made more intelligible by it to the ancient readers, who knew the processes of Olive-culture, and esteemed them as sacred and divinely revealed. Here, as often in the Bible, the reverence of the ancients for the divine life of the trees of the field must be borne in mind in order[1] to appreciate properly the words of the Biblical writers. It is proverbially difficult to make an allegory suit in every part; the restoration of the amputated branches of the Olive cannot actually take place; but here St. Paul invokes superhuman agency, for God can regraft them on the stock, if they recover faith. Does he mean to suggest that, while this is possible with God, it is not likely to take place in practice, for the ejected Jews show no more sign of recovering faith and so establishing a claim to restoration than the amputated branches show of recovering vigour and deserving regrafting on the

[1] On this subject I may be permitted to refer to *The Letters to the Seven Churches*, 1904, p. 247.

old stock? Just as the process does not occur in nature, so
the spiritual process is impossible except as a miracle of
God's action.   If we could press this suggestion, then the
allegory would suit with quite extraordinary completeness.

The reference to nature in xi. 24 is probably to be
understood as we have explained it in the preceding paragraph.   Commonly, the produce of grafting was spoken of
by the ancients as contrary to nature, and was compared
with the adoption of children by men, which also was contrasted with the natural process of generation.   But here
the ordinary and invariable process of grafting with a noble
scion is called natural, while the unusual and exceptional
process of grafting with the Wild-Olive is said to be contrary to nature.   The changed point of view is obviously
justified, and needs no further explanation.

I do not know certainly how far it is safe to press the
expression used by St. Paul, "some of the branches were cut
off".   It is a well-known and familiar fact that every young
Olive-tree, when grafted with a shoot of the cultivated Olive,
is pruned and cut down so thoroughly that hardly anything
is left of it but one bare stem, on which the new scion is
grafted.   Thus the entire energy of the young tree is directed
into the new graft.   Does St. Paul imply that, in the process of grafting at a later period of growth, when the tree
has become enfeebled, only some of the old branches were
cut away, while others were allowed to remain?   Both
Columella and Palladius seem favourable to this interpretation.   I should be glad to receive correction or additional
information on this point; and I mention it here chiefly in
the hope of eliciting criticism.   What is the exact process,
when this exceptional kind of grafting takes place?   How
far is the fruitless old tree cut down?   Is the tree left still

a tree with some branches, or is it cut down to a mere stock? It is well established, according to Professor Fischer p. 31, that every fifty years the Olive ought to be closely pruned and thoroughly manured in order to give it fresh vigour; and it is natural to suppose that the still more drastic method of regrafting with Wild-Olive was connected occasionally with this process of rejuvenating and reinvigorating the worn-out tree, and that it would be accompanied by a thorough pruning and cutting down, though this does not imply a reduction of the tree to a single stem, as in the first grafting of the young tree at the age of seven to ten years.[1]

The idea in this regrafting evidently is that reinvigoration will be best accomplished by mixture with a strange and widely diverse stock; and this idea has sound scientific basis. It is not strange that the ancient rules of culture implied the knowledge of such secret and obscure facts. The account given in the present writer's *Impressions of Turkey*, p. 273, of the rules for maintaining the highest quality in the Angora goat (as observed in its original home) may be compared here. It is necessary to recur occasionally to the natural ground-stock, the original and fundamental basis of the Olive; and though the existing Wild-Olive is not exactly the fundamental and original stock, it is as near it as the possibilities of the case permit, and crossing with the Wild-Olive is the only way possible now of replacing the weakened original elements in the cultivated tree.

Most of the modern writers on this subject have been betrayed by the assumption (which they almost all seem to

---

[1] The nature of the Wild-Olive is discussed in Part II.

make [1]) that in this passage of Romans St. Paul is speaking of the ordinary process of grafting the young Olive-tree. This grafting is a necessary and universal fact of Olive-culture. An ungrafted tree will never produce really good fruit, however noble be the stock from which it is derived. The process is familiar ; and yet it must be briefly described in order to eliminate a certain error. The Olive is grown from a shoot of a good tree, planted in well-prepared ground, carefully tended and treated. When the young tree is seven to ten years old, it is grafted with a shoot from the best stock procurable. The Wild-Olive plays no part whatsoever in the life of the ordinary Olive-tree, which is of noble stock and grafted anew from noble stock.

St. Paul was not referring to that process when he used the words of xi. 17. He was quite aware of the character of that process, and clearly refers to it in xi. 24, when that verse is properly understood. But in xi. 17 he describes a totally different and, as he clearly intimates, unusual process, employed only in exceptional circumstances (as Columella also implies), when the Wild-Olive was called in to cure the inefficiency of the cultivated tree.

Two different kinds of unfavourable comment are made on this passage. Some writers consider that St. Paul is merely supposing a case, and does not intend to suggest that this is a possible or actually used method of grafting ; this supposed case illustrates his argument, and he moulds his language accordingly. Other writers consider that St. Paul was wholly ignorant of the nature of the case ; that he had heard vaguely of the process of grafting, and fancied that a wild shoot was grafted on a good tree ; and they

---

[1] Ewbank (quoted by Howson in Smith's *Dictionary of the Bible*, ii., 622) has taken so far the right view; but I have not access to his Commentary.

rightly add that such ignorance would prove him to have
been wholly uninterested in the outer world.

The first view—that St. Paul merely takes this impossible
and unused method of grafting as an illustration of his argument, without implying that it was actually employed in
Olive-culture—has been widely held by British scholars.   It
is stated very strongly and precisely in what may fairly be
styled the standard Commentary on Romans, by Professors
Sanday and Headlam, and we shall have their work chiefly
in mind in this connection.[1]

This view seems unsatisfactory.   St. Paul is attempting
to describe a certain remarkable spiritual process, to make
it clear to his readers, to enable them to understand how it
was possible and how it was brought about.   The spiritual
process was in itself, at first sight, improbable and difficult
to reconcile with the nature of God, who in it cuts off some
of the people that He had Himself chosen and puts in their
place strangers of a race which He had not chosen and
which therefore was inferior.   This seemingly unnatural
process is, according to the view in question, commended to
the intelligence of the readers by comparing it with a non-
existent process in Olive-culture—" one which would be
valueless and is never performed," to use the clear and
pointed words of the two above-named authors.   They say
that "the whole strength of St. Paul's argument depends
on the process being an unnatural one ; it is beside the
point, therefore, to quote passages from classical writers,
which even if they seem to support St. Paul's language

---

[1] I hope that I shall not misrepresent their view.   Owing to certain
widespread misapprehensions about Olive-culture (described in the sequel),
I have found some difficulty in catching their real meaning, in spite of the
apparent clearness and sharpness of their language.

describe a process which can never be actually used. They could only show the ignorance of others, they would not justify him."

It is, however, hard to see how a spiritual process, confessedly contrary to nature and improbable, is made more intelligible by comparing it with a process in external nature, which is never employed, because it would be useless and even mischievous if it were employed. Other writers have tried to make spiritual processes credible by showing that similar processes occur in external nature. St. Paul, according to this view, proves that the spiritual process is credible, because it resembles a process impossible in and contrary to external nature.

We cannot accept such a view—in spite of our respect and admiration for the distinguished scholars who have advocated it. Nor can we admit that they are justified in setting aside the statement of a writer like Columella with the offhand dictum that it "shows his ignorance". Columella, in a formal treatise on horticulture (v., 9), describes very fully the process, stage by stage. He describes it as unusual and exceptional; and he describes in another chapter (v., 11) the usual and regular process of grafting. The fact is that it is the modern commentators who have misunderstood and misjudged. Columella, Palladius and St. Paul agree and are right: and modern science has justified them, as we shall see.

Rejecting this first view, and concluding that St. Paul was here quoting what he believed to be an actual process used in external nature in order to make intelligible a spiritual process, we may for a moment glance at the other view, that his belief was wholly wrong. Thus, for example, Mr. Baring-Gould, in his *Study of St. Paul*, p. 275, finds

in this passage of Romans the occasion for one of his contemptuous outbursts against the narrowness, dulness and
ignorance of the Apostle. " Inspiration," he says, " did not
prevent him from bungling in the matter of grafting of an
Olive-tree, and from producing a bad argument through
want of observing a very simple process in arboriculture."

It would certainly be a very strong proof of blindness to
the character of external nature, if St. Paul had been mistaken in thinking that this process was used ; and it would
fully justify some strong inferences as to his character and
habit of mind.   This point is one that deserves some notice.
Olive-culture may seem to the northern mind a remote and
unfamiliar subject, about which a philosopher might remain
ignorant.   Even in the Mediterranean lands it is now very
far from being as important as it was in ancient times.   It
was practically impossible for a thinker, at that time, if
brought up in the Greek or Syrian world, to be ignorant of
the salient facts about the nature of the Olive, and yet to be
abreast of the thought and knowledge of his time.   So
important was the Olive to the ancient world, so impressive
and noteworthy were its nature and culture, so much of
life and thought and education was associated with it, that a
gross mistake about the subject would imply such a degree of
intellectual blindness as is quite inconsistent with the conception of St. Paul which the present writer believes to be right.

About three years after grafting the young tree begins
to bear fruit ; but eight or nine years are required before it
produces plentifully.   Thus Olive-trees require from fifteen
to nineteen years before they begin to repay the work and
expense that have been lavished on them.   Such a slow
return will not begin to tempt men except in an age of
peace and complete security for property.   The cultivation,

when once established, may last through a state of war and uncertainty—if not too protracted or too barbarous in character—but it could not be introduced except in an age of peace and security. The Olive was the latest and highest gift of the Mother-Goddess to her people.

The Olive has therefore always been symbolical of an orderly, peaceful, settled social system. The suppliants who begged for peace, or sought to be purified from guilt and restored to participation in society, according to Greek custom (probably derived immediately from Asia Minor),[1] carried in their hands an Olive-bough. On the other hand, a district which was dependent for its prosperity on Olive-cultivation suffered far more than others from the ravages of war, when the war, as was not uncommon in a barbarous age, was carried to the savage extreme of destroying the fields and property of the raided or conquered country. At the best the ruin was practically complete until the new Olive-trees which were planted had time to grow to the fully productive stage about seventeen years later. But, if security was not felt, if people were afraid to risk their labour and money in outlay which might be seized by others long before it could begin to be remunerative, the ruin was permanent, and the country sank to a lower economic and social stage; it was impoverished, and could only support a much more scanty population. As an example of the effect of the Olive-cultivation on the density of population Professor Fischer[2] mentions that in the arrondissement Grasse in the south of France, one-third of the land, in which Olives were produced, contained in 1880 a population

---

[1] See an article on the " Religion of Asia Minor " in Hastings' *Dictionary of the Bible*, v., p. 127.

[2] In his already quoted treatise *Der Oelbaum*, p. 2.

of 60,000, while the other two-thirds, where no Olives grew, supported only 10,000 people. The importance of this production becomes more evident when one remembers that the Olive grows excellently on hill-slopes, where the soil is thin and scanty and otherwise of little value; while the rich soil of well-watered plains produces fruit large in size, but poor in oil. Abundant air, light and sunshine are necessary, and these can be best obtained on sloping ground, while artificial enriching of the soil supplies all the needed nourishment to the tree.

Several passages in the Bible refer to the uncertainty of possession in Olive-trees that results from war. The Israelites were promised the ownership of Olive-trees in Palestine which they had not planted (Joshua xxiv. 13, Deuteronomy vi. 11). Such is the invariable anticipation of the tribes from the desert, which from time immemorial have been pressing in towards the rich lands of Syria, eager to seize and enjoy the fruits of the cultivated ground which others have prepared. The anticipation can be best realised if the conquest is quick and sudden. In case of a long resistance and a tedious evenly balanced contest, the land is injured more and the fruit-trees are cut down ; the inhabitants of a besieged city may cut down the fruit-trees to prevent the enemy from sheltering behind them in their attack, or the besiegers may cut them to make engines and other means of attack (as the Crusaders did at Jerusalem in 1099). Invaders who were repulsed, or were not strong enough to hope for permanent possession of the land, were the worst of all in ancient warfare. They commonly burnt, ravaged and destroyed from mere wanton desire to do as much harm as possible to the country and the enemy who possessed it.

As the cultivation of the Olive requires so much prudence, foresight and self-denial in the present for the sake of gain in the distant future, it belongs to a higher order of civilisation, and in modern times it has almost entirely ceased in many Mohammedan countries, and where it persists in them it is practised, so far at least as the present writer's experience extends, almost solely by Christians. In part this is due to the savage nature of the Mohammedan wars ; but that is not the whole reason. The Olives were not wholly cut down at the conquest, for it was too rapid and easy, but they suffered terribly in the Crusaders' wars ; though even so close to Jerusalem as the Garden of Gethsemane there are still some trees which, according to common belief, pay only the tax levied on Olives that existed before the Moslem conquest, and not the higher tax levied on those which were planted after the conquest.

But Mohammedanism is not favourable to the quality of far-sighted prudence needed in Olive-culture: the Mohammedan tends to the opinion that man ought not to look fifteen or nineteen years ahead, but should live in the present year and leave the future to God. Where this quality of prudence fails, Olive-culture must degenerate, since the outlook to a distant future, which is needed at every stage, becomes neglected more and more as time passes.

The cultivation of the Olive therefore has practically ceased wherever a purely Mohammedan population possesses the land. This arises not from any inherent necessity of Mohammedanism, but from the character which that religion gradually wrought out for itself in its historical development. No Mohammedan people, except perhaps the Moors in Spain, has ever constructed a sufficiently stable and orderly government to give its subjects confidence that they will retain their possession long enough to make it worth while to cultivate the Olive. As confidence grows less, the outlook over the future is narrowed, the Olive is more and more neglected, and the spirit of fatalism grows stronger.

Similarly, even in Corfu, it is said, the culture has much degenerated, owing to the people becoming idle, careless and improvident. At Athens the Olives of the famous groves are now oversupplied with water, and the fruit has become large and oil-less: whereas in ancient times that grove produced finer and more abundant oil than any other trees.

In short, the Olive is a tree that is associated with a high order of thought and a high standard of conduct. It demands these; it fosters them; and it degenerates or ceases where the population loses them. In the beginning the collective experience and wisdom of a people living for generations in a state of comparative peace [1] formulated the rules of cultivation, and impressed them as a religious duty on succeeding generations.

So important for the welfare of ancient states was the proper cultivation of the Olive, that the rules were prescribed and enforced as a religious duty; and, as gradually in Greece written law was introduced in many departments, where previously the unwritten but even more binding religious prescription had alone existed to regulate human action, so in respect of the Olive law began in the time of Solon to publish and enforce some of the rules to be observed. The Olive-tree requires a certain open space around it to admit freely the air and light which are indis-

[1] Hastings' *Dictionary*, v., p. 133.

pensable for its growth, and in Solon's time the principle
was that there must be a space of at least eighteen feet
between two trees.[1] The wood of the Olive was extremely
valuable, and there was a danger that short-sighted selfishness might cut down trees for immediate profit regardless
of the loss in the future; therefore an old law in Attica
forbade any owner to cut down more than two Olive-trees
in a year.

Dr. Post and others have well described the usefulness
of the Olive in modern life in Mediterranean lands. Study
of the inscriptions and authors shows that its usefulness to
the ancients was far more highly esteemed, just as it was far
more abundantly and widely cultivated. It was regarded as
being more than useful; it was necessary for the life of man,
as life was understood by the ancients.

Such was the lofty conception which the ancients, especially the Greeks, entertained of the sacred character of
the Olive; and a modern writer might be justified, if he
tried to describe in more eloquent terms than mine the importance of the tree. St. Paul might well go to the Olive-
tree for explanation and corroboration of his argument; but
the effect of his illustration would depend with his ancient
readers entirely on the correctness of his facts. They
respected and venerated the tree: to make an absurd suggestion or display an erroneous belief about the culture of
the tree would only offend the ancient mind. We, who have
to go to books in order to find out the elementary facts
about the Olive, and who regard the whole subject as a

[1] Plutarch, *Solon*, 23. The distance is inferred from the form of the
order; a man must not plant a fig or Olive within nine feet of his neighbour's
boundary. Professor Fischer, p. 30, has incorrectly apprehended the rule;
he says that Solon ordained that Olives must be nine feet distant from one
another, which would be far too close.

matter of curiosity, will naturally be lenient on a writer
who errs where we feel that we should ourselves be prone
to make errors; but the ancients did not judge like us in
this case.   This is one of the many cases where ancient
feeling and modern are widely separated; and St. Paul
must be judged by the requirements of his time.   I almost
cease to wonder that Mr. Baring-Gould became so severe a
critic of St. Paul's character and intellect, after he had persuaded himself that the great Apostle had made such a
blunder in such a matter, for Mr. Baring-Gould is a man
who has observed and judged frankly for himself.

If the process of grafting with the Wild-Olive shoot was
a known one in ancient Olive-culture, the question may be
asked how it happens that Origen was ignorant of it, since
he asserts positively that St. Paul in this passage is putting
a case which never actually occurs.[1]

In the first place, it is evident from the nature of the
case that this kind of grafting was not very frequent: only
in exceptional cases was a tree in such circumstances as to
need this surgical treatment.   It might therefore quite well
happen that Origen might know about the ordinary process
of grafting and yet be ignorant of the extraordinary process,
so that he declares as emphatically as most modern writers
except Professor Fischer, that there was no grafting with
Wild-Olive but only with the cultivated Olive.

In the second place, Origen lived in Egypt, and this
explains his ignorance.   The Wild-Olive was and is unknown
in Egypt.[2]   It does not grow in the country naturally; and,
of course, only the cultivated Olive would be introduced
artificially.   Origen, therefore, could never have seen the

---

[1] The passage is quoted in the edition of Professors Sanday and Headlam.
[2] Fischer, p. 10.

process in Egypt, where Olive-culture must have made shift without this surgical treatment. Similarly, the modern scholars, who assert so positively that there is only one kind of grafting, are all ignorant of the practical facts, because they belong to lands where Olive-culture is not practised, and they speak all from theory, or as the result of questions which they have put to Olive-growers during their travels. Now, it is very easy for misunderstanding to arise on this subject: the practical growers even in Palestine assured Mr. W. M. Thomson [1] frequently that all grafting was done with cultivated shoots, because they were speaking of the regular grafting: the extraordinary process for surgical reasons was not in their mind at the time. Moreover, those men are always extremely unwilling to reveal the secret and exceptional processes of their occupation. An example of this unwillingness, connected with the breeding of the mohair goat, is described in the present writer's *Impressions of Turkey*, p. 272.

In the third place Origen evidently was entirely ignorant of Olive-culture as it was conducted in Egypt, and knew it only from literature, not from observation. He says that the cultivators grafted the cultivated Olive on the Wild, and not *vice versâ*. But, as we have seen, the Wild-Olive is unknown in Egypt; and the Olive there, both root and graft, was the cultivated Olive.

Finally, as the most important reason of all, St. Paul introduced the illustration from the spontaneous fountain of his own knowledge; he selected a good illustration where he found it. But Origen is here the commentator toiling after his author and forced to go where the author leads him, whether or not his own experience and knowledge are

[1] *The Land and the Book*, p. 53.

competent. In such circumstances the author's knowledge
and statement must be reckoned higher than the commentator's, even if they were both equally unconfirmed from
external sources.

It may also be added here that, not merely is the cultivation of the Olive now carried out on a very much smaller
scale than in ancient times, having entirely perished in many
districts and entire countries where formerly it was practised
on a vast scale; it is also, in all probability, done now in
many districts (though certainly not in all) after a less
scientific fashion and with less knowledge of the possible
treatment of weak and exceptional cases than in ancient
times.

The method of invigorating a decadent Olive-tree, described above as practised in Palestine, is, I believe, not
employed now in Asia Minor. I have consulted several
persons of experience, and they were all agreed that this
process is unknown in the country. But this forms no proof
that the method was unknown there in ancient times. The
culture has entirely ceased in many districts, and where it
remains the methods are, as I believe, degenerated in several
respects (as in many other departments of the treatment of
nature for the use of man) from the ancient standard.

II

The slight account given in the first part of this paper of
the importance of the Olive-tree in the economy of an Olive-
growing country brings into clear relief the meaning of many
passages in the Bible. Only one of these will be touched
on here. When in Revelations vi. 5 f. the rider on the black
horse, who symbolises famine resulting from invasion, goes
forth, scarcity is announced with dearness of wheat and

PLATE X.

Fig. 16.—Falls of the Cydnus on the North side of Tarsus
(Mrs. W. M. Ramsay).

To face p. 240.   *See p.* 279.

barley, but the oil and the wine are not to be injured. The standing crops shall be wasted by the Parthian invaders, but the fruit-trees shall not suffer. The raid shall be a passing one, and shall not do permanent and lasting destruction. The land shall be able to recover with the coming of the next summer harvest, according to the facts stated above, p. 234.

In view of modern opinion it is advisable before concluding to say a word about the Wild-Olive. So far as ancient literature is concerned there is no special need of much explanation. The ancients clearly distinguish between two trees—the cultivated Olive-tree, and another which is always regarded as different in kind, called *kotinos* in Greek and *oleaster* in Latin, terms which are ordinarily and (as I believe) rightly rendered Wild-Olive by modern students of ancient literature. As was pointed out in the first part of this article, p. 221, these are mentioned separately in lists of different trees; they were regarded as different and distinct in kind; and they were sacred to different deities. Zeus was the god to whom the Wild-Olive was sacred; but Pallas Athenaia presided over the cultivation of the Olive, she produced the tree from the ground, and the Olive-garland was the symbol of her worship. In the following remarks the term Wild-Olive is used to designate the tree which was called by the ancients κότινος and *oleaster*. The ordinary unscientific, yet not unobservant, traveller,[1] or the ordinary inhabitant of the Olive-growing districts of Asia Minor, would have no doubt as to what tree is meant by these terms: he is familiar with both: they are both ex-

---

[1] Throughout these articles I have been indebted to the observant eyes and retentive memory of my wife for such facts, though she must not be held responsible for any mistakes I may make.

16

tremely common, yet different in appearance and character.
He cannot doubt that these two trees would both be frequently mentioned by the ancients, and would be regarded
by them as separate and distinct kind of trees.

The case of the Wild-Olive is totally different from
that of the Wild-Fig : this is a false name, a mere expression of ignorance, denoting the male Fig-tree (called ἐρίνεος
by the Greeks, and *caprificus* by the Latins). The Wild-
Fig tree, or Male Fig, is in appearance exactly like the
Fig-tree, so far as the ordinary person can detect. It very
often grows in walls or stony places. The fruit is smaller,
and drops off about two months before the edible figs ripen.
This fruit is full of dust and flies; the flies carry the dust
to fertilise the edible figs. I have been told in Asiatic
Turkey that unless fertilised by this dust or pollen the figs
do not ripen ; but I believe that this is not strictly correct.
The pollen quickens the growth and improves the fig ;
but is not absolutely necessary. The statements made by
some modern writers that ripe figs can be found on the
trees for many months [1]—statements which so far as I know
are quite incorrect—perhaps originate from a confusion between the two kinds of fig.

It is different when one comes to investigate modern
opinion on the subject. Then one is involved in endless

---

[1] Canon Tristram says that in the hot and low lands beside the Dead
Sea the figs are ripe during most part of the year. Even if this be so it
does not affect the case of the barren Fig-tree mentioned in Matthew xxi.,
Mark xi., which was nearly 4,000 feet above the Dead Sea, where no person
could dream of finding fruit at Easter. That incident is one of the most
difficult in the New Testament ; and nothing that has been written about
it seems of any value; but I am not prepared to offer any opinion. I do not
see the way open to any explanation of the difficulty, whether in the way of
moral teaching or of erroneous popular mythology affecting in this case the
Gospels. The passage is to me utterly obscure.

difficulties and differences of opinion, amid which it is extremely hard to pick and choose.

There is a great deal of misapprehension about the relation between the Olive and the Wild-Olive. As a general rule recent writers in English seem to have missed the truth owing to the erroneous idea that a much closer similarity exists between these two trees than is really the case. It would almost seem as if many of them thought that the Wild-Olive is simply an ordinary Olive-tree in its natural state before it is grafted, and that it is made into a true Olive by the process of grafting. That is erroneous, as Mr. W. M. Thomson recognises, in the book which we have often quoted with admiration above. So much I think it is quite safe to say, though I may not be able to state the facts as I have seen them without falling into mistakes due to unscientific habits of mind and the inevitable inaccuracy of the mere untrained observer.

The Wild-Olive is a distinct kind of tree, which even the superficial observer would not mistake for the true Olive. It bears small fruit, which produces little oil;[1] it has ovate leaves of a greener colour than the grey Olive-tree, while the leaves of the Olive are more pointed and lancet-shaped; the bark of the Wild-Olive is smoother, and the twigs are thorny and more square in section, whereas the Olive has no thorns and the twigs are round. The Wild-Olive is usually only a bush, which grows very widely in all those parts of the Mediterranean world that I am acquainted with (except Egypt). Where it has room and good soil, however, it grows to be a considerable tree, as is mentioned below; and its wood is tough, hard, and useful.

[1] The oil, though small in quantity, is perfectly good.

The Wild-Olive grows in many regions where the cultivated Olive is now entirely unknown; and it grows abundantly in regions which are so high and inclement that,
according to modern statements, the cultivated Olive could
never have flourished in them. The modern opinion which
I have heard is that the Olive requires a temperate and even
warm climate; and, as far as the facts of the present day
go, it never grows on the high central plateau of Asia Minor.
But this modern opinion seems to be unjustifiable. The
failure of the Olive on the plateau is only an example of
the general fact that the tree is never cultivated where a
purely Mohammedan population possesses the soil. Strabo
mentions that the mountain valley in front of the Phrygian
city of Synnada was planted with Olive-trees. Now this
plain lies very high, and lofty mountains surround it.
It must be one of the most inclement districts in central
Anatolia, and is not much below 4,000 feet above sea-level.
Formerly, misled by the modern idea, I proposed to alter
the text of Strabo's account of Synnada, supposing that the
original epithet ἀμπελόφυτον had been corrupted by losing
the first three letters into ἐλεόφυτον for ἐλαιόφυτον; but
now I follow Strabo, and understand that, where the Wild-
Olive grows, the Olive can be cultivated.

The *kotinos* is never mentioned by Homer; and, considering the importance in Greece of the tree alike in religion
and in wide diffusion, this is strange. It is, however, probable that in some cases, where he speaks of the Olive-tree
ἐλαία, he means the Wild-Olive, κότινος; and Professor
Fischer seems to hold this opinion (unless he has made a
mere slip, for he says that the marriage-bed which Ulysses
constructed in his palace was made in the stem of a Wild-
Olive, but Homer uses the name ἐλαία for that large tree

(Odyssey, xxiii., 190 ff.). The description given in that passage certainly suggests Wild-Olive rather than Olive.

The ancients were quite familiar, as might be expected, with the difference between the *kotinos* and the cultivated Olive; for Theophrastus, in his *History of Plants*, II., 3, states the principle that the *kotinos* can never develop into a true Olive-tree. This seems to imply that the ancients did not graft the true Olive shoot on the *kotinos*, though the modern cultivators in France and Spain, as well as in Greece and the islands of the Ægean Sea, often do so: yet Origen says that the process was common in his time, but (as we saw) Origen is probably speaking not from personal knowledge.

The relation of the true Olive to the Wild-Olive is very far from certain; the most diverse and very contradictory opinions are stated, sometimes with diffidence, sometimes with unhesitating confidence, by different modern authorities; and it is extremely difficult to know what to believe. While the appearance of the two kinds of tree is very different, yet the fact is indubitable that a Wild-Olive stock, grafted with a shoot from a cultivated Olive, produces a good and productive true Olive-tree. The two species are certainly very close to one another; and it is quite possible that to the scientific mind they may be much more nearly akin than they seem to the ordinary unscientific observer.

The young Olive-tree is, in course, selected from a good stock, and is a true Olive from the beginning. It is, however, the case that the true Olive can be obtained by grafting a noble scion on a Wild-Olive, and this process has been frequently employed in modern time in the Mediterranean, where groves of Wild-Olive have thus been utilised on a large scale. But, where cultivation is long settled and Olives are planted and tended from the beginning, the young stock is noble ; and this beyond all doubt was the regular ancient practice.

This leads up to a misapprehension, into which Canon Tristram has fallen in his *Natural History of the Bible*, p. 377, and which has been commonly repeated on his authority by English writers subsequently (*e.g.*, by Messrs. Sanday and Headlam in their commentary). Canon Tristram asserts that there are three different kinds of Olive : (1) the ungrafted tree, which is the natural or Wild-Olive, ἀγριέλαιος; (2) the grafted tree, the cultivated tree, ἐλαία ; (3) the oleaster, "a plant of a different natural order" (Sanday and Headlam), which "has no relationship to the Olive" (Tristram), yielding inferior oil, bearing long, narrow, bluish leaves, *viz.*, the bush or small tree called *Eleagnus angustifolia*.

There is just sufficient resemblance to the truth in this account to make it peculiarly dangerous. The ungrafted Olive is, of course, different from the grafted tree ; and it would in its natural ungrafted condition produce inferior fruit, containing little oil. That is the almost universal rule among cultivated fruit-trees : they must be grafted to produce well.[1] But this natural ungrafted Olive-tree is not ἀγριέλαιος, and is not the tree which St. Paul here has in mind.

Canon Tristram does not mention the Greek name for the shrub which he identifies with his oleaster. He could hardly avoid the view that the Greek *kotinos* is the Latin *oleaster ;* but if he stated that, he would be face to face

---

[1] The fig-tree is one of the few exceptions. It may be grafted, but grows quite well from shoots alone.

with a serious difficulty. Many Greek authorities [1] say that
κότινος and ἀγριέλαιος denote the same tree, and most add
that κότινος is the name used in the Attic dialect. There
can be no doubt that this tree is the Wild-Olive, *oleaster* in
Latin ; and the Latin version of Origen states that this was
the ground-stock on which the true Olive was grafted (an
erroneous statement as regards Egypt, but correct in regard
to some places).

It is, as Fischer says, still a matter of dispute among
botanists whether the cultivated Olive and the Wild-Olive
(*Oleaster*) are entirely distinct species, or whether the Wild-
Olive is only the original and natural tree out of which the
Olive has been gradually developed by generations of cultivation : or, thirdly, whether the Wild-Olive is the form into
which any ordinary specimen of cultivated Olive degenerates
when it is left neglected for a long time.

Professor Fischer (p. 4 f.), who takes no notice of the
second alternative, but only discusses the question between
the first and third alternatives, inclines to the view that
Olive and Oleaster are distinct species, though he admits
that the grafting of the true Olive on the *Oleaster* produces
a perfectly good productive Olive-tree. Though I have no
claim to be a scientific observer, yet one argument, which
Professor Fischer does not notice, seems to me conclusive
against his view. This argument was stated to me by the
late Mr. George Dennis, author of that excellent book *Cities
and Cemeteries of Etruria*, whom I had the advantage of
knowing well about 1880 to 1882, when he was H.B.M.
Consul in Smyrna. Mr. Dennis was an extremely accurate
observer, and his great book derives its value from its trust-

---

[1] Suidas, Hesychius, Etym., Dioscorides, i., 136, Pollux, i., 241, Schol.
Theocr., v., 32, etc.

worthiness and accuracy, not from learned theories or ingenious combinations.   Moreover, he was familiar for many
years with Spain, Italy and Sicily; and he had travelled
widely in the Greek world.   He said that in the neighbourhood of Çyrene, where he had travelled and excavated, the cultivated Olive no longer exists, but the Wild-Olive abounds ;
and since Cyrene was once rich in Olives, he inferred that
the Olive, when left uncared for during many centuries, went
back to its original and natural condition as a Wild-Olive.

If this observation is correct, it seems to demonstrate
that, when the cultivated Olive is left uncared for during a
series of generations, it gradually relapses into a form which
is closely similar to the Wild-Olive or Oleaster (though I
am assured that probably a scientific observer would find
differences, proving that the line of descent had been modified by generations of cultivation) ; and the easy explanation
of this appears to be that the Wild-Olive or κότινος is very
closely akin to the original natural tree out of which the
cultivated Olive was developed by generations of care.

On the other hand Professor Fischer (p. 5) quotes Von
Heldreich, who in a letter written from Athens in 1882
declares that the Olive in countries like Barka (the district
of Cyrene), where it has been uncultivated for so many centuries, does not degenerate into a Wild-Olive, but remains
a true Olive, though becoming poorer and less productive.
This statement does not seem to rest on observation, but on
theory.   It cannot be denied that the Wild-Olive is abundant all over the Cyrenaica ; and Professor Fischer's account
of the Cyrenaica, p. 69, is hardly consistent with Von Heldreich's words, though he does indeed quote some allusion
to true Olives still surviving in small numbers there.

The facts are that (1) the Wild-Olive, when properly

grafted with the nobler shoot, gives rise to the true Olive (though of course when ungrafted it can, as Theophrastus says, never become a true Olive): see examples in Fischer, p. 5. (2) The cultivation of the Olive, which originated in Western Asia several thousand years ago, has produced a well-marked difference in the tree. (3) The Olive, if neglected, would naturally revert to the primitive type in the course of centuries, though not completely so, for it would still retain distinguishable traces of the cultivated tree; and thus both Mr. Dennis and Von Heldreich may be correct in their statements about the Cyrenaica, from different points of view. (4) A shoot of the finest cultivated Olive, if planted, will not grow into a good and productive Olive unless it is grafted just like a Wild-Olive. The essential and indispensable fact is everywhere and in all cases the grafting of the young tree. (5) The ordinary practice in the Levant regions is to plant shoots of the cultivated Olive, and not to graft the Wild-Olive.

The conclusion is unavoidable that the Wild-Olive or Oleaster is the tree here referred to by St. Paul and contrasted with the true Olive, which is essentially a cultivated tree. It may indeed be conceded to Canon Tristram that the ungrafted young tree, even if grown from a noble shoot, may probably have been sometimes loosely called by the Greeks ἀγριέλαιος because it had not yet been ennobled;[1] but this furnishes no proof that such was the regular and ordinary use of that word.

The opinion of Canon Tristram that the ἀγριέλαιος is

---

[1] Theophrastus seems to use ἄγριος ἐλαία in this way. Pausanias, ii., 32, 10, seems to distinguish three classes of Wild-Olive, κότινος, φυλία and ἀγριέλαιος; but the best authority on technical matters, Blumner, refuses to pronounce any opinion on the passage. Presumably, the second term was used by Pausanias to indicate the ungrafted tree.

totally distinct from the *oleaster* of the ancients has been
widely adopted by English writers; but there seems to be
no authority for it. Several passages in Latin (for example,
Virgil, *Georgics*, ii., 182) seem to demonstrate that the
Oleaster was the *kotinos* or ordinary Wild-Olive; and in
Hastings' *Dictionary of the Bible*, art. "Oil-Tree," an argument is advanced about the corresponding tree in Hebrew,
which seems to dispose entirely of the proposed identification
with *Eleagnus angustifolia*, which is a mere bush and not a
real tree. Dr. Post says (iii., 591), "The oleaster [which he
assumes to be the *Eleagnus*] never grows large enough to
furnish such a block of wood as was required for the image
[ten cubits high, to be placed in the Holy of Holies]. It is
also never used for house carpentry." These statements are
doubtless quite true in the modern state of the country: Dr.
Post is a thoroughly satisfactory authority for what comes
in the range of his experience in the present time. But the
Oleaster or Wild-Olive (Greek κότινος ἀγριέλαιος) was far
more widely used and more useful in ancient times. It grew
sometimes then, and grows sometimes still, to be a stately
tree, though generally it is only a bush ten to fourteen feet high.
Professor Theobald Fischer, one of the leading authorities of
the day, mentions that it grows in suitable circumstances to
a height of fifty to seventy feet and forms large forests.

In this difficult subject, in regard to which I find hardly
any statement made by any authority which is not flatly
contradicted by some other equally great authority, I cannot hope to have avoided error. I have no botanical training; and when I was in Asia Minor I had never any
occasion to pay attention to Olive cultivation, but merely
picked up by chance some information. I shall be grateful
for correction and criticism.

X

QUESTIONS

PLATE XI.

FIG. 17.—American Missionary on the Roman Road (Mrs. Christie of Tarsus).

To face p. 252. *See p.* 280,

X

QUESTIONS

AT the urgent request of the Editor, I began to string together a few suggestions, or rather questions, about the interpretation of passages in the New Testament, which have been scattered over many publications; and, further, at his special wish, some disconnected impressions of some of our great scholars, now passed away, are interwoven, just as they rose to my mind and slipped to the tip of the pen.

I. The riches hid below the surface of the earth belonged to the Emperor. All quarries were managed and worked by his own private officers for his private purse. Every block that was quarried was inspected by the proper officer, and marked by him as approved.[1] Our knowledge of the subject has been for the most part derived from blocks actually found in Rome, and which, therefore, were choice blocks sent to the capital. But at the Phrygian marble quarries there have been found many blocks, which had been cut, but not sent on to Rome. These are never marked as approved; and some of them bear the letters REPR, *i.e.*, *reprobatum*, "rejected". These were considered as imperfect and unworthy pieces, and rejected by the inspector.

This explanation of the letters REPR, which passes under my name, was published in the *Mélanges d'Arché-*

---

[1] *Probante.*

ologie et d'Histoire of the French School of Rome, 1882 ; but I am glad to take the opportunity of giving the credit where it is due. It was suggested by that excellent scholar, the late Father Bruzza ; but, as the proof-sheets of my paper passed through his hands, he did not allow the acknowledgment to stand in print. It was he who perceived that this custom of testing, and sometimes rejecting, blocks for building purposes was connected with the words of First Peter, "the stone which the builders rejected," ii. 7.

These words (derived from *Psalm* cxviii. and applied to himself by Christ, *Matthew* xxi. 42) are quoted by Peter in his speech to the Sanhedrin, *Acts* iv. 11. But in *Acts* he uses the verb ἐξουθενέω, "to despise and regard as valueless," while in the *Epistle* he uses the verb ἀποδοκιμάζω, "to test and reject". It is an interesting point that the former is the more accurate translation of the Hebrew word, while the latter is the word used in the Septuagint.[1] Why should Peter sometimes use the one word and sometimes the other? The view is, apparently, held by some that Luke is here translating from a Hebrew authority, and that he is responsible for the rendering. But Luke can hardly have been ignorant of the Septuagint rendering ; and it is improbable that on his own authority he should have selected a different word. On the view which I have maintained of Luke's character as an historian, I feel bound to think that he used the verb because Peter used it ; and, therefore, Peter addressed the Sanhedrin in Greek. But further, Peter must have been thinking of the Hebrew text of *Psalms*, and have rendered the Hebrew word direct into Greek.

May we not infer that the change of verb in the Epistle

[1] See Hort's notes on 1 *Pet.* ii. 4 and 7.

corresponds to a change that occurred in Peter's mind and circumstances in the interval between *Acts* iv. 11 and 1 *Peter* ii. 7 ? He had become more Græcised; he now used the Greek Bible in place of the Hebrew (or at least in addition to it), and he recognised that the verb ἀποδοκιμάζω, "to reject after actual trial," though not a strictly accurate rendering of the Hebrew word, corresponded better to the actual customs known to those whom he addressed.

Further, may this progress towards Greek and Western ways and speech be taken as a proof that Peter moved westwards in the direction of Rome, and did not go away to the East and direct his work to the city of Babylon ? Had that been the course of his life, there could have been no such progress as is evinced in this little detail and in many more important ways.

It is satisfactory to see that Dr. Hort decisively rejected that most perverse of ideas—that this Epistle was written from the city of Babylon. They who hold such a view, however great they may be as purely verbal scholars, stamp themselves as untrustworthy judges in all matters that refer to the life and society of the Empire. The Jew who wrote this Epistle must have lived long amid the society of the Empire ; and he could never have acquired such a tone and cast of thought, if he had spent his life mainly in Palestine and Mesopotamia.

II. The variation in the power and success of missions in different countries is obvious to the most casual observer. Missionary work does not radiate steadily forth from a centre. It moves along the lines of least resistance, and its course is determined by many conditions, which the historian must study and try to understand, while the men who are actually engaged in the work obey them, or are compelled by them, often without being fully conscious of them.

Now, let us apply this to the book of Acts. One of the most striking features in the book is the apparently restricted view that is taken of the spread of Christianity. We read of the way in which it was carried north to Antioch, and then north-west and west to the South Galatian cities, to Macedonia and Achaia, to Asia and to Rome; and when we have crossed the limits of the land of Rome, and approach the city,[1] the brethren come forth many miles to welcome us, and convoy us into the midst of an already existing Church in Rome. The news has reached the heart of the Empire long ago.

There is no reasonable possibility of doubting that Christian missionaries went in other directions and by many other paths than those described in Acts. We can trace the activity of nameless missionaries in many places, *e.g.*, in *Acts* xi. 19, in *Acts* xxviii. 15. Among them we must class the Judaising missionaries who troubled Paul, in South Galatia, in Rome, and probably everywhere. These unknown workers doubtless tried literally to "go forth into all the world".

The question is whether we are to class the silence of Luke about almost all this mass of active work among the "gaps," which so much trouble many scholars, or whether we should not rather look to discover some reason for his silence? It is plain that, in Luke's estimation, all the other missionaries sink into insignificance in comparison with the one great figure of Paul. They become important in proportion as they agree with his methods, and are guided

[1] Οὕτως εἰς τὴν Ῥώμην ἤλθαμεν *Acts* xxviii. 14, and εἰσήλθαμεν εἰς Ῥώμην xxviii. 16. On the distinction between these two phrases, which with singular blindness the commentators still persist in regarding as exactly equivalent, see *St. Paul the Traveller*, p. 347.

by his spirit. When they differ from him, they become
secondary figures, and disappear from Luke's pages.

Was Luke's vision restricted in this way merely because
he was dazzled by the brilliancy of Paul? Or may he have
had some better ground to stand on? One may speculate
on these alternatives in an abstract way ; but the more profitable method is to seek for some concrete facts on which
to found an hypothesis. Some facts bearing on the subject
are, I think, furnished by the distribution of second and
third century Christian inscriptions in Central Asia Minor.
Elsewhere it is pointed out that these inscriptions fall into
three groups, clearly marked off from one another both by
geographical separation and by style and character, pointing
to "three separate lines of Christian influence in Phrygia
during the early centuries".[1] . . . "It seems beyond question that the first line of influence spread from the Ægean
coastlands, and that its ultimate source was in St. Paul's
work in Ephesus, and in the efforts of his coadjutors during
the following years; while the second originated in the
earlier Pauline Churches of Derbe, Lystra, Iconium and
Antioch." The third belongs to the north-west of Phrygia,
and, by a remarkable coincidence, to the country which
Paul traversed between Pisidian Antioch and Troas (*Acts*
xvi. 6-8).

We possess only one document long enough to show
anything of the spirit of these early Churches, the epitaph
which a second-century presbyter or bishop[2] wrote "to be
an imperishable record of his testimony and message which
he had to deliver to mankind"; and it mentions (besides

[1] *Cities and Bishoprics of Phrygia*, pt. ii., p. 511.
[2] *Op. cit.*, p. 722 ff., where the voluminous literature about Avircius
Marcellus is described.

the main truths of his religion) the ever-present companion-
ship and guidance of Paul. It has survived to bear witness
that the Churches of Central Asia Minor continued to look
to Paul as their pattern and their guide more than a century
after his death.

Must we not take these facts as a sign that, so far as
Asia Minor is concerned, Luke perceived the truth? It was
the influence of Paul's spirit, acting directly or through his
followers and pupils, that was the really powerful force in
the country. Everything else becomes insignificant in comparison. So Luke thought: and so the facts bear witness.

Further, may this not have been the case elsewhere?
Perhaps Luke perceived the essential facts, and recorded
them. Perhaps it was only in the Roman world that men's
minds were ready for the new religion. If that religion
came "in the fulness of time," was not that "fulness of
time" wrought out by the unifying influence of Roman
organisation, and by the educating influence of Greek philosophical theory, so that it was only within the circle of these
influences that the Church grew? May it not be the case
that the pre-Pauline Church in Rome was recreated by
Paul, and acquired its future form and character from him;
and that thus the historian is justified in leaving its earlier
existence unmentioned until it came forth to welcome him
as he was approaching the gates of Rome? Certain it is
that Christianity was made the religion of the Roman
Empire by Paul, and by Paul's single idea; that Luke's
mind, as he wrote, was filled with that idea; and that he
fashioned his history with the view of showing how that idea
worked itself out in fact. Hence after A.D. 44 all other
missionary work, except what sprang from Paul, was unimportant in his estimation.

Is it so certain as many seem to hold that Luke's conception was inadequate? Would any extra-Roman spread of Christianity have been permanent? Would even the non-Pauline propagation southward towards Egypt (which may be assumed as certain) have been successful and lasting, had it not been reinforced by the Pauline spirit? Is not the case of Apollos in *Acts* xviii. 24 ff. really a typical one, as Luke evidently considered it?

A phrase which often occurred to me when, as an undergraduate, I was studying Greek philosophy for the schools, bears on this. As I tried to understand the character of those later systems in which the earlier and more purely Greek thought, when carried by the conquests of Alexander into the cities of the East, attempted to adapt itself to its new environment by assimilating the elements which the East had to contribute and which the Greek mind could never supply, the expressions often rose to my lips that these were the imperfect forms of Christianity, and again that Paul was the true successor of Aristotle.

The phrases were probably both caught from some source that I was studying (though I was never conscious of having read them); and, if so, I should be glad to learn where they occur. At the time, in 1875-1876, the writers who most influenced me were T. H. Green and Lightfoot. To both I owe almost equally much, though in very different ways. My debt to Green is similar to that of many Oxford students; though I never heard him lecture, and only twice or thrice was so far honoured as to be allowed to talk with him. The quality in Lightfoot's work that most impressed me was his transparent honesty, his obvious straining to understand and represent every person's opinion with scrupulous fairness. In him I was for the first time conscious of coming in contact with a mind that was educated, thoughtful, trained in scholarship, perfectly straight and honest, and yet able to accept simply the New Testament in the old-fashioned way, without refining it into metaphysical conceptions like Green, or rationalising it into commonplace and second-rate history like my German idols. The combination had previously seemed to me impossible in our age, though possible at an earlier time; and its occurrence in Lightfoot set me to rethink the grounds of my own position.

III. Why is Peter silent about Paul, when he is writing to so many of the Pauline Churches? This question is briefly touched by Hort; and, while saying nothing positive, he obviously inclines to the view that Paul was dead. He explains away the obvious remark, that some reference to the recent death of their great founder would seem imperatively demanded from Peter in writing to the Churches, by the supposition that the "sad tidings of Paul's death had been already made known to the Asiatic Christians by their Roman brethren or by St. Peter himself".[1]

But is it not clear in this Epistle that the writer is clad with authority, as the recognised head to whom the Pauline Churches looked for guidance and advice in a great crisis? The writer evidently speaks with full and conscious deliberation, because he feels that a serious trial awaits the Churches, and that he is the person to whom they look. This is distinctly inconsistent with the idea that Paul was living; and we need not doubt that this was the argument which weighed with Hort, and made him place the letter after Paul's death. The authority which Paul exercised over his Churches, and the discipline on which he laid such stress, would be violated,

[1] Hort, *First Epistle*, p. 6.

if another stepped in to address and comfort and encourage them, without a word of apology or explanation, without even a reference to Paul. That would be the act of a rival and not of a friend ; but it seems to me beyond all question that Peter was the most cordial and hearty supporter of Paul among the older Apostles, and the one with whom Paul felt most kinship in spirit. Especially is it clear that the author of this Epistle, whoever he was, must have been in the most cordial relations with the Pauline policy.

But is this letter conceivable even after Paul's death, except at some considerable interval? An analogy will help us in this question. Paul's silence about Peter in the letters to and from Rome is, in my estimation, a conclusive proof that Peter had never been instrumental in building up the Church of Rome, until after the last of these Epistles was written. Similarly, Peter's silence about Paul is to me con-clusive that Peter was now the recognised successor to Paul's position in relation to the Asian Churches ; [1] that he is not simply putting himself into that position without a reference to his dead friend ; but that he can look back over a lapse of some years, during which his standing had become es-tablished, and Paul's followers, Silas and Mark, had attached themselves to the company and service of his successor. So Rev. F. Warburton Lewis pointed out to me.

This view is not wholly inconsistent with the theory that First Peter was composed before the Apostle suffered under Nero, supposing that Paul suffered in 62 or even in 64, and that Peter survived till 67 or so. But, for my own part, I can see no ground for believing that Paul died before 66 or

[1] What ground is there for the general view that Peter was older than the Saviour, and much older than Paul ? It might be argued that he was four or five years younger than Christ, and nearly of an age with Paul.

even perhaps 67 ; and in that case the life of Peter must have lasted into the time of Vespasian, as no persecution can have occurred while the wars of the succession absorbed Roman attention.

IV. Now that Hort has laid down with a precision characteristic of himself, and with a decisiveness and finality that is almost rare in his work, the principle that the Churches of Asia Minor are classified according to the provinces of the Roman Empire, and not according to the non-Roman national divisions, and has stated positively and unhesitatingly that the Pauline Churches in Phrygia and Lycaonia [1] were classed by St. Peter as Churches of Galatia, it is to be hoped that the progress of study will no longer be impeded by laboured attempts to prove that it was impossible or inaccurate for Paul to class them as his Churches of Galatia, or by equally futile attempts to prove that the name Galatia was never applied to the great Roman Province of Central Asia Minor, stretching across nearly from sea to sea. It will remain as one of the curiosities of scholarship that in this last decade, after these points had long been taken as settled by all historical students, so many distinguished theologians, after casting a hasty glance into the antiquities of Asia Minor, should print discussions of the subject proving that that which was could not possibly have been.

But if Peter, as Hort declares, classed Antioch, Iconium, Derbe and Lystra among the Churches of Galatia, must not Paul have done the same thing? Is it likely that First Peter, a letter so penetrated with the Pauline spirit, so much influenced by at least two Pauline epistles, composed in such close relations with two of Paul's coadjutors, Silas and Mark,

---

[1] Hort, *First Peter*, pp. 17, 157 ff.

should class the Pauline Churches after a method that Paul would not employ?

Further, Hort lays down as a matter of certainty that Asia throughout the New Testament means the Province, therein contradicting the recent ideas of Professors Blass and Zahn. Must we not then take Galatia in Paul on the same analogy, and admit that when he wrote to the Churches of Galatia he included among them all Churches within the bounds of the Province?

It has just been said that Hort speaks on this subject with a decisiveness and finality that is not so common in his work. It is characteristic of him, rather, never to reach decisiveness. He seems always to have been keenly conscious how much subjectivity is liable to be admitted into the judgment of the most careful, cool and mature scholar, and to have often shrunk from feeling confident in his own best proved conclusions. One of our best scholars told me in a different connection a story which illustrates this quality. Speaking of the authorship of Second Peter, he said he had once spoken to Hort on the subject. Hort replied somewhat to this effect: My first impulse is to say that the same hand which wrote the first epistle could not have written the second. But, then, my second impulse is to doubt whether I can be right in thinking so.

Was it not this quality, which is closely connected with his love of perfect truth and his unwillingness to leave the smallest trace of error in his work, that prevented him from writing more, and deprived us of much that we had almost a right to expect from his admirable scholarship, his wide range of knowledge, and his clear judgment? He that is never content till he has risen superior to the weakness of humanity, who is unwilling to print anything till he has purged it of the minutest trace of error, will write little. But, worse than that, it is very doubtful whether he will ever write his best. While he spends his time polishing up the less important details, he sometimes loses his grasp of the essential and guiding clue. Truth will not wait to be wooed after we shall have finished the accessories. We must press forward, when the goddess allows a glimpse of her face to be visible for a moment; it will be veiled again immediately; it may be never again unveiled to the too cautious seeker. He who attempts the pursuit must be content to arrive bearing the stains and mud and dust of travel; and, if he is too careful to avoid soiling his feet, he is less likely to reach his aim.

It seems a sort of retribution on the man, whose too delicate and overstrained love of perfection deprived the world of the work it had always expected from him, that his manuscripts should be published after his death by the piety of his pupils—a piety so reverent that they apparently shrink even from the thought that anything in his work could need correction. For example, in his too short edition of the opening chapters of First Peter, there is an essay on the provinces of Asia Minor. It was written, apparently, in the year 1882, for I see no reference to anything not accessible in that year. Hort was lecturing on the Epistle as late as 1887; but it may be doubted if he did anything at this essay during the intermediate years. He evidently studied carefully the inscriptions bearing on this subject, while preparing the essay; but he studied them in 1882, and shows no knowledge of several inscriptions which (with Mommsen's commentary on them) would have materially modified his statements on some points. The essay is, indeed, remarkably accurate, considering when it was composed. It is, of course, founded on Marquardt's *Römische Staatsalterthümer;* but it tacitly avoids several of Marquardt's mistakes, and shows an admirable tact in selecting what was permanent and true in the views current at that period. There are few statements that could have been called erroneous at that time;[1] but, surely, there might have been found among his pupils some one who would take the trouble to look over at least the parts of the Berlin Corpus that have been published since Hort's death, and mingle sufficient courage with his piety to correct (or at least to omit) the statements which the progress of discovery has shown to be inaccurate. Thus, for example, the old statement (founded on Dion), that Claudius instituted the province of Lycia-Pamphylia in A.D. 43, appears on p. 162, though the difficulties of this view are plainly stated. It is now established by Mommsen's commentary on a recently discovered Pamphylian inscription that Pamphylia was a distinct procuratorial province for some time later, then was connected with Galatia for a short time, and at last was united to Lycia by Vespasian.

But enough of the ungrateful task of pointing out faults! Yet it is regrettable that Hort's work should be treated with such undutiful dutifulness; and that English scholarship should be exposed to the just criticism of the foreigner, that it seems to be ignorant that some errors have been eliminated between 1882 and 1898 and that these should not appear any longer in print under the patronage of an honoured name.[2]

[1] I quote one to justify the criticism. On p. 162, note 3, he treats as part of the reorganisation of the East by Pompey in B.C. 64 the gift of parts of Pamphylia to Amyntas, which was really made by Antonius in 36.

[2] In i. 7 Hort sees that an adjective is needed, and is inclined to accept the poorly attested reading δόκιμον. Why should not an editor indicate that Deissmann has discovered the adjective δοκίμιος, and thus justified Hort's inclination in an unexpected way.

V. Did early Christian travellers pack their baggage?
This question is suggested by *Acts* xxi. 15, where Dr. Blass
rejects the reading ἐπισκευασάμενοι [1] on the ground that (1)
there are no other cases where this verb means "collecting
one's baggage" (*sarcinis collectis*), and (2) it is strange that
packing up should be mentioned here and nowhere else on
the journey. But, on the contrary, it seems only natural
that the equipment should be mentioned here and nowhere
else. Dr. Blass has taken too narrow a view of the process
of equipment. The company was changing from sea-voyage
to landfaring. Equipment was needed to perform the
journey of sixty-four miles to Jerusalem in two days, and
this was provided in Cæsareia, and was brought back to
Cæsareia by the disciples from the night's halting-place.
Let us look into this carefully and from the proper point
of view, and not as travellers in trains or by Cook's excur-
sions, for whom everything is arranged with the minimum
of exertion on their part. The company had spent in
Cæsareia the time during which they might have been
making their journey quietly and easily to Jerusalem; yet
they were pressed for time, if they were anxious to arrive
before a near day. If they waited till the last moment at
Cæsareia, as they obviously did,[2] this implies that they were
calculating their journey very nearly, and reckoning it to a
matter of hours. Now it is an elementary principle of right

[1] He proposes the conjecture ἀπασπασάμενοι, but wisely refrains from
putting it in the text.

[2] On the one hand it is clear that the fifty days had not elapsed between
the start from Philippi and the arrival at Cæsareia, and that, after reaching
Cæsareia, they had it in their power to reach Jerusalem in time for Pentecost.
On the other hand, by waiting several days (πλείους ἡμέρας) at Cæsareia, it is
equally clear that they were running it very fine, and were leaving themselves
no margin.

living in southern countries that one must avoid those great
exertions and strains which in northern lands we habitually
take as an amusement. The customs of the modern people
show that this principle guides their whole life ; and it may
be taken for certain that in ancient time the same principle
guided ordinary life. Moreover, Paul was accompanied by
his physician, who fully realised the importance of the
principle, and knew that Paul, subject as he was to attacks
of illness and constantly exposed to great mental and emotional strains, must not begin his duties in Jerusalem by a
hurried walk of sixty-four miles in two days.

In a word, they arranged for horses or conveyances to
take them without fatigue over a great part of the long
journey ; and they had been able to stay so long in Cæsareia
because it had been settled with the disciples there that this
should be done. The whole journey must have been discussed and planned ; and it is just because the method was
unusual for that company of travellers, and because it had
therefore taken time to settle details, that it is so pointedly
mentioned in the narrative.[1] The horses then conveyed
the company rapidly along the level coast road to a point
where the ascent to the highlands of Judæa began,[2] probably
to Lydda, a distance of forty miles. The disciples returned
to Cæsareia, taking the animals with them ; and Paul's
company could safely perform the twenty-four miles' walk

---

[1] One other case occurs in which, as I think, Paul's disciples sent him on
by horse or carriage (see *Church in Rom. Emp.*, p. 68), where the evidence is
contained, not in *Acts*, which was written by one who had not been present,
but in Paul's own words to his entertainers. In this case, also, the conveyance was, I doubt not, provided by the Cæsarean disciples, and not hired by
Paul himself. They brought Paul to the village, and took home the horses.

[2] Every reader of Professor G. A. Smith's *Historical Geography* will recognise how much his lucid pictures help in conceiving this journey properly.

to Jerusalem on the following day. So far, then, from ἐπισκευασάμενοι being used, as Dr. Blass thinks, in an unexampled sense here, it is probably used in its proper and commonest sense, " having equipped (animals)" ;[1] and, when we translate it in its ordinary sense in classical Greek, we find the journey described exactly as any common pagan traveller would have made it. But many people write and think about *Acts* as if the early Christians never could have lived or travelled like ordinary men.

VI. As this Article has been largely devoted to Dr. Hort, the following brief estimate and reminiscence of that great scholar may be added.

It may be not unbecoming for one who cannot pretend to estimate Dr. Hort's merits as a theologian, to venture to add a word on the loss which ancient history has sustained by his death. In an epoch of surpassing interest in the history of the world, his work is a sure and strong foundation for the historian to work on ; and it could never have been so if he had confined his survey to the Christian documents alone, and had not been guided by a wide outlook over the whole field of contemporary history. The early Christian writers were environed by the Roman Empire; and one could not talk for half an hour with Dr. Hort without seeing how clearly he realised that fact and the necessary inference from it, that the want of a vivid and accurate conception of the Roman world as a whole is certain to produce distortion in one's conception of the historical position of the early Christian writers. Many of

---

[1] Chrysostom clearly understood the word so. He explains it as τὰ πρὸς τὴν ὁδοιπορίαν λαβόντες (*i.e.*, ὑποζύγια) ; cp. Pollux, x., 14, quoted by Wetstein (with a misprint), ἐπεσκευασμένα ἦν τὰ ὑποζύγια, οἶον ἐστρωματισμένα. The ellipsis of ὑποζύγια is natural, when we take the word, with Pollux, as " having saddled ".

PLATE XIV.

Fig. 20.—Sarcophagus in the Ruins near the Arch of Severus
(Mrs. Christie of Tarsus).

To face p. 268.

See p. 281.

the modern so-called "critical" theories about them could never have been proposed, had the authors possessed a clear idea of the whole life and history of the period. From such falseness of view, and from other possible distortions in a different direction, Dr. Hort was saved, partly of course by his natural genius, but to a considerable extent by his university training; and I hope the day is far distant when theologians will start without such preliminary discipline in historical facts and method. Perhaps also one may express the hope, with which I know that Dr. Hort strongly sympathised, that the day will soon come when the historians will recognise how much they sacrifice by their almost complete overlooking of the early Christian writers as authorities for the general history of the period.

The first time that I had the opportunity of meeting Dr. Hort—in Dr. Westcott's house at Cambridge in 1887— was only sufficient for me to learn what a vigorous, sympathetic, wide and masculine intellect his was. But the only occasion on which I could really profit by his knowledge was in June, 1892, when his health was already broken. Dr. Sanday ordered me (for his advice I accepted as a command) to call on him, and had arranged that my call should not seem an intrusion. The conversation was entirely about the lectures which I had just had the honour of giving at Mansfield College; and I was much encouraged to find that many of the views I had expressed met with his cordial approval, and that his criticisms on matters of detail as a rule only strengthened the general position. In one point I owe him eternal gratitude. I mentioned that the period to which tradition assigned the New Testament documents seemed to me to be correct in all cases except one: First Peter appeared to me to be fixed inexorably to a period A.D. 75-85. Before I could go on to state the inference which appeared to me necessary, and which I had drawn in one of my lectures—that the Epistle could not be the work of the Apostle—he broke in with much animation that he had always felt that there was no tradition of any value as to the date of Peter's death : the martyrdom was clearly and well attested, but its period rested on no authority. I caught from him at once the idea, which I have since worked out at some length, that First Peter, though composed about A.D. 75, is still a genuine work. At the time he seemed very favourably inclined to this date, and suggested several points bearing on it. Perhaps on subsequent reflection he may have seen objections to it which did not come up in conversation ; nor do I wish to claim him as finally supporting this view, because he for a short time busied himself in suggesting circumstances that told in its favour, several of which were of a kind that I cannot myself use, as I restrict myself to external and archæological evidence. But certain it is that I left him (after he had kept me so long that I feared it would do him harm in his obviously weak state) with the impression in my mind that he would work out the idea in lines different from mine, and in a way that I could not attain to. Whether he afterwards rejected it or not will now perhaps never be known.

PLATE XV.

FIG. 21.—Looking up towards the Cilician Gates (Mrs. W. M. Ramsay).

See p. 282.

PLATE XVI.

FIG. 22.—In the Cilician Gates (Mrs. W. M. Ramsay).

To face p. 270.

See p. 283.

XI

ST. PAUL'S ROAD FROM CILICIA TO ICONIUM

XI

ST. PAUL'S ROAD FROM CILICIA TO ICONIUM

THE western part of Cilicia is a triangular plain, whose base is the sea, and whose apex lies in a corner formed by the Taurus Mountains bounding Cilicia on the north. In the apex the river Saros issues from its wonderfully romantic course of more than a hundred miles through the lofty Taurus and enters the low sea plain. There was a time when this level plain was a great gulf of the sea. The gulf has been gradually filled up by the two great Cilician rivers, the Pyramos and the Saros, probably aided by slight elevations of the level of the land;[1] and of the two rivers the Saros has been the chief agent in determining the character of the plain.

The road from Syria and the East enters the western Cilician plain by a pass through which the Pyramos also enters the plain. At the western end of this pass the river turns down towards the south, and the road crosses it by a large bridge (Fig. 10). The crossing has always been a highly important point in all military operations in Cilicia. A garrison and a fortress had to be placed there to guard the passage of the river. Thus arose the city of Mopsou-Hestia, "the Hearth of Mopsus" (the Greek prophet and interpreter of the will of the Greek god Apollo, who marks the advance of the old Ionian colonists into the Cilician land). In this

---

[1] Dr. Christie of Tarsus has observed a series of raised sea beaches.

exposed situation Mopsou-Hestia, whose name has gradually degenerated into the modern form Missis, was exposed to the force of every invasion. Every enemy that would enter the fertile plain must first capture the city, whose situation was not susceptible of any strong defence in ancient warfare. Every successful invader first destroyed the city, and then restored it to guard the passage against future invaders. No city has experienced a more calamitous history and been more frequently captured than Missis.[1]

The road passes on over the plain to Adana on the Saros, which again is crossed by a long bridge (Fig. 11). Adana is situated near the apex of the plain. It is the natural centre of distribution for the whole plain, and capital of the country. In the beginning it must have been the capital of Cilicia ; it has a splendid acropolis ; and the natural path across Taurus leads up from Adana into Cappadocia. But it is far from the sea, and the mouth of the Saros has never been navigable, so that, when maritime intercourse was important, the presidency of the country passed either to Mallos on the Pyramos, or to Tarsus on the small river Cydnus. Those two disputed the primacy for centuries. In the Turkish period, when navigation ceased to be of any importance, the primacy in the country passed again to Adana.

From Adana the road goes on to Tarsus. In modern time it crosses the river Cydnus just before entering the city (Fig. 12). But in ancient time the river flowed in a different channel through the heart of the city. The change in its course was the work of Justinian in the sixth century after Christ. The channel of the Cydnus required to be carefully kept, in order to provide for the unimpeded course

---

[1] Langlois, in *Revue Archéologique*, 1855, p. 410 ff., describes the remains of the city.

PLATE XVII.

Fig. 23.—In the Vale of Bozanti (Mrs. W. M. Ramsay).

To face p. 274.   *See p.* 284.

of the water ; as the energy and prudence of government degenerated in later Roman time, the channel was allowed to get into bad order, and part of the city was liable to be flooded. Justinian cut a relief channel, which was intended only to carry off the surplus water in time of flood and pour it into the channel of a small stream (dry except in time of rain) which flowed parallel to the old Cydnus on the east side of the city. But gradually the bed of the Cydnus within the city was blocked ; and the new channel carried more and more of the water. In early modern time travellers saw both channels flowing; but now only the new channel carries any permanent flow of water. An artificial watercourse for purposes of irrigation diverts part of the Cydnus through the gardens on the north and west of the modern town ; but it does not coincide, either in its exit from the main stream or in its channel, with the old Cydnus bed, which can be traced in the southern part of the city.

The walls of Tarsus have been pulled down in comparatively recent time. There remains now only one fragment, a gateway on the west side of the town with a small part of the wall adjoining. A second gate on the east side, which was in even better preservation, was destroyed only a few years ago. The one remaining gate is popularly called "St. Paul's Gate" (Fig. 13), but there is no justification for attaching the Apostle's name to it. The walls and gates were wholly a work of the mediæval period; and at "St. Paul's Gate" one sees fine stones of the Roman time embedded in the centre of the masonry. The work though late is of good character ; and it is probable that these walls were substantially the defences built by Haroun-al-Raschid, when he restored and refortified and repeopled Tarsus about A.D. 780-800, to serve as basis of operations in his attempt to concentrate the military power of the Khalifate on the conquest of the Roman Empire, though they were often injured and repaired since his time.

The building of the walls implies that Tarsus had sunk into decay. The reason lay in the growth of a second Tarsus on the hills in front of Taurus, about ten to twelve miles north of the city of the plain. The old Tarsus had been defenceless, without a citadel and without strong walls. In the later Roman Empire, when these lands became exposed to invasion, the situation was too unsafe ; and a more defensible city gradually formed itself on the high ground, as will be described below. The modern Tarsus on the ancient site was the creation of Haroun-al-Raschid. It has retained the ancient name, which has lasted with only the slightest change from the Tarshish of Genesis x. 4 in the second millennium B.C.[1] to the Tersous of the present day.

The most striking episode in the wars of Haroun, " Aaron-the-Just," is associated with the writing of one of the most remarkable letters in all history. The Romans were in the habit of paying a yearly tribute to the Khalifs ; Irene, who made herself Empress by assassinating her own son the Iconoclast Constantine and with difficulty maintained herself in that position through the strenuous support of the Orthodox party, had so slight a hold on the reins of power that she had submitted to accept this mark of servitude. When Nicephorus I. succeeded her in A.D. 802, he wrote to Haroun, refusing to pay any longer the tribute which only a timid woman would have consented to pay, declaring that the rightful relation between the Empires was that the barbarians ought to pay double that tribute to the Roman

[1] On the identity of Tarshish and Tarsus, see the discussion in *Expositor*, April, 1906, p. 366 ff.

PLATE XVIII.

FIG. 24.—Looking up towards White Bridge (Mrs. W. M. Ramsay).

See p. 286.

PLATE XIX.

FIG. 25.—Looking down towards White Bridge (Mrs. W. M. Ramsay).

To face p. 276. See p. 287.

sovereign, and appealing to the issue of war. The ambassadors, after delivering his letter, which was expressed in the form " From Nicephorus, Emperor of the Greeks, to Aaron, King of the Arabs," were instructed to throw down a bundle of swords before the steps of the Khalif's throne.

The Khalif, according to the story of the Arabs, drew his scimitar of supernatural fabric and hacked the Greek swords in twain without turning the edge of his weapon. Then he dictated his answer to the Emperor's letter—an answer whose brevity left nothing omitted :—

> In the name of God the All-Gracious, the All-Merciful, Aaron-the-Just, Commander of the Faithful, to the dog of the Greeks. I have read thy letter, thou son of an infidel mother. The answer thou shalt not merely learn, thou shalt see with thine own eyes.

The answer appeared in the march of a mighty army.

Owing to that apparently complete break in the history of Tarsus, there was necessarily an interruption in the continuity of Christian tradition. No memory of Pauline sites could have survived, as there was no continuous Christian society to preserve the recollection. Besides the false " St. Paul's Gate," there is a " Well of St. Paul " shown in the courtyard of a house in Tarsus ; but the owner of the house, an educated and intelligent Syrian, of a family settled for three generations in Tarsus, who speaks English with ease and exceptionally good accent, told me that the sole foundation for the name was that a marble plaque bearing the name of the Apostle had been found when his father had had the well cleared out. The plaque was discovered in a small cell or chamber which opened on to the shaft of the well.

The road from Tarsus to the West and to Rome by Derbe and Ephesus has to cross the lofty mountains of

Taurus, snow-clad during great part of the year, as they
are seen from the little hill beside the American College (in
Fig. 15). This hill is really formed by the accumulation of
soil over ancient buildings, and is not a natural elevation.
The pass by which the road crosses the mountains carries
the only road practicable for wheeled traffic from Cilicia to
the central plateau of Asia Minor. The importance of
Tarsus in history was to a great extent due to its position
at the end of this great historic road. The road had to be
cut by hand through the rock for a considerable distance at
several points; and it was the energy of the Tarsians in
making the road many centuries before Christ which laid
the foundation for the future greatness of the city. It was
probably the enterprise of the early Greek colonists that
planned and undertook this really great engineering work.
This artificial road was far superior to the natural path
from Adana across the mountains; and there is no proof
that the people of Adana ever seriously tried to improve
their road.

If the primacy of Cilicia passed from Adana to Tarsus,
the reason lay in the superior energy and enterprise of the
Tarsians, which counterbalanced the superior natural advantages of Adana. The same activity and boldness were
shown by the Tarsians in opening their city to the sea. The
Cydnus ran through the centre of Tarsus and entered a
shallow lagoon a few miles below the city; it had no direct
navigable communication with the sea. A bank of sand
over which the sea broke barred the communication. Engineering operations assisted nature, defined the lagoon,
formed it into a lake which made a splendid land-locked
harbour for ships, cleared and deepened the lower course of
the river, embanked and bordered the river and the lake with

PLATE XX.

FIG. 26.—Above White Bridge : Rock-gate cut to take the Ancient Road
(Mrs. W. M. Ramsay).

See p. 288.

PLATE XXI.

FIG. 27.—At Twin Khan, looking up the Water of Bulghar Maden
To face p. 278. (Mrs. W. M. Ramsay). See p. 288.

piers and docks. Thus Tarsus, like modern Glasgow, made its own river and its own harbour.

Just as the cutting of the road over Taurus gave Tarsus the advantage over Adana, so the great engineering operations in its river and lake made it superior to Mallos, and ousted that city on the great river Pyramos from its old rank as the chief port of Cilicia. In the making of the harbour it stands out clear that the Greek maritime colonists in Tarsus again played the leading part. It was as a meeting-place of oriental Cilicians and occidental Ionians that Tarsus became great. Hence it is mentioned in Genesis x. 4 as Tarshish child of the Ionian (Javan).

The crossing of Taurus is made by way of the great historic pass called "the Cilician Gates," which lies about thirty miles north of Tarsus. The road therefore issues from the city on the north side, and immediately crosses the new channel which Justinian made for the river Cydnus and which is now the only channel. Close above the little bridge is a waterfall, where the river flows over a ledge of rocks in a picturesque and irregular cascade of about ten to fifteen feet in height (Fig. 16). Before the river was diverted into this course the rocks were cut to form graves; and when the water is low many of these graves can be seen, which are hidden from view when the Cydnus is swollen by the melting snows of Taurus.

The modern road was constructed by Ibrahim Pasha of Egypt during his gallant attempt in 1832-1840 to overthrow the Ottoman Sultan and to make his father the supreme ruler of Turkey, an attempt in which—after inflicting on Von Moltke, then an officer in the Turkish service, the only defeat which that great general ever sustained—he was finally foiled by the British guns under Sir Sidney Smith and the bombardment of Acre. The road fell into disrepair after 1840, and was restored by a series of spasmodic efforts made from time to time during the last twenty-six years. It ascends the valley of the little stream, into which Justinian conducted the surplus waters of the Cydnus, and then turns in a winding course west across the undulating hills to enter the glen of the Cydnus at about thirty-seven kilometres (twenty-four miles) from Tarsus, and keeps on up a branch of the Cydnus to the Cilician Gates, fifty-four kilometres (thirty-four miles) from Tarsus.

The Roman road followed a straighter line. It went nearly north over the plateau that divides the glen of the Cydnus from the more open valley which the modern road prefers. Its course can be traced for miles in this part, and the surface is sometimes quite good, being formed of rectangular slabs of stone (Fig. 17). About twelve miles from Tarsus, near the village of Bairamli, it is spanned by a triumphal arch (Figs. 18 f.), which I conjecture to have been built in honour of the Emperor Septimius Severus, who marched down this road towards his final victory over his rival, Pescennius Niger, in the battle near Issus, A.D. 194. A four-horse car, Quadrigæ, once stood on the top of the arch; and the place is mentioned on coins of Tarsus under the name Kodrigai (in Greek letters).[1] Langlois, in his excellent paper, *Revue Archéologique*, 1856, p. 481, is disposed to date the arch under Constantine.

The arch is near the highest part of a broad ridge, about 1,400 feet above the sea; and it commands a magnificent view of the entire Cilician coast with the gulf of Issus, the

---

[1] I have described the evidence in the *Bulletin de Corresp. Hellén.*, 1898, p. 234. A different view was taken by Professor Kubitschek, *Numismat. Zeitschrift*, xxvii., p. 87 f.

PLATE XXII.

FIG. 28.—Old Turkish Bridge in the Gorge above Twin
Khan (Mrs. W. M. Ramsay).

  See p. 288.

western plain, and the mountain-wall of Taurus on the north.

Around the arch, and especially on the west, stretching as far as the gorge of the Cydnus, is a bewildering mass of ruins, temples, houses, tombs, sarcophagi, etc., overgrown with brushwood and difficult to traverse. These form a city, strongly fortified by great walls which skilfully take advantage of the hilly ground. We have here a second Tarsus, belonging to the late Roman period, not a mere adjunct to the city of the plain, but a really great city, which however was not independent but merely part of Tarsus, for it stands within the territory of that city. It is shown by the coins that all the territory up to the " Bounds of the Cilicians " belonged to Tarsus (Fig. 20).

Originally, this second Tarsus was doubtless a mere summer city and country residence for the population of the lower town. But, when the danger of invasion made the Tarsians seek for stronger defences, it is probable that this hill city became the principal place, as being a great walled city offering military strength and safety to the whole population of Tarsus. The Jerusalem Itinerary, which belongs to the fourth century, puts Tarsus twenty-four Roman miles south of the Cilician Gates ; and probably this hill city was the Tarsus which the Jerusalem pilgrim [1] saw. From this city, then, he turned east to Adana, and never went south to the Tarsus of the plain.

The Roman road must touch the modern road somewhere near the thirty-third kilometre from Tarsus. It is still undetermined whether it thereafter followed the winding modern line, or went straight on over the hilly ground direct towards

---

[1] He travelled by land from Bordeaux to Jerusalem and back, A.D. 333.

the Gates. On the modern road, in the Cydnus glen, about thirty-eight kilometres from Tarsus, is a khan called Mazar-Oluk with a large fountain of water. If the Roman road took this course, the fountain would have to be regarded as the ancient Mopsou-krene, Fountain of Mopsus, often mentioned as a station between Tarsus and the Gates, whose name furnishes the proof[1] that Ionian Greek colonists were (as we have said) instrumental in building and cutting that great Tarsian road. But I am disposed to think that the ancient road crossed the modern road at right angles and went straight on over the hills northwards. In that case Mopsou-krene would have to be sought in the hilly ground east of the Cydnus gorge ; and its discovery by some explorer may be hoped for.

The whole of this ground over which the road winds is undulating, and the valleys between the rising grounds are cultivated, fertile and well-watered. The wild olive and wild vine abound. The gorge of the Cydnus is very picturesque, and becomes wilder and grander as we travel northward. The country is well-wooded with wild olive, various kinds of fir, plane trees, oaks, cedars, etc.

About kilometre forty-four we reach Sarishek-Khan. Here the Roman road, if it took the short route over the hills, would join the modern road ; and here a road comes in from Adana. This is an ancient site.

Thereafter we ascend rapidly, and the scenery becomes grander. We have reached the steep slopes of the Taurus proper. After a few more kilometres, the Cilician Gates (kilometre fifty-four) appear in front of us (Fig. 21), 3,750 feet above the sea. The Gates are a deep gap, worn by the Cydnus through a lofty wall of rock that runs athwart our

[1] See p. 273.

PLATE XXIII.

Fig. 29.—The Castle of Loulon (Mrs. W. M. Ramsay).

To face p. 282.   *See p.* 289.

path. Originally there was only room for the stream, until the Ionian Tarsians cut out of the rock on the west bank space for a waggon-road. The pass is singularly grand; and a strong wind seems always to blow up it from the hot country of Cilicia to the cold summit of Taurus. A mediæval castle crowns the rock wall at the western edge of the Gates; and there is a path across this mountain wall, by which it would be possible in ancient times for an enemy to turn the flank of the defenders in the Gates. Inscriptions of Roman time on the rocks place here the "Bounds of the Cilicians" (Fig. 22).

That narrow gorge must have been a serious obstacle to the first Crusaders, one of whose armies at least, under Tancred and Baldwin, passed this way. They called it "the Gate of Judas," because it was the enemy of their faith and the betrayer of their cause.[1]

North of the Gates the road rises rapidly for a few kilometres until it reaches a bare broad pass, now called Tekir, about 4,250 feet high, bounded right and left by hills a few hundred feet higher, behind which the mountains rise still more. While the Gates were the natural point of defence in ancient time, the Tekir summit is the line of defence in modern warfare; and here Ibrahim Pasha drew his military lines, when he was compelled to abandon his conquests farther north. On the sides of this bare summit the snow must be deep and even dangerous in winter. In B.C. 314 Antigonus attempted to march from Cilicia northwards, but lost many of his soldiers in the snow, and had to return into Cilicia. A second attempt at a more favourable opportunity was successful.[2] Haroun-al-Raschid crossed the pass in the early winter of A.D. 803-804, and thus took the

[1] *Letters to the Seven Churches*, p. 10.   [2] Diodorus, xix., 69, 2.

Byzantine Emperor Theophilus unawares.[1] A hardy traveller, by watching his opportunity, can cross the pass even in the winter season. But the peaceable population in ancient times seem to have regarded the mountains as closed (like the sea) in winter, and to have expected the return of summer before attempting to traverse them.[2] And, in truth, there are times when it would be dangerous for any traveller to attempt the crossing.

Somewhere on the sides or top of the Tekir summit there was a large khan in ancient times for the benefit of travellers. It was probably maintained by the State, and hence is specially mentioned under the name Panhormus.

From Tekir the road, which hitherto has had a northerly direction, descends rapidly towards north-east, down a narrow glen beside a little stream. At kilometre seventy-three we enter the Vale of Bozanti, the ancient Podandos (2,800 feet), a little valley about two and a half miles long from north to south, and one and a half broad, entirely surrounded by lofty mountains (Fig. 23). Basil describes it with horror in his *Epist.*, 64 : " When I mention Podandos, suppose me to mean the pit Ceadas at Sparta or any natural pit that you may have seen, spots breathing a noxious vapour to which some have involuntarily given the name Charonian ". It is a very beautiful little valley, as we have seen it, in bright sunny weather.

High over us on the right, as we enter the Vale of Bozanti, perched on the summit of the mountains is a Byzantine castle, Anasha-Kale, described by Langlois [3] as

---

[1] Weil, *Geschichte der Khalifen*, ii., p. 159.

[2] See the quotations in Art. XV. from Basil, describing a country more open and less exposed to snow-drifts than the Taurus Pass.

[3] His paper in *Revue Archéologique*, 1850, p. 481 ff., is well worth study.

PLATE XXIV.

FIG, 30.—Looking South-East up the River towards the Snowy summit
of Taurus ; Ibriz on the right.

To face p. 284.   *See p.* 261.

built of black marble. This castle, called Rodentos by Constantine Porphyrogenitus, was held by the Crusaders for a time, and their historians call it and the vale beneath it Butrentum. On a rock near the castle, overhanging the precipice, are the little crosses which many of the Crusading warriors cut as memorials of themselves. "Those armies were led by the noblest of their peoples, by statesmen, princes and great ecclesiastics. Yet not one written memorial of all those Crusading hosts has been found in the whole country."[1]

The castle of black marble among the lonely mountains beyond the frontier of the Mohammedan land is familiar to every reader of the *Arabian Nights*: it occurs in more than one of the tales, if I remember rightly, but the story whose scene is most evidently laid in the Vale of Bozanti will be mentioned on the following page.

Through the Vale of Bozanti flows a river, called Tchakut-Su or Bozanti-Su, which runs away south-eastwards to join the Saros a little above Adana. The mountains close in around it below the Vale, and its course cannot be followed except by wading through the water, which is too deep for comfort and even safety in some places. Colonel Massy, formerly Consul in Mersina, informed me, on the authority of the engineers who made the survey for the Bagdad Railway, that the mountains actually close in overhead and the river runs through a tunnel; but neither he nor I can vouch for this from eye-witness. This seems to be the only possible route for the Railway, which will be very expensive in this section.

---

[1] *Letters to the Seven Churches*, p. 10, where the illiteracy of the Crusaders, A.D. 1100, is contrasted with the general power of writing possessed by Greek and Carian mercenaries in the Egyptian service B.C. 600.

The Tchakut-Su rises on the central plateau south of
Tyana and west of Ulu-Kishla, and offers an easy gradient
for the Railway through the Taurus, though much rock-
cutting and building for protection against loose rock will
be necessary in some parts of its course.

Our road goes north two miles along the western edge
of the vale and then turns westwards up the glen of the
Tchakut-Su, which is singularly grand and picturesque.
The gorge narrows and the mountains rise more and more
steep as we advance. After kilometre eighty we cross to the
north bank by the White Bridge (Ak-Keupreu), which in
1890, when I first saw it, was a quaint little mediæval bridge
with pointed arch and low parapet, but was soon afterwards
rebuilt in incongruous style with considerable stone em-
bankments on each side concealing one of the springs of
water that rise close to it on the southern side. In Fig. 24
the White Bridge is hid from view at the left side of the
picture.

Space does not permit me to repeat here the legends
which are told about these fountains, the Black Water (Kara-
Su) and Sugar Spring (Sheker-Bunar), and the tale of the fish
which caused the death of the Khalif Al-Mamun in A.D. 883.[1]
But the connection of the localities with a tale in the *Arabian
Nights* demands a word of notice. The tale of the fisherman,
who caught the strange fish of four colours, Christian, Moslem,
Jew and Magian, had its origin in Tarsus, the city of the
Sultan Al-Mamun (who died there). The fish were caught
"in a pond situated betwixt four hills, beyond the mountain
which was seen from the city". These are the fish of the

---

[1] They are narrated in an article " Cilicia Tarsus and the great Taurus
Pass " (*Geograph. Journal*, Oct., 1903, pp. 391-393) ; the last also in *Impressions of Turkey*, p. 288 f.

PLATE XXV.

Fig. 31.—The Sarcophagus of Sidamaria.

To face p. 286.
See p. 293.

Sugar Spring beside White Bridge (now destroyed, but still a picturesque pond as late as 1891, when I saw it for the second time). In the tale the Sultan encamped beside this pond, just as the Khalif Al-Mamun encamped beside White Bridge ; and from the pond the Sultan went away alone, " till he saw before him a great building: when he came near he found it was a magnificent palace, or rather a very strong castle, of fine black polished marble," the castle of Butrentum. The crossing of the mountain of Taurus, visible from Tarsus, the descent into the plain between mountains on all four sides, the pond with the marvellous fish, the castle of black marble among the mountains—all these are true details of the Vale of Bozanti.

The ancient road did not cross at White Bridge, but kept on the north bank for some distance down the river. Much cutting was needed to carry it through the rock below White Bridge, and three " Gates " were carved through projecting spurs of the northern cliffs. At the western end of the western " Gate " is an early Byzantine inscription, probably the work of some pilgrim bound for Jerusalem, " Lord! help Martyrius the Deacon ". The northern pier and part of the roadway of another mediæval bridge, narrower and older than White Bridge and about one hundred yards below it, can be seen in Fig. 24. At no other place can the work of the ancient road be better studied.

The White Bridge is now the boundary of Cilicia, dividing Adana Vilayet from Konia Vilayet ; and it was also the boundary between Ibrahim Pasha's country and the Ottoman territory as fixed in 1839 for a short time.

Above and west of this bridge the gorge grows deeper and gloomier (Fig. 25). On the south a wall of rock, which one would guess to be 1,500 feet in sheer perpendicular height,[1] borders the stream for more than a mile.

The road follows the north bank, and frequently traces of ancient cutting can be observed beside the easily distinguished blasting for the modern road (Fig. 26). The ancient road was destroyed during the Arab wars between A.D. 660 and 960 in order to render the passage between Arab Cilicia and Byzantine territory more difficult.

The road passes the Wooden Bridge (Takhta-Keupreu), which spans an affluent from the plateau on the north; and goes on due west, until after six or seven miles we reach Twin Khan (Tchifte-Khan), one of the most beautiful spots I have ever seen (Fig. 27). Two waters meet at the Khan, one coming from the south-west down an open glen from the old Hittite silver-mines of Bulghar-Maden, and one from the west through a gorge so narrow that in some places it looked as if one could jump across it a full hundred feet above the water. The water here has cut its way so sharp and clean through a bed of rock, that the walls on each side are perfectly perpendicular and apparently about twelve feet apart.[2] At the bottom of this narrow cleft the water foams and rushes. The road keeps near this water, but ascends to a higher level. Farther on the river-bed opens out a little, and an old Turkish road crosses it (Fig. 28). The modern road, which was excellent in 1902, keeps on a much higher level. In this part the scenery is very desolate and bare for some distance.

---

[1] It seems actually to overhang, as if from the summit one could drop a stone clear of the rock wall; but the eye is a fallible judge of height and character.

[2] We overlooked the cleft from the road, but did not go down to it: the estimate is mere guesswork.

PLATE XII.

FIG. 18.—The Arch of Severus with Students of the American College in Tarsus (Mrs. Christie of Tarsus).

PLATE XIII.

FIG. 19.—The Arch of Severus at Bairamli (Mrs. Christie of Tarsus).

 See p. 280.

PLATE XXVI.

FIG. 32.—The Castle of Karamanat Laranda.

To face p. 288.

See p. 294.

After four miles we reach a point whence we see the Castle of Loulon in the distance, and overlook the Vale of Loulon, into which the road now descends. This vale is very narrow at the eastern end, but opens out as we go on.

We are now some ten miles north of the front main ridge of Taurus, and are thus able to get a view of it. Previously we were too near to see its summits. It runs east and west, a long ridge about 9,000 or 10,000 feet in height, making an imposing background to the view over intervening hills. Snow lies on it through great part of the year. In June, 1902, with the clouds covering its shoulders, and its long snowy summit rising above them, it offered a strikingly beautiful picture, which a photograph reproduces only imperfectly.

After a few miles the vale forks, where two streams meet : one glen runs up south-west into the hills, the other ascends in a direction slightly north of west and along this goes the road. At the apex of the low hills, which divide the two streams, a little plateau faces us on the left; this is the site of the Roman Colonia Faustiniana, called in Greek Faustinopolis; and two miles up the northern stream we find the site of the old village Halala [1] adjoining the road. When the Emperor Marcus Aurelius was travelling along this road, his wife Faustina died at Halala, and the Emperor made a new city to perpetuate her name.

Standing on the road beside Halala, we look up to the Castle of Loulon, on a lofty peak which rises above the village on the north. This castle commands the northern end of the pass which we have just traversed from Tarsus ; and hence it played a very important part in the Saracen

[1] See p. 182.

19

wars, A.D. 660-965. When it was in Byzantine possession, Arab armies could not use the pass except with considerable difficulty, and would have to leave a strong force to confine the garrison of Loulon. When the Saracens held it, the Roman armies could not traverse the pass towards Cilicia; hence Al-Saffsaf (as the Arabs called Loulon) was to them the "Bulwark of Tarsus". The possession of this critical fortress was keenly contested. It often changed hands, but was generally Byzantine, for the Arabs never succeeded in permanently holding any point north of Taurus. The Arab geographer of the ninth century, Ibn Khordadhbeh, calls it[1] "the camp of the King of the Romans". Here was the first beacon-fire on the line of communication with Constantinople. As soon as a Saracen army was known to be crossing the pass, Loulon lit its beacon, and flashed the news along a series of fires to the capital. In the photograph, Fig. 29, the tall peak is dwarfed.

A few hundred yards farther on towards the west, the ancient and the modern road alike fork. One branch goes off at right angles to the north through a break in the hills at the western foot of the castle-peak to Tyana and Cappadocia generally. The other keeps straight on for four miles along the river to Ulu-Kishla, where the hills on the north end ; and the road enters on the open central plateau of Anatolia and attains its highest elevation, about 4,600 feet above the sea. The "long barracks," Ulu-Kishla, are one of the most remarkable old Turkish buildings.

The traveller who is making for Iconium and the West has a choice of routes from this upland to the next important station, Herakleia-Cybistra, about thirty miles west of

[1] Or perhaps a camp in the low ground beneath the castle. The localities need careful examination.

PLATE XXVII.

To face p. 290.

FIG. 33.—The " Pilgrim-Father " above Derbe (Mrs. W. M. Ramsay).

See p. 294.

Ulu-Kiskla. In modern time waggons keep well out to the
north into the open plain ; but I believe that the Roman
road continued straight on over undulating and hilly country,
until it entered a valley with a stream which flows direct
to Cybistra. Horses can now use this route ; but it could
easily be adapted to wheeled traffic, and the Roman road
ought to be traced.

Where the valley, just mentioned, opens on the main
Lycaonian and Cappadocian plain, about six miles south-
east of Eregli (now a railway station), it is joined on the
left by the water of Ibriz, and above it on the right rises the
last of those outlying northern hills, a peak bearing the
strong Castle of Herakleia, called Hirakla by the Arabs.
The beautiful glen of Ibriz, with its remarkable Hittite
sculpture, is described in Article VI., p. 172 f., of this volume.
Hirakla was one of the fortresses most disputed in the
Saracen wars, as it guarded and commanded the road to the
West ; it was often captured, *e.g.*, by Haroun-al-Raschid, and
always retaken by the Greeks. Looking back towards
south-east, as we stand at the entrance on the Lycaonian
plain, we have the view shown in Fig. 30.

Cybistra is generally identified with the modern town
Eregli (*i.e.*, Herakleia) ; but perhaps it may hereafter be
found more correct to say that Eregli stands among the
gardens of Cybistra, and that the ancient city occupied a
stronger position on the hills (perhaps somewhere as yet
undiscovered near the Castle of Hirakla).

From Eregli onwards the general character of the road
does not vary. It runs on an almost dead level, hardly
varying from the elevation of 3,100 to 3,300 feet. The route
keeps to the southern edge of the great central plateau. On
the left hand rises the outer front of Taurus like a great

wall. On the right spreads out the boundless level plain of Lycaonia. But amid this uniformity there is constant variety in the picture presented to the traveller's eyes. Taurus is sometimes nearer, sometimes more distant, as the road winds; in some places it seems to rise like a continuous wall, in other cases it is broken into distinct peaks of varied forms. The level plain to the north is never monotonous, for it is dotted with lofty islands of mountain that spring bold and sharp from the sea of plain. Due north of Eregli, at a distance of forty to fifty miles, are the beautiful double cones of Hassan-Dagh, the ancient Argeos or Argos,[1] nearly 11,000 feet high. Thirty miles to the west of it, Karadja-Dagh looks like a low blue island on the horizon. In front, about forty miles from Eregli, barring the view to Iconium, is Kara-Dagh, a black volcanic jagged mass, behind which in dark nights of May or June the lightning plays with strangely beautiful effect during the frequent thunderstorms of those months. In the intervals between these mountains stretches the dead level plain, over which nothing except its own weakness appears to prevent the eye from looking away to infinity.

Beyond Eregli the road in ancient times passed along the south-eastern end of the White Lake, close to the hole under the mountains into which the lake discharges its waters,[2] crosses a rocky ridge, where the ancient cutting to carry it is well marked, to a village called Serpek or Ambararassi, the site of the ancient town Sidamaria. Here was found the immense sarcophagus of late Roman time adorned with

---

[1] It is to be distinguished from Mount Argaios farther east and out of sight.

[2] See p. 172 f. The modern road and railway go direct to Karaman by a more southerly route, shown on the map, p. 48.

PLATE XXVIII.

FIG. 34.—The Acropolis of Derbe.

See p. 295.

To face p. 292.

elaborate sculptures—probably the largest known sarcophagus of Greek or Roman time—which is now in the Imperial Museum at Constantinople. When I was travelling with Sir Charles Wilson in 1882 he had this monument dug up; and, as the heads of the two colossal figures on the top of the sarcophagus have long since disappeared, we are assumed to have broken them off and carried them away. The sole foundation for this idea, which is openly declared by high Turkish officials, is that there were two ancient heads and two Englishmen. As a matter of fact there were no heads on the figures when we uncovered them; and had there been, the art of the two figures is so bad, and the heads would have been so weighty (as the figures must be about twelve feet long) that there would have been no temptation to carry them away. Their sole interest would lie in keeping them attached to the bodies (Fig. 31).

The character of the subject shown in the accompanying photograph of one side of the sarcophagus is discussed in *Studies in the History and Art of the Eastern Provinces,*[1] p. 59.

Ambararassi lies in the level plain, but three miles on to the west is the true ancient site, a fortress on a hill at Kale-Keui (Castle Village). Beyond this the road, which hitherto has been going straight towards the dark mass of Kara-Dagh, turns south-west, passes the old fort of Sidero-palos on a mound in the plain, now a formless ruin two miles from the railway station Sidirvar (Sidivre), and reaches Karaman, the ancient Laranda, metropolis of South-eastern Lycaonia from the beginning of history, now a railway station, 103 kilometres from Iconium and 87 kilometres from

---

[1] London, Hodder & Stoughton, 1906. See also M. Th. Reinach in *Monuments Piot,* and M. Mendel in *Bulletin de Correspondence Hellén.,* 1902.

Eregli.[1] It lies in a triangular recess of the Taurus, where the mountains recede and the level plain stretches far south; and the road makes a great southward bend in order to reach it, attracted by its economic importance. The view of the castle on a hill in the centre of the city is given as a specimen of a kind of military architecture common in this country, and probably early Turkish in origin. The old name Laranda is known to the Greeks, a small body of whom preserved a continuous existence through the Turkish period; but the name of an old Seljuk chief, Karaman, has replaced it in Mohammedan use (Fig. 32).

We now turn north of west past Ilistra (which keeps its ancient name) to Cassaba, the old Pyrgos, a picturesque little town, in the open plain, entirely surrounded by high mediæval walls.[2] Thence the modern road goes straight over the plain north-north-west to Iconium; but the Roman road in the first century went on a little north of west past the villages Passola or Possala (which retains the ancient name) and Losta, which are one ancient town, to Derbe. Over all three towers a huge conical mountain of bare limestone rock, of singularly grand and bold outline, which presides like a giant guardian over Southern Lycaonia, and assumes an element of personality even to the unimaginative Turks. This mountain is called the "Pilgrim Father," Hadji-Baba; and it is a striking feature in the view from all Southern and Central Lycaonia, until one crosses the ridges of Boz-Dagh, behind which it is concealed from view; but if the traveller continues to go north, it emerges

[1] The road by Ambararassi is distinctly longer than the railway line.

[2] That was the case when I saw it in 1890; but old walls are frequently pulled down, and sold as building material; the price passes into the pocket of officials [an isolated case of local resistance to such jobs, by a Protestant native, is described in *Impressions of Turkey*, p. 233].

PLATE XXIX.

FIG. 35.—Walls within the Hill-fortress above Derbe (Mrs. W. M. Ramsay).

See p. 295.

To face p. 294.

again after some distance and rises sharp over the long low line of the Boz-Dagh as one looks back from the higher ground in Northern Lycaonia. As is usual with photographs, the effect of its height is dwarfed in Fig. 33.

Near Derbe on the east, close to the road, lies a tombstone with a dedication to Paul the Martyr. The Christians of the district regard this stone as a proof that Paul visited the place, but are ignorant that it is the site of Derbe. The place was deserted, and the tradition perished [1] (see Fig. 38 on p. 322). A view of the deserted site is given in the *Church in the Roman Empire*, page 55, and is here repeated. The Byzantine ruins shown in the photograph (Fig. 34) have all been pulled down to get building material for the new village.

There are at least three cities or settlements connected with Derbe: the Greek and early Roman Derbe on a mound in the plain, the late Roman and Byzantine city at Bossala and Losta, and an early hill-fort high above the plain on a peak of Taurus (west of the Pilgrim Father), a view in which is shown in Fig. 35.

The great Roman Imperial road during the first century went north-west from Derbe, entered the Isaurian hills after a few miles, and reached Lystra in the most northerly valley of those hills, about twenty-five miles from Derbe. From Lystra it went to Pisidian Antioch, passing a few miles to the south-west of Iconium, with which it was connected by a side-road. As one approaches from Derbe, the first glimpse of Lystra and Khatyn Serai, " Lady's Mansion," the modern village a mile south-east of the ancient site, is picturesque with trees and greenery to a degree rare in Lycaonia (Fig. 36). The hill of Lystra, very similar to the

---

[1] The modern village is a recent erection by refugees from Roumelia.

site of Derbe, is shown in Fig. 37, taken from the *Church
in the Roman Empire*, page 47, where a description is given
(as also by Rev. H. S. Cronin in *Journal of Hellenic Studies*,
1904).

But the importance of Iconium was far too great to
allow it to remain on a mere branch-road. Lystra was only
a hill town, whose sole claim to importance was that it had
been selected as a Roman garrison and colony at the time
when the Pisidian and Isaurian mountaineers were a pressing danger. When that danger passed away, not even the
honour of a Roman colony could maintain its consequence
in the country. Even Derbe was only a second-rate city.
Iconium was the natural and inevitable metropolis of Western
and Central Lycaonia. Derbe and Lystra therefore passed
out of the system of Roman roads, and the line of communication went direct from metropolis to metropolis, from
Laranda by Pyrgos to Iconium, across the level plain.
About half-way, or a mile beyond half-way, is a low ridge,
from which the traveller gets the first view of Iconium.
Straight behind the city rises a remarkable conical peak,
about 2,000 feet above the level of the plain, called Takali
by the Turks, Dakalias by the Saracens in the ninth century,
and St. Philip by the Greeks at the present day. If we
now look back towards Laranda, the Pilgrim Father attracts
and fills the view. As we look east the Kara-Dagh shuts
out everything else from sight. Away to the north of
Iconium, above Laodicea (Ladik), and screening it from
view is a massive peak, conspicuous alike from the south
and the north. In Byzantine times all these doubtless got
Christian titles; but long before that they were probably
considered to be the guardians of the land. The belief in
the divinity of mountains is as natural as in the divinity of

PLATE XXX.

Fig. 36.—Distant View of Khatyn-Serai and Lystra from the South-East (Mrs. W. M. Ramsay). *See p.* 295.

To face p. 296.

rivers, and is attested for the Anatolian land. Argaios towers over Cæsareia-Mazaka and is represented on all the city-coins. Mount Viaros (probably the tall peak of Egerdir) is a common type on coins of Prostanna.

Those four mountains of Western Lycaonia are the most prominent and imposing,[1] and the Christian names of three are known or can be guessed. The Christians celebrate a Panegyris of Araba Georgi, St. George of the Car, near the peak over Ladik annually on 23rd April; and there as the story goes, "at dawn water and milk flow in a dry place" (see p. 188). St. Philip still dominates Iconium, and the Greeks hold a Panegyris there on 24th November. Hadji-Baba may be taken as a Turkish rendering of a title describing the travelling Apostle Paul as the guardian of Derbe. We remember how Ephesus extended from St. Paul by the sea to St. John on the eastern hill; and we may look for similar cases in many parts of Anatolia. The Christian names exemplify the permanence of older religious feeling under Christian forms (Article VI.).

A mile farther on towards Iconium the road descends a hundred feet to a river which flows from the heart of the Isaurian mountains, and is lost in the plain north-east of Kara-Dagh. The water of the Lystra Valley would flow into it, if it could reach so far; but it is dissipated in the plain and used up for irrigation or to supply the villages. The Arabs called this stream Nahr-el-Ahsa, the River of Subterranean Waters. This is doubtless a reference to the fact that the water of the great lake Trogitis (Seidi-Sheher-Giol) was formerly brought into it by a cutting through the

[1] They are not the loftiest, but they dominate the plain. Ala-Dagh is loftier than Hadji-Baba, and Elenkilit than the other three; but both are far from the plain, in the heart of mountainous districts.

rock. The purpose of this cutting was partly to keep the lake low and set free a large tract of fertile soil for agriculture, partly to supply water for irrigating the great plain of Iconium. The latter project has been revived in recent years, and the engineers who surveyed the route for connecting the lake with the river discovered the old cutting, which is now blocked. In 1905 the water of the lake Trogitis rose so high that villages and a great deal of cultivated land around it were submerged. From the bridge which carries the road over this river it is about twenty-four miles to Iconium, whose acropolis is crowned with the church of St. Amphilochius (Plate III., p. 170).

Between Iconium and Derbe lies a region rich beyond all others in early monuments of Christian art. Four examples are given in Figs. 7 (p. 162), 9 (p. 216), 14 (p. 300), 31 (p. 322) and 39 (facing p. 1), taken from Miss Ramsay's article on Early Christian Art in this region, *Studies in the History and Art of the Eastern Provinces*, 1906, pp. 23, 34, 38, 54, 61.

PLATE XXXI.

To face p. 298.

Fig. 37.—The Acropolis of Lystra.

See p. 296.

XII

THE AUTHORSHIP OF THE ACTS

ΕΝΘΑΔΕΓΗΚΑΤΕΧΙΑΥΡΠΡΙΣΚΟΝΕΙΗΤΡΟΝ
ΕΟΝΤΑΕΞΟΧΟΝΗΛΙΚΙΗΣΕΠΙΕΤΕΣΙΕΞΗΚΟΝ
ΑΝΕΣΤΗΣΕΝΔΕΑΥΤΟΝΤΙΜΟΘΕΟΣΥΙΟΣ
ΑΥΤΟΥΣΥΝΤΗΙΔΙΑΣΥΜΒΙΩΑΛΕΞΑΝΔΡΙΗΤΙΜΙ

Tomb of a Christian Physician (see p. 298).

XII

THE AUTHORSHIP OF THE ACTS

RECENTLY a friend, in whose judgment I place great confidence, remarked in a letter to me that Dr. McGiffert's book on the *History of Christianity in the Apostolic Age* contained the most powerful .statement known to him of the view that the *Acts of the Apostles* could not have been written by Luke, the friend and pupil of St. Paul; and he urged that I should state clearly and precisely the attitude which I hold towards the argument so ably stated by the distinguished American Professor. The very fact that in several important points, such as the Galatian question, Dr. McGiffert has come to the same opinion as I hold, makes the difference between us as regards authorship all the more marked; and, as the Editor also asks me to write a review of this important book, it seems advisable to state why I remain unconvinced by its arguments against the Lukan authorship. It is rather confusing that Luke is spoken of as "the author" in many pages of Dr. McGiffert's book; but this is merely done for brevity, and the Professor is most clear and emphatic in denying the Lukan authorship.

The judgment which has been quoted in my opening sentence may be taken as a proof that the book is characterised by deep study and knowledge, long deliberation, and remarkable dialectical skill. I do not, however, intend to write a review of the book as a whole; but content myself with a brief statement of the strong qualities shown in it. I should mention, as an example of the book at its best, the defence of the Pauline authorship of the Epistle to the Colossians, which is an admirably concise and powerful piece of reasoning. And there occur many other similar passages, some of which critics may rank higher than the one which I have selected. The same qualities appear everywhere throughout the book. It will, however, be better to confine myself to one subject—the authorship of the Acts of the Apostles (with which of course goes the Third Gospel).

Dr. McGiffert goes over the book of *Acts* paragraph by paragraph, dissecting every statement; and with remorseless logic piles up argument upon argument. The cumulative effect of these is to show such a series of erroneous statements in the book as are absolutely inconsistent with the idea that the writer could have been an intimate friend of Paul and of other actors, or himself an actor, in the events described. The book of Acts is pronounced to be a second-hand work throughout: and the proper and only profitable method of historical study and criticism in reference to it is found to be an analysis of its sources.

On any theory as to the authorship of *Acts* and the Third Gospel, the question of sources is one of great importance. The author is almost universally admitted to be a Greek, a stranger to Palestine (which he knew only from a visit), probably born after many of the events which he records had occurred; and he expressly states that many written accounts of the period treated in his First Book (*i.e.*, the Third Gospel) were known to him. The question as to his sources is of prime consequence; and we all admit that some of his sources were written. But I have been concerned to maintain that great part of *Acts* is not dependent on written sources, but is partly gathered from the mouths and from the oral accounts of actors (especially Paul), and partly written down from personal knowledge (in which case the author uses the first personal form of narrative). The author's view as a whole throughout the book is, as I maintain, Paul's view; and in great part of it we must trace the hand of a pupil of Paul's, accustomed to hear Paul's opinion and to be largely, almost entirely, guided by it. But, in certain cases, I think that statements resting on other authority are admitted: in chaps. i. and ii. traces of popular traditions are visible, in chap. xii. 12 it is distinctly given the reader to understand that John Mark was the authority: the comparison of viii. 40 with xxi. 8, 10 gives an equally distinct hint that Philip was the authority for chap. viii. In the Ephesian narrative, chap. xix., I recognise probably a statement of popular Asian belief in verses 11-19, and in verses 1*b*-7 a narrative of non-Pauline tone, intended by an admirer of Paul to bring out that Apollos was indebted to Paul's teaching (conveyed through Aquila and Priscilla) for a great advance in his spiritual knowledge and power: the author was fully aware of Apollos' gifts and grace, but he was clearly desirous that it should be known that these were acquired only after Apollos had come in contact with Pauline influence. I cannot recognise any hint conveyed by the author as to the source of his narrative about Peter ; but probably a better knowledge of the author's life and circumstances would reveal some hint as plain as that in xii. 12, or that which lies in the comparison of viii. 40 and xxi. 8, 10.

These may serve as examples to show how it would be possible to draw out a detailed argument that the author of

Acts, while sharing the general carelessness of ancient historians as to stating precisely their sources of information, does nevertheless suggest intentionally to the reader in various cases the idea that definite persons were the authorities for certain statements. Further, the author's style marks the difference between those parts where he had been a witness and those where he was dependent on the reports of others. Studied according to the canons of criticism which govern the study of the ordinary classical authors, *Acts* must be recognised as a work in which the expression is perfectly clear and natural in the person to whose pen it is attributed by tradition, and is unexplained and unintelligible in any other person. Further, the tradition makes clear the genesis of much of the book, and enables the reader to follow back most of the statements to their exact source. In the case of any ordinary classical author, this line of reasoning would be treated as conclusive, and the inference would never have been doubted. The literary history of the book in its growth stands before us clear, simple, self-consistent and harmonious with the facts known from other sources,[1] provided one does not twist it, or squeeze it, or thrust into it such absurdities as the North-Galatian theory (pardonable and hardly avoidable when Phrygia and Galatia were unknown lands, but now persisting only through the strength of prejudice).

From the literary point of view, the proper object of study is the author, his attitude towards his sources, and his method of using them; and I believe that that method of study is the most profitable as regards *Acts*, as is recognised

[1] That difficulties remain to be elucidated and obscurities to be illuminated, I have always declared; but that is universal in classical literature, and the discovery of new documents, while solving many old questions, adds continually to the number of difficult points in all departments of ancient scholarship.

in the case of every other book. But the " Source-Theory,"
as one may term it, turns the study of that book into a mere
analysis of Sources ; it proceeds as if the author's method
and personality had no significance except as a cause of error,
and makes it a fundamental principle that the one and only
important question in every case is whether the author had
a good or a bad, an early or a later, Source for every statement.

Dr. McGiffert has not convinced me : in other words, I
think his clever argumentation is sophistical. In examining
it, I should like as much as possible to concentrate attention
on the impersonal aspect as a problem in history ; and, to
avoid obtruding the personal reference on the reader, it will
be better to speak as far as possible of "the Source-Theory,"
meaning always the special form set forth in the work under
review. Dr. McGiffert and I are desirous of reaching the
truth, starting from different sides.

A true critical instinct makes Dr. McGiffert recoil from
the extremest form of the " Source-Theory ". The fundamental difference between the Source-Theory and the literary method of study is that, wherever any characteristic
is observed in the book, the former attributes it to the
" Source," while the latter sees in it an example of the
author's method and style in using his sources. Take, for
example, the transition from the name Saul to the name
Paul during the interview with Sergius Paulus (*Acts* xiii. 4
ff.). Dr. McGiffert rightly says, on page 176, that in this
case " the author, with the instinct of a true historian, evidently felt the significance " of the interview. On the other
hand, many scholars see there only the transition from a
" Source," in which the Apostle was called by the name Saul,
to another " Source," in which he was called Paul. Now

20

what authority have we for the confidence (which Dr. McGiffert rightly entertains) that the author of *Acts* "felt the significance" of the situation?   What reason is there for rejecting the theory that the peculiar constitution of the text at this point springs simply from the " Sources "?   Our only ground is the literary instinct which recognises with absolute and unfaltering force that here the author is not dominated by his sources, but dominates them and moulds them into a powerful narrative, showing the hand of a master, not of a mere editor.

On the other hand, we find the statement on page 257, "There are certain features in his report of Paul's stay in Athens which can be explained only on the supposition that he had in his hand an older document which he followed in the main quite closely". But we search in vain for any reasoning to prove that the literary skill which was recognised in the Paphian episode was inadequate to frame the Athenian narrative out of information which the author received and moulded to his own purposes. It is simply assumed that, because the narrative is at this point generally trustworthy, therefore it uses "an older document". The same assumption is made time after time in the course of the keen scrutiny to which the narrative of *Acts* is subjected. In this scrutiny, as a rule, the "Source-Theory" starts by begging the whole question; and the admission which has just been quoted from page 176 is a temporary divergence from the regular method.

It is a rule of criticism that when a theory of authorship is propounded, the supposed author must be a conceivable and natural personality. It is not admissible to make the imagined author in one place of one character, and in another to attribute to him different qualities. But this compiler of *Acts* is never presented to us as a self-consistent and possible and imaginable character. Inconsistent and contradictory qualities are assigned to him. " He was keenly alive to the dramatic possibilities of the position in which the Apostle found himself placed" at Athens (p. 257); but he sternly resisted the temptation to work up those possibilities in a way contrary to the real facts recorded in his sources. Now, only a person endued with considerable literary feeling and historical sympathy is able to be " keenly alive to the dramatic possibilities" of a situation in past time and in a strange country; and only a person who has a strong sense of veracity will resist the temptation to touch up the situation whose possibilities he is so keenly alive to, and will rigorously deny himself the slightest embellishing touch which does not stand in the record.   Yet this person did not shrink from the most shameless and stupid mendacity in other cases : he found in two " Sources " accounts of a visit of Paul to Jerusalem, and he thought they described two separate visits, and invented a whole chapter of false history in order to work in the second visit which his stupidity had conjured up :[1] he invented a Decree (or rather made up a Decree from real materials which belonged to another time and situation), and placed this Decree in the mouth of the Apostles assembled at Jerusalem (xv. 22-29) : he invented, without justification or suitability, two sentences (xix. 28, 29), which he put in Paul's mouth in the same incident where otherwise he showed such self-denial and rigorous adherence to truth and the record ; and so on in endless succession.   How reconcile these contradictions? Who is this author, who shows at once such literary feeling and such helplessness in literary expression, such scrupulous

---

[1] See below, p. 310 f., on this point, and p. 311 on the Decree.

veracity and such unscrupulous disregard to truth? Who is it that sometimes transfers to his pages fragments of a "Source" more awkwardly than the feeblest Byzantine compiler, for he forgets to change a first person to a third, at another time selects and remodels till he has constructed a narrative which shows "the instinct of a true historian," "keenly alive to the dramatic possibilities of the situation"?

The charge is frequently brought against the author of *Acts* that he gives a false picture of Paul's sphere of work in the cities of Asia, Galatia, Macedonia and Achaia, describing Paul's work as conducted largely among the Jews, whereas Paul's own words show that it was mainly among the Gentiles. This is not taken by the critics as a proof of mendacity: but as simply the result of ignorance; and the inference is that, if the author had really been a friend of Paul, he would have known better. It is indisputable that in *Acts* the reader's attention is always pointedly drawn to Paul's work among the Jews. Dr. McGiffert draws from this the inference that the author knew no better. Mr. Baring-Gould, on the contrary (as we shall see in the following article), draws the inference that Paul misstated or misjudged the facts, when he represents himself as the Apostle of the Gentiles. To me it seems that Luke, while devoting most space to the account of Paul's work among the Jewish part of his audiences, makes it clear that the Gentiles were vastly more numerous than the Jews in the Churches of Galatia, Thessalonica,[1] Asia, etc. I find no such contradiction between Paul and *Acts* as Dr. McGiffert does. Paul speaks more of the Gentiles and to the Gentiles, because they were the most numerous, but usually makes it quite clear that

[1] The question of reading comes in here: *St. Paul the Traveller*, p. 235 f.

there were Jews also in the Church which he is addressing. Luke speaks at greater length of the appeal to the Jews because he lived through the struggle against the Jews, and sympathised with Paul under the attacks made against him as unfriendly to his own nation, and was keenly desirous to prove that Paul always gave full opportunity and welcome to the Jews in every city. Such a desire is very natural in a personal friend of Paul ; but we see no reason why a stranger, writing after the conflict was long past, should be so eager to defend Paul against dead enemies and a buried enmity and a people which had ceased in A.D. 70 to be a nation.

In this connection, take one example. In *Acts*, Paul is represented at Corinth as going to the Jews, and only after their refusal, turning to the Gentiles, and doing so at first by means of the half-way "house of a certain proselyte, Titus Justus".[1] But, "in Paul's own epistles there is no hint of any such procedure"; and his statement "is hardly calculated to confirm Luke's account" (p. 268). And yet, "it must be recognised that there are some striking points of contact" between Luke's and Paul's accounts of Corinthian affairs (p. 269). Crispus is common to both accounts; and though Paul does not mention that his Crispus was a Jew, "there is no reason to doubt that he is the man whose conversion Luke reports". Obviously Paul is not concerned to

[1] It is unfortunate that the bare term "proselyte" is sometimes inaccurately used in the book under review to designate a "God-fearing" Gentile. In a question so delicate and so vexed, it is desirable to use the technical term very strictly. In my *St. Paul*, p. 43, I used "proselyte" in the same loose way, to indicate a "God-fearing" person, because I had not yet defined the terms, and added the definition in the next paragraph; but friendly critics pointed out that it was best to avoid absolutely this loose use of "proselyte". Titus Justus (rather Titius Justus) was not a "proselyte," but only one of the "God-fearing" Gentiles, who had been attracted to the circle of the Synagogue.

mention the nationality of the persons whom he names among the Corinthians—he is entirely absorbed in a different purpose; and it is mere hypercritical special pleading to argue that Luke is inaccurate, because Paul gives no account of the stages by which his mission in Corinth developed. If he converted a ruler of the Synagogue (and Paul does not himself think it necessary to mention that Crispus was so), it is pretty clear that he must have addressed himself directly to the Jews. He would never convert a Jew, if he addressed only Gentiles.

But I cannot stop to show, step by step, how unfair and sophistical the "Source-Theory" is: to do so would need a book. I can only ask the "Source-Theorists" what points they lay most stress on, and examine these.

Beyond a doubt, the one serious reason which must weigh heavily with every reasoning man, and make him doubt whether the author of *Acts* could have been an intimate friend and companion of Paul, is the topic discussed on pages 170-172, 194-201, 208-217. Paul, in his letter to the Galatians, speaking with the strongest emphasis, and with a solemn adjuration that he is speaking the absolute truth —"touching the things which I write unto you, behold, before God, that I lie not"—declares that in his first two visits to Jerusalem after his conversion, he learned nothing from the older Apostles, that he carried no message from them to his own Churches, that they imparted nothing to him, but merely approved of his schemes and ratified his mission.[1] Now the second visit is by most scholars identi-

---

[1] Dr. McGiffert puts this clearly and well, p. 211: "It is a point of the utmost significance that Paul distinctly asserts that those who were of repute in the Church of Jerusalem imparted nothing to him (*Gal.* ii. 6) . . . in other words, he was left entirely free by them to preach to the Gentiles exactly as he had been preaching".

fied with the visit described in *Acts* xv. But, in that visit, so far from the Apostles imparting nothing to Paul, as he declares, they, according to *Acts*, were the supreme authority to whom he referred a question for decision; they imparted to him a Decree on this question. He carried this Decree to his Churches, and "delivered them the Decree for to keep, which had been ordained of the Apostles and Elders that were at Jerusalem" (*Acts* xvi. 4). Rightly and honestly, Dr. McGiffert is revolted by this contradiction between Paul and *Acts*: rightly and honestly, he refuses to shut his eyes to it, or to whittle it away and minimise it, and delude himself into the idea that he thereby gets rid of it: the clear contradiction exists in a most vital and serious matter. If *Acts* is right, and if the common theory is to be followed, Paul was throwing dust in the eyes of the Galatians; therefore, the inference is drawn that *Acts* is wrong, and that the supposed Decree was never issued by the Council, or carried by Paul to his Churches. The "Decree" is a mere fabrication by the compiler of *Acts*; or, rather, "it is impossible to suppose so peculiar a document an invention of the author of *Acts*," and, therefore, "some historic basis for it must be assumed". The basis is found by supposing that it was probably made up out of James's speech (*Acts* xv. 13-21), or that it was promulgated at some other time, and wrongly attributed by the author to this Council (p. 212 f.).

Another difficulty exists in this connection, and the "Source-Theory" is again invoked to solve it. "It is clear that Paul intended the Galatians to understand that during the fourteen years[1] that succeeded his conversion, he had been in Jerusalem only twice." But in *Acts* three visits

---

[1] Or, as some hold (wrongly, in my opinion), seventeen years.

are mentioned, according to the ordinary view; and Dr. McGiffert rightly refuses to accept the sophistical excuse that the middle visit was only a little one, or an unimportant one, and might therefore be omitted by Paul, even though he takes his oath to the Galatians that he is telling them the absolute truth. Once more the explanation is sought in an error of the author of *Acts*. He found in two "Sources" two different accounts of the same visit, *viz.*, a visit paid in A.D. 48, in which Paul and Barnabas carried to Jerusalem the money collected by the Antiochian Church (*Acts* xi. 29), and at the same time propounded the difficulty as to Gentile Christians for solution by the Apostles and Elders (*Acts* xv.). These accounts were so different that the author mistook them for accounts of two separate visits, for one Source "might well be interested to record only the generous act of the Antiochian Church, while another might see in the settlement of the legitimacy of Gentile Christianity the only matter worthy of mention". Inasmuch as the Gentile question fell immediately after the first missionary journey, the compiler made the unhappy guess that the money had been carried to Jerusalem before that journey, and thus falsely evolved an intermediate unhistorical visit of Paul and Barnabas to Jerusalem.

If this view hits the truth, then assuredly *Acts* was not written by Luke, the friend of Paul. It is impossible that a companion of Paul in many journeys and for many years should be so ignorant of a most important epoch in Paul's life as this theory makes out. But there are difficulties besetting the theory. We may well grant that the author of *Acts* may have "found two independent accounts of the same journey in his sources". But these accounts would not be divorced from all surroundings; each of them would necessarily relate the events before and after, and would make the succession of events moderately clear, for these sources were historical narratives traversing part of the same ground that *Acts* treats of. I can find no fair parallel in literary history for a supposition so violent. One is used to such maltreatment of history among ignorant students, who are experimenting to discover what is the minimum of knowledge which will be accepted for a "pass" by an examiner. But except among the examination papers of passmen, I have seen nothing to parallel the audacious and shameless ignorance which is thus attributed to the compiler—an ignorance which might almost suggest the theory that *Acts* is the rejected examination paper in history of some lazy candidate for matriculation in an ancient University. The compiler is supposed by Dr. McGiffert to have written under Domitian, between 81 and 96, at a time when one Christian had been martyred in Pergamos and none in Smyrna,[1] when many pupils and friends and associates of Paul and the Apostles were still living, when the real facts must have been known to great numbers of persons, and when any doubt could have been cleared up with the utmost ease. We are asked to believe either that the compiler was so extraordinarily stupid as to imagine that the accounts of one event given in two historical narratives were accounts of two different events, feeling no doubt, and boldly lifting one account out of its place and thrusting it in at a point several years earlier, or that he was so careless and

---

[1] On the date see page 437 f. ; on the view that so few martyrs suffered in Asia under Domitian, see page 635 (where it is apparently implied that there had been no serious persecution in any of the seven Churches of Asia, except the martyrdom of Antipas : that is as much as to say there had been no persecution in Asia, against which see *Letters to the Seven Churches*, ch. ix).

lazy that he would not test by a very easy process the doubts which did suggest themselves to him.

While the form which is given to the "Source-Theory" in this work is in many respects most ingenious and able, the early date assigned to the compilation involves the Theory in many difficulties, which it was free from on the old supposition of second-century authorship. But that supposition in its turn is involved in difficulties which have led Dr. McGiffert to abandon it.

My own theory of the visits to Jerusalem—that the second visit of *Acts* is the second visit as described by Paul in *Galatians* ii. 1 ff., and that the third visit of *Acts* lies outside of Paul's argument (because he is merely discussing what was his original message to the Galatians, whether of God or from the Apostles, whereas the third visit did not occur till after the Galatians were converted)—is briefly dismissed as impossible on page 172 *note*. The reason is noteworthy: "The discussion recorded in *Acts* xv. can have taken place only on the occasion which Paul describes in *Gal.* ii. 1 *sq.*," and neither earlier nor later. We ask how and where Dr. McGiffert acquires the knowledge of that obscure period which enables him to pronounce so absolutely that, on a subject which (unless *Acts* is hopelessly wrong) was debated for years with much bitterness, the particular discussion mentioned in *Acts* xv. can have occurred only in A.D. 48 and at no other time. His authority is *Acts* itself, an authority which he discredits at almost every point to some greater or less degree; yet from this poor authority he can gather absolute certainty as to the exact period when alone one discussion of this much-debated topic can have occurred. The fact is that unless *Acts* is accepted as a good authority, we must resign ourselves to be ignorant about the Apostolic period, and must cease to make any dogmatic statements as to what is possible or impossible.

Every reader must be struck with the enormous part that is played in the discussion of the *Acts of the Apostles* by the argument from the author's silence. Wherever we learn from any other source of any incident or detail, however slight it may be, which is not recorded in *Acts*, the inference is almost always drawn that the author was ignorant of it, or rather that he had an inadequate or inaccurate "Source". For example, in the Athenian narrative "his account betrays a lack of familiarity with some of the events that transpired at this period" (p. 257); and yet the author here "followed in the main quite closely" a document, which is stated in the following pages to be old and trustworthy. Moreover, the author "was keenly alive to the dramatic possibilities of the position in which the Apostle found himself placed"; which implies a high degree of historical insight and sympathy. Here, then, we have a case in which an author, who possessed great literary and historical power, and had access to a good and early authority of Athenian origin, is pronounced ignorant of certain *minutiæ* of the going and coming of Timothy, because he does not enumerate them. Surely the supposition should here be entertained that he thought these *minutiæ* too unimportant to deserve enumeration in a highly compressed history of the developing force of Christianity within the Roman Empire.

Many critics seem to have failed utterly to realise that the author of *Acts* is not a biographer but a historian, that he selects the points which are important in his conception of the developing Church, and stands quite apart from little details regarding the precise number of times that Timothy went back and forward between Achaia and Macedonia. It is enough that the author says nothing that is contradictory of what Paul mentions in writing to the Thessalonians (as is frankly conceded on p. 257); beyond that it is mere pedantic niggling to insist that, if the author had known how many times Timothy went to and fro, he must have told it.

It is impossible in a necessarily short paper to touch on every point raised as regards *Acts*. But I have taken those which seemed most characteristic. Let me add one only. On page 280 f. the Ephesian residence is discussed. From the word used by Paul himself, " I fought-with-beasts at Ephesus " (ἐθηριομάχησα, 1 *Cor.* xv. 32), it is inferred that the Apostle had been condemned to death, exposed to wild beasts in the amphitheatre, and escaped in some way from death. This penalty could only be inflicted by the supreme official of the province, the Proconsul; and therefore it is maintained that "an uproar resulted, and he was arrested and condemned to death as the cause of it"; the Proconsul had the power, "when the contest in the arena did not result fatally, to set him free". As Dr. McGiffert rather humorously observes, "doubtless he was convinced that Paul would avoid creating any more disturbances".

When Paul recounts to the Corinthians his sufferings, 2 *Cor.* xi. 23 f., he did not think it worth while to mention that most remarkable of all escapes and dangers, though he mentions many far less striking and impressive, because he had already mentioned it in the first Epistle, and it "may have seemed unnecessary to do so in the second". Why not apply the "Source-Theory" here? The two Epistles use different Sources!

I need not discuss such a shadowy and hypothetical substitute for the realistic and impressive narrative of *Acts*.[1] I venture to doubt if any two scholars in the whole of Europe will accept this interpretation of the fundamental word "fought-with-beasts". The sketch of the supposed trial and condemnation and fight in the amphitheatre and pardon is too false to Roman habits of administration, and to the surroundings of Epheso-Roman society, to have any claim to be taken seriously. It is simply a blot upon a very clever and learned book.

The conclusion from a long examination of the Ephesian incident is that "it is impossible to discover a satisfactory reason for the omission of" so many occurrences as are known to us from Paul's own words, or why the author failed to relate the events which were of most interest and concern to Paul himself (p. 283), except that his "Sources" are to blame. But why was Luke bound to guide his history according to the thread of interest which guided Paul in writing to the Corinthians? Paul was arranging his topics to suit the special circumstances of the Corinthian Church; Luke was arranging his history according to his idea of the real importance of the topics.

This method of studying the *Acts*, and distinguishing between what is true and what is false or only half-true in it, is generally practised with a view to eliminate the "miraculous" element, and leave a solid basis of non-miraculous facts. The miraculous element is, undoubtedly, a serious difficulty; but no honest process of criticism can get rid of it. It is implicated in the inmost structure of the

[1] Dr. McGiffert himself says about part of it, "The general trustworthiness of Luke's account cannot be questioned. The occurrence is too true to life and is related in too vivid a way to permit a doubt as to its historic reality" (p. 282).

whole New Testament, and in the very nature of the men
who wrote its books.   Dr. McGiffert sees clearly and
frankly recognises that the miraculous element cannot be
expelled from *Acts;* that Paul, and his contemporaries, and
the oldest and best "Sources" of *Acts,* all believe and
accept and record miraculous events and miraculous powers.
He leaves the marvellous element in *Acts.*

Accordingly, the miraculous healing of the lame man at
Lystra "is too striking and unique to have been invented"
(p. 189).   Some of the accompaniments, however, are pronounced doubtful.   There are analogies to *Acts* iii. 2 ff.
and x. 26 ; and the words of xiv. 15*b*-17 "are much like
Paul's words in his address to the Athenians recorded in
the seventeenth chapter of *Acts*".   Therefore these touches
are declared to result from the author's feeling "the influence of other accounts given elsewhere in his work".   If
I understand this phrase rightly, it means that the author
could not resist the temptation of touching up his narrative
here by introducing words and details from other incidents
belonging to other years and countries.   This is the same
author, who, as we saw, so sternly resisted the temptation
to touch up his narrative at Athens (except the speech of
Paul, which he did embellish).

Moreover, when we turn to the passages which are said
to have furnished the materials which are worked up in the
Lystran incident, we find that they also have themselves
been touched up, and are not pure, unadulterated early
sources.   How marvellous is the unerring art which can
distinguish every layer in this complicated construction, and
can determine how far the Lystran incident is taken from
a good and trustworthy source, what details are added, from
what secondary source each added detail is derived, what is

the character of the secondary sources, and what elements in them are good and what are bad! But this elaborate process is not recognised as permissible by profane historical critics: it is too clever for us.

The term "an older source" is used in a very vague way, which defies strict analysis, throughout the book. Where-ever there is found in *Acts* any fact which can be accepted as true, it is attributed to the use by the author of "an older source". As the author was not the pupil and friend of Paul, we get the general impression that his authorities about events, none of which were known to him on his own authority as an actor in them,[1] were partly older and good, and partly later and bad.

With this classification of the authorities in our mind, we turn to page 647 ff. There we find that the term "the Apostles" is used by the author of *Acts* in a peculiar and narrow sense, *viz.*, denoting the primitive body of Twelve Apostles (to whom Paul is added as an equal, though of later appointment); whereas "in the Gospels of Matthew, Mark, and John, and in the Epistle of Barnabas," as well as in the Apocalypse and the *Didache*, the term "Apostles" is used in a broader sense (which was the common use of the word, while the original Apostles are "the Twelve").

"In the book of Acts, on the other hand, the broader meaning appears only twice (xiv. 4, 14), and that apparently under the influence of an older source." In contrast to that "older source," the ordinary Lukan use of Apostles in the narrower meaning of "the Twelve" with Paul is, as we must understand, under the influence of a later source. This "later source" was, however, of strongly Pauline character, for the narrower sense occurs during the first century "only

---

[1] On that point Dr. McGiffert is quite clear and emphatic.

in the writings of Paul himself, and of those authors who had felt his influence ". Now the "older sources" described events in almost every stage of Paul's life, and therefore those on which chapters xiii. to xxviii. were founded can hardly have been written before A.D. 60-70. The "later source" is closely connected with Paul and under his influence, and, as it was employed by an author who composed his history between A.D. 80 and 95, it must have been written as early as A.D. 70-80. The distinction is remarkably subtle between the two classes of "source," and does great credit to the acumen of the scholar, who can preserve his balanced judgment as he walks along this sharp knife-edge, and can unhesitatingly distinguish between the older and the later source.

In the time of Bentley it was a proof of genius, a matter requiring great acuteness and wide knowledge, to distinguish, as earlier and later, between works whose time of composition was divided by centuries. In the present century, after discussion and minute examination by many generations of scholars, opinions vary widely as to the period to which many works belong. The *Nux* is taken by some critics for a youthful work of Ovid, while others would refer it to a time after Ovid's death. One of the greatest of modern scholars considers that the *Epicedion Drusi* was composed in the fifteenth century after Christ; many believe that it was written in the first century before Christ immediately after the death of Drusus (B.C. 9).

But, although the original works are lost, the "Source-Theorist" decides with unhesitating confidence whether the source for some half-sentence or half-paragraph of Luke is old, dating from 60-70, or later, dating from A.D. 70-80. We humble students of history cannot come up to such skill as that; and we are so rude and barbarous as to smile at it and disbelieve in it. We think that, if the "Source-Theorists" had spent twenty years in the school of Mommsen and the great pagans, instead of among the theologians, they would see that they are attempting an impossibility, and would be as much amused at it as we profane scholars are. All theories of Acts, except one, result in hopeless confusion.

We have in Dr. McGiffert's work a book which shows many very great qualities, and which might have ranked among the small number of really good books, if it had not been spoiled by a bad theory as to the fundamental document, on which it must rest. But it will do good service in bringing home to us that, if the author was Luke, then the acknowledged difficulties in *Acts* must not be solved by the theory of insufficient information. Whom should we look to for knowledge of Paul, if not to Luke, his companion in so many captivities and journeys (the times when Paul would be least occupied with the daily cares of preaching and teaching)? Those who contend for Lukan authorship must deny themselves the easy cure of inadequate knowledge. There was abundant opportunity for Luke to acquire exact information, if on any point he lacked it, for intercommunication was the life of the early Church, and numerous witnesses were living. Dr. McGiffert has destroyed that error, if an error can be destroyed.

21

XIII

A STUDY OF ST. PAUL BY MR. BARING-GOULD

XIII

A STUDY OF ST. PAUL BY MR. BARING-GOULD

IN my *St. Paul the Traveller* a conception of Paul's character is stated, which seems to me to be so patent in the narrative of *Acts*, that it must have been the conception entertained by the author. My aim in that book was rather to show clearly what was Luke's conception of Paul than to state my own views of the Apostle's character; though, to a certain extent, my own conception necessarily tinges the picture. The attempt was, of course, a delicate and difficult one; it is founded on a certain theory of Luke's own character and action, and partakes of the uncertainty that attaches to that theory. The evidence of the *Epistles* is interpreted according to my conception of the situation, as they would appear to Paul's contemporaries, not as they appear to us in the nineteenth century. This whole process is so delicate that the opportunity of weighing and pondering over a conception of the Apostle's character, formed by one who takes much the same view as I do of the historical facts and incidents and dates, is valuable; and I am indebted to Mr. Baring-Gould for several good ideas [1] and much interest; but also I must confess that I have often felt repelled by the way he belittles

---

[1] *E.g.*, that the loss of the offerings of the "God-fearing," whom Paul tempted away from the synagogues, annoyed the Jews (p. 180, etc.).

and (in my opinion) misrepresents a great man. The passage at foot of page 327 is a libel on Paul: "Paul is thoroughly Oriental in his indifference to the welfare and sufferings of the brute creation. . . . He imputes to the Almighty the same insensibility to pity and care for the dumb beast that he possessed."

Mr. Baring-Gould defines his aim in this book as follows: "The line I have adopted is that of a man of the world, of a novelist with some experience of life, and some acquaintance with the springs of conduct that actuate mankind"; and he describes the novelist as "one who seeks to sound the depths of human nature, to probe the very heart of man, to stand patiently at his side with finger on pulse. He seeks to discover the principles that direct man's action, to watch the development of his character, and to note the influence that surroundings have on the genesis of his ideas and the formation of his convictions."

The programme was quite fascinating to one who, like myself, has attempted (in a humbler way and on a less ambitious plan than Mr. Baring-Gould) "to take Church History for a moment out of the hands of the theologians," and treat it on freer lines. I have none of the prejudice, which he anticipates, against a novelist's attempt to understand and depict the mind of Paul. On the contrary, the most illuminative page that I have ever read about the central scene of Paul's life, that scene whose interpretation determines our whole conception of Paul's work, the appearance of Jesus to him "as he drew nigh unto Damascus," is in a tale by another novelist, Owen Rhoscomyl.[1] Hence I welcome the application of Mr. Baring-Gould's method, as he defines it, to the personality of Paul. He has, however,

---

[1] This illuminative page is quoted in *The Education of Christ*, p. 9 f.

not given himself fair play. Instead of trying simply to present his own view to the reader, he tries too much to correct the views of others ; he lays so much stress on those sides of Paul's character which have, in his opinion, been too little regarded, that his picture of the Apostle is one-sided. The qualities on which he insists, and to which he returns with painful frequency, are so unpleasant that the character which he sets before us is repulsive and almost detestable. It is rare that any sentence is devoted to the good or great qualities of Paul's mind.[1] His blunders, his failures, his weaknesses, his domineering nature, fill up most of the book. Mr. Baring-Gould knows that he was even a bad workman (p. 296).

My objection to Mr. Gould's book as a whole is, not that it *is* a novelist's view, but that it *is* *not* a novelist's view. I have not been able to feel that he presents Paul as an intelligible character, clearly understood by the author, and therefore easily recognisable by the reader ; and he leaves Paul's work and influence more completely a riddle than before. One seems in this book to see two Pauls, sometimes coalescing more or less into a single picture, sometimes separate from one another, as if one were looking through a badly focussed optical instrument; and neither of the figures of Paul, which thus dance before one's eyes, seems to suit the work and life that are shown us in *Acts* and the *Epistles*. The author describes his aim in the words, " I treat the great Apostle as a man ". I went to the book, hoping to find a man there. I found much that was interesting; I found a view so different from my own that it was bound to be instructive by forcing me to try to understand the causes which had produced it. But I do not find in it a man: I

[1] Examples on pp. 127, 434, 436 f.

find a conception, half double, half single, like the Siamese twins. Now, as I have been requested, I shall state the reasons for this opinion, though I feel as if it were ungrateful to do so, after the kind terms in which he has referred to my work on the subject. I would not have promised to write this paper, had I not thought at first that it was likely to be far more laudatory than it is.

Briefly, I may say at the beginning that on almost all the main controversies as to the facts of Paul's life, I find myself in agreement, or nearly so, with Mr. Baring-Gould. It is in the general conception that he does not persuade me. I do not insist that I am right, and I am eager to study any view that differs from mine, but I feel very sure that his view is not right, because it fails to make history intelligible.

To make Mr. Gould's position clear, it should also be mentioned that the author accepts all the Epistles attributed to Paul as his genuine work, and as divinely inspired writings, and that he is fully convinced of the miraculous character of Paul's conversion. He accepts the Divine element in the narrative of the early Church, holding "that to eliminate that is to misconceive the story of Paul altogether". But he is "indisposed to obtrude the Divine and miraculous, wherever the facts" can be explained without such a supposition.

Before criticising details, I will quote what I thought one of the best passages in the book: " As the moon has one face turned away from earth, looking into infinity, a face we never see, so it is with the mystic. In him there is the spiritual face—mysterious, inexplicable, but one with which we must reckon. And this it is that makes it so difficult to properly interpret the man of a constitution like

Paul. We have to allow for a factor in his composition that escapes investigation " (p. 138).

We must try to put shortly the character of the man Paul according to Mr. Baring-Gould, and it will be best to do so as much as possible in his own words. The central point in his theory is thus stated : " The generally entertained idea of St. Paul as the Apostle to the Gentiles, preaching to the unconverted, drawing the net of the Church in untried waters, must be greatly modified. He did not carry the Gospel to the heathen, though he certainly travelled among them" (p. 417, compare 148, 435, etc.).

Paul was, it seems, rarely able to persuade others fully as to his sincerity or his authority as an Apostle. "Obviously the Apostles did not altogether trust Paul's account of his vision seen at Antioch. They thought he had unwittingly coloured it to suit his own wishes" (p. 121). "It must be allowed that he possessed a faculty of giving these matters a partial aspect, and embroidering them to suit his purpose, which is calculated, if not to awake suspicion, at all events to call forth reserve" (p. 122). "Were they (*i.e.*, the elder Apostles) to accept the assurance of a man of whom all they knew was that he was a weather-cock in his religious opinions, and that in a matter of supreme importance?"

Extreme and ill-regulated statements of this kind prevent the author from achieving a fair presentation of his own case, and will tend to prevent the good points in the book from being appreciated.

Further, the author seems sometimes almost to doubt if Paul had any faith in his mission. For example, on page 239, he asks, "could Paul have thought, could these shallow sciolists have conceived it possible, that the badly expressed words in which he professed his convictions would outlast and overmaster all their cobweb-spinning, and that, in a few years, deep into the rock where Paul stood and received their jeers, the cross would be cut?" I should have believed that Paul thought, and was even firmly convinced, that his words would last; but Mr. Gould apparently leads up to a negative answer.

The reasons why Paul could never convert any of the Gentiles, except certain God-fearing proselytes who had been already half-converted by the Jews, were various; but the chief were, first, his ignorance and utter want of education in anything except the narrowest and straightest Judaic legal teaching; secondly, his utter inability to argue.

As to Paul's ignorance of all things Greek, except a certain fluent command of a vulgar provincial dialect, so bad that it made, his language in speaking a subject for contempt and ridicule in Athens and Corinth (p. 226, etc.), Mr. Gould speaks with remarkable emphasis in various passages.

Paul had been altogether outside the circle of Greek studies; and had no knowledge of Greek philosophy or thought. "Paul was as incapable of appreciating the art treasures of Athens as he was of giving proper value to its philosophy." "As he had no appreciation of art, so had he none for Nature" (p. 227). "So, he was ignorant of Greek history, and out of sympathy with the noble struggles of the past" (*ibid.*); for "the entire system of training under Gamaliel had been stunting to the finer qualities of the mind" (p. 228). "He had no knowledge of geography" (p. 317).

In Tarsus during boyhood he did not attend Greek schools, and was never allowed to come "in contact with the current and eddies of thought among the Greek students".

He was even kept by his strict father from associating with such Jews as were not strict in their adherence to the Law and to the traditions of the rabbis. He learned nothing of Greek thought; and, inasmuch as "it is not probable that there was an elementary school at Tarsus" (*i.e.*, a Jewish school), "he learned texts of his mother and the interpretation from his father". "As he worked at the loom, the old Pharisee laboured to weave as well his prejudices, interpretations, hatreds and likings into the texture of his son's mind." Thereafter, as he grew old, Paul "would be placed under instruction in the traditions with the ruler of the synagogue".

In this narrow system of education, "which had tortured his growing mind," Mr. Gould finds the explanation why Paul went "to the opposite extreme," when he "deserted the religion of his youth".[1]

Not merely was Paul kept from any share in Greek education; but also the amusements of the city were forbidden to him. "As Jews, the tentmaker and his son abstained from theatrical and gladiatorial shows"; but at this point the author remembers, apparently, how frequently Paul took his illustrations from the games, and he makes an exception as regards the circus. Probably "he took advantage of having a seat[2] in the circus, and followed the contest with zest".

But why should we consider that the circus was permitted to Paul, and not the other amusements of the

[1] See pp. 51-53.

[2] The idea that Paul had a seat in the circus by right (for which I know of no justification) seems to spring from the mistaken idea (p. 60) that the Roman citizenship and even equestrian rank were gained by Paul's father from his having held office in the city. See the remarks below, on p. 340.

stadium and the amphitheatre? He very often takes his illustrations from the foot-races and athletic sports of the stadium. Once at least he uses an expression which derives its force from the *venationes* in the amphitheatre.[1] Are we not as fully justified in supposing that attendance at the stadium and amphitheatre was permitted to Paul as at the circus? Is it not obvious that, if we once admit the principle that Paul's illustrations and comparisons and metaphors give a clue to his own early experiences and education, it becomes difficult to draw any such hard line of demarcation between the Jewish boy Paul's surroundings in Tarsus and those of the young Greeks? Canon Hicks says well: "See how essentially Greek is his perpetual employment of figures drawn from athletic games. . . . Not less essentially Greek are his metaphors from the mysteries, or from civic life, or from education. It is plain that St. Paul's mind is stored with images taken from Græco-Roman life; he calls them up without effort. He returns to some of them again and again. Even when a metaphor is suggested by an Old Testament text like *Isaiah* lix. 17 and xi. 5, he works up the illustration (1 *Thess.* v. 8; *Eph.* vi. 13) after the manner of a pure Greek simply describing a Roman soldier."[2]

Those whose intellectual life has been chiefly spent in Greek, like Professor Ernst Curtius, or Canon E. L. Hicks (who knows as much about the Greek cities of the Asian coast at the period in question as any living man), recognise in Paul a man whose mind is penetrated with Greek thoughts and familiar with Greek ways. Those who are come to him fresh from Roman surroundings recognise in

[1] *St. Paul the Traveller*, p. 230.
[2] *St. Paul and Hellenism*, p. 7 f. (*Studia Biblica*, iv.).

him a mind which works out in practical life many of the guiding ideas of Roman organisation, and which often expresses itself in words whose full meaning is not apparent without reference to Græco-Roman Law.

That Paul was, above all things, a Jew trained in the Mosaic Law and its scholastic or rabbinical interpretation is quite true ; but the old-fashioned (unfortunately not wholly old-fashioned) idea that he was nothing more than that is miserably inadequate and utterly misleading. It has maintained itself so long, because Pauline study has usually been almost exclusively in the hands of men whose education has been directed in their early years to classical Greek authors, and then to Jewish life and history. The life of the Græco-Asiatic cities, a life inarticulate to us because its literature has wholly perished (and perished unregretted) —a life known only to the antiquary through the laborious piecing together of scattered fragments of stories, inscribed and uninscribed—is a subject which the Pauline interpreters, as a rule, only enter [1] in search of illustrations ; but he who is to appreciate Paul rightly must first make himself as familiar as Hicks and Curtius have been with the life and surroundings and education, amid which he worked and preached, and then proceed to study his works, instead of regarding Paul always as the Jew, and reading him with a mind always on the outlook for Judaic ideas, and with the vague prepossession that nothing is Greek which does not resemble the Greece of Demosthenes and Plato.

The author has on page 277 ff. an interesting comparison between the Roman *Jus Gentium* (a statement of those elementary and universal principles of equity which were recognised, or supposed to be recognised, by all nations,

[1] Even the best seem to enter with minds already made up.

and which lay at the basis of all right law) in its relation to the statute law, and the Gospel principles of justice and duty in their relation to the Mosaic Law.[1] In each case the modification of hard, inelastic, formal laws was sought in a return to first principles, in an appeal to fundamental and elementary conceptions of moral rectitude. The comparison may be considered perhaps a little fanciful; but I do not think so. The distinction between principles of right and rigid regulations was in the air at that period; and the educated men were thinking of it, or, at least, were in that line of thought.

This comparison illustrates a point on which Mr. Baring-Gould differs diametrically from me; and the comparison which he himself here draws seems to tell strongly against his view and in favour of mine. It is impossible to determine how far Paul was distinctly conscious of the analogies that exist between his conception of Christianity and certain features of the Imperial system; but, if he had any consciousness of these analogies, he must have been far more familiar with the Roman world than Mr. Baring-Gould is willing to acknowledge. And, even if he were not conscious distinctly of the Roman analogies (though, for my own part, they are so numerous that I cannot believe them to have been hit upon ignorantly by him), yet at any rate his point of view is that of the educated men of the period; he is not

---

[1] Dr. E. Hicks refers to the same subject less fully in his suggestive little book on *Greek Philosophy and Roman Law in the New Testament*. See also *Hist. Comm. on Galatians*, pp. 337-374. Mr. Gould speaks, not quite accurately, of the *Edictum Perpetuum* as issued by the *prætores peregrini*; but it was specially the declaration by the *prætor urbanus* of the principles on which he intended to interpret justice (*jus dicere*). It is inferred that the final codified *Edictum Perpetuum* includes the equity of the peregrine prætors; but the record is that it was the codification of the *Edictum Urbanum*.

a mere narrow and ignorant Pharisee, as Mr. Gould regards him, but a man familiar with the thoughts and questions of the time.

In that antithesis lies the crucial fact on which Mr. Gould and I are opposed to one another. Regarding Christianity as having come "in the fulness of time," when the world had been in part brought to that stage of education and thought in which the new religion was comprehensible, and regarding the organisation of the Church as arising naturally out of, and excellently suited to, the facts of the time, I cannot consider Paul as being wholly ignorant of, and out of sympathy with, the Greek and Roman world.

Mr. Baring-Gould does not consider that the facts and surroundings of Paul's life are of supreme importance. "I put aside," says he, "details unnecessary to my purpose, archæological, epigraphical, historical, geographical. My book is not, therefore, a life of St. Paul, if incidents and accidents make up a man's life, but a study of his mind, the formation of his opinions, their modification under new conditions, and the direction taken by his work, under pressure of various kinds and from different sides. At the same time I have done my best endeavour to be accurate in such details as were to my purpose to mention, having had recourse to the latest and best authorities " (p. ix.).

After this depreciation of historical study we are rather surprised to find that there is contained in chaps. i. and ii. a general sketch of the character of Jewish education, thought and society—such a sketch as few would attempt to write who had not made long and careful study of the evidence. From some pages we get the impression that, in this author's estimation, when you have seen one Jew you have seen all Jews ; and the Jew whom he has seen is the Jew in whom the Talmud finds delight, and whom the rabbis of the early centuries of our era tried to train. Chap. i. describes the Palestinian Jews according to that type; and chap. ii. paints the extra-Palestinian Jews as much the same: "All the Hellenistic Jews, to the number of three millions, who made the annual pilgrimage to Jerusalem to keep the Passover,[1] differed from the Jews resident in the Holy Land in no other particular than that of language" (p. 50). One rubs one's eyes after reading such a statement, and goes over it again in order to see if one has read aright, and has not omitted a negative, or in some other way got the wrong sense.

But it is an error to take the Talmudic picture of a perfect Jew for a portrait of the actual Jew of Palestine in Paul's time; and it is a still greater error to think that the foreign Jews were not often strongly affected by Greek and Roman education.[2] In other places the author speaks more correctly on this last point.

Mr. Baring-Gould has not much doubt that Paul married Lydia at Philippi, or would have done so "but for untoward circumstances," falling "under the more or less despotic control[3] of the rich shopkeeper," like Hercules in the palace of Omphale, "and delivered from it by a very peculiar circumstance," *viz.*, the adventure with the slave girl. On the whole Mr. Gould concludes that it is more

---

[1] Taken literally, this seems to imply that 3,000,000 Jews annually came to Jerusalem from abroad for the Feast. "A man of the world" would hardly make such a statement; but probably the author has here merely made one of those awkward sentences which sometimes obscure his real meaning, and are apparently due to haste (see below).

[2] Many examples in my *Cities and Bishoprics of Phrygia*, ch. xv.

[3] He thinks that the money which Paul evidently had command of at Cæsarea and in Rome was all supplied by Lydia (p. 402).

probable that the marriage did not actually come off. It was, according to him, a lucky accident that Paul had to leave hurriedly, so that "the Church of Philippi was given a chance of growth independent of his presence"; for the idea seems to rule through this book that Paul ruined every Church which he founded or interfered with, partly by his lack of ability to convert, partly by the bad influence which he had on those whom he converted. The only persons on whom he could exercise much influence were, apparently, women : in Macedonia "he liked . . . the independence of the women and their amenability to his preaching". Timothy, "evidently a tender-hearted, gentle, sensitive person, whose bringing up by two women, and whose delicate health, made him wanting in initiative, . . . was precisely the sort of person Paul liked to have about him ; one who would obey without questioning and follow without murmur" (p. 206).

The author recurs frequently to his idea of a feminine element in Paul's nature. I believe he is right, for there is always something of that element in every great nature ; but Mr. Gould gives an unpleasant, gibing turn to his expressions on the subject. He points out that, if Christianity was to be trammelled by being bound to the text of the Judaic Law, it never could become a religion for the world, nor one of progress. As for Paul, "this he did not see,[1] but he felt it by a sort of feminine instinct, and what he felt, that he was convinced was right". The closest analogy which he can find to illustrate Paul's character is in St. Theresa, who "was a female counterpart of St. Paul" (p. 127, a very interesting passage, well worth reading).

Mr. Gould seems more than half inclined to think that

[1] I should have thought that, if there were anything in the world that Paul saw more clearly than another, it was this.

22

Stephen and Paul were wrong in method, and that their action was a misfortune to Christianity. The older Apostles preferred the wise and calm course of work. " They strewed the seed over every tidal wave that rolled to Jerusalem at every feast, and then retreated to the ends of the earth, whereas Paul darted about dropping grains here and there " (p. 259). Paul has had the luck to be the " most advertised," and his " comet-like whirls" are more " striking in story" than the quieter but more effective work of the other Apostles, who " sat at the centre, forming as it were a powerful battery sending out shock after shock to the limits of the civilised world" (p. 259 ; see also pp. 200, 300). But Paul, " as he had no knowledge of geography, supposed the world was very small, and that he could overrun and convert the whole of it in a very few years " (p. 317).

Even the blame of Nero's persecution is laid on Paul. " So little did Paul conceive of the possibility of Nero becoming a persecutor, that apparently he took the occasion of his appeal to detach the Christian community from the Synagogue, to organise it in independence, and so place it in such a position that, after the fire, the tyrant was able to put his hand down on it, and select his victims. . . . But for this step taken by Paul, it would have been difficult to distinguish them from the Jews."

Still more strange than the oft-repeated diatribes against Paul's inability to convert the heathen, or to make himself intelligible to them, are the passages in which the author describes the evil consequences of Paul's work. These culminate in the sentence: " His model Churches either stank in the nostrils of the not over nice pagans through their immoralities, or backed out of antinomism into Judaic observance " (p. 316, compare p. 304 ff., etc.).

I have left myself no space in which to speak of the many pages in which ridicule is poured on Paul's argument. " His reasonings convinced nobody, and he was himself conscious at last how poor and ineffective they were " (p. 317). Nothing is more difficult than to understand or sympathise with the style of argumentation current in ancient times. Take Plato's arguments in *Republic* I. Nothing could well seem on a superficial view more pointless or more unfair, except some of those which Plato elsewhere puts into Socrates's mouth. Yet it would be hardly more foolish to consider Plato as incapable of arguing in a style which his public could understand than it is to pour contempt on Paul's reasoning. Mr. Gould has not taken enough time to understand it.

It must be frankly stated that Mr. Baring-Gould seems not to have given himself the time to do justice to his own thesis. He has made a number of slips in details, both of fact and of style, which are hardly explicable except on the supposition of extreme hurry.

As to errors of fact, he considers that the breaking of bread, etc., at Assos (*Acts* xx. 7 f.) took place on the Saturday afternoon and evening, not on the Sunday, as the words plainly imply and the commentators whom I happen to have at hand all [1] understand; and on this, apparently, he founds an elaborate theory as to the origin and nature of the Agape-meal. [2] On page 74 he maintains that the seven deacons (*Acts* vi. 5) were " all Hellenistic Jews. It is hardly likely that as yet a place in the ministry would be given to a proselyte."

---

[1] Doubtless some others take the same view as Mr. Baring-Gould, for nothing in Luke or Paul is so clear, that some will not misunderstand it.

[2] See pp. 188, 253, etc. The Agape-meal had, as he thinks, a totally different meaning and origin in Jerusalem and in Antioch.

But it is expressly said by Luke that one of them, Nicolas, was a proselyte Antiochian. On page 79 he finds significance in the fact that Stephen's burial "was not conducted by the believers, though they lamented his death; but by 'devout men,' a term specially applied to the uncircumcised proselytes". Apparently, he has been content with the English version, and has not consulted the Greek Text: the "devout men," who buried Stephen, were εὐλαβεῖς, a term perfectly applicable to the believers, and not σεβόμενοι, which is the term applied to "uncircumcised proselytes". On page 242 Diolcus seems to be spoken of as a harbour on the Saronic Gulf. On pages 224-226 it would almost seem that Thessalonica and Berœa are treated as one and the same city. Mr. Baring-Gould describes the coming to Thessalonica and the riot; and "the result was that Paul and Silas were expelled from Berœa"; and this is not a mere slip of the pen, for there is no allusion to any visit to Berœa; and the confusion between the two cities continues through pages 225 and 226. On page 60 there occurs a strange sentence: "As his father was a citizen, and he likewise, they were not mere residents of Tarsus, but enjoyed the privileges and position of Roman citizenship". Taken strictly, this implies an idea that Paul's Roman rights belonged to him in virtue of his Tarsian citizenship.[1] That would, of course, be quite erroneous; but the following paragraph seems to prove that such was the author's idea, for he goes on to speak as if the enjoyment of office in the city would carry with it equestrian rank.

I cannot close without protesting against a passage on page 418: "The Americans send out and maintain missions

---

[1] On p. 47 he speaks more correctly on this subject; but his words there are discordant with p. 60. The view stated on p. 60 has been often maintained by writers on Paul.

to the Mohammedans in Mesopotamia and Asia Minor, but the missionaries have long despaired of making one convert of the disciples of Islam, and they poach for congregations among the historic Christian Churches". In every point of view this sentence is false. The missionaries to whom Mr. Baring-Gould refers were sent out from the first for the purpose of educating the Christians, and never with the intention of converting the Mohammedans. They were welcomed and protected by the three reforming Sultans, Mahmud and his two successors, which would never have been the case had their action been in any way directed to convert the Turks or other Mohammedan peoples. Further, their primary object is not to proselytise among the Armenians, but to provide an educational system of schools and colleges for a people who had been so repressed and degraded that they were wholly without the humblest educational organisation. To this day members of many Churches attend these schools, knowing, after sixty years' experience, that no attempt will be made to interfere with their religion. I have talked frequently with members of the Armenian and the Greek Church who have been educated at the missionary schools; and speak on their authority, as well as on that of the missionaries themselves. Moreover, every one who has even the most superficial acquaintance with the facts of recent Turkish history and life knows that a great number of Bulgarians were educated at the Mission College in Constantinople, Robert College. Was Mr. Gould ignorant of this, and of the part they have played in emancipated Bulgaria, or does he think that M. Stoiloff (who succeeded Stambuloff as Prime Minister) and the other Bulgarian College students were converted, or that the missionaries aimed at converting them? In the following sentence he betrays

some apprehension that he may be ignorant : he proceeds,
" these missionaries, I daresay, give themselves out as labour-
ing among the unbelievers, but all their efforts are directed
in quite another direction ". This is all dragged in, without
being relevant in any way to the subject, simply in order to
give Mr. Baring-Gould the opportunity of showing his dislike
for people of whom he has heard vaguely, but about whose
work he knows nothing, and has not thought it necessary to
inquire. They seem to him to resemble Paul. In their
inability to convert unbelievers, they try to pervert Christians ; and so " Paul would have liked to convert the
heathen, but he could not do it ; he had not the faculty.
He proposed it more than once, but there it all ended."

We should have expected that a writer about St. Paul,
who adopts " the line of a novelist with some experience of
life," would take some trouble to familiarise himself with the
general facts and situation of the country where his scene
lies. Mr. Baring-Gould prefers to be ignorant of the modern
facts, though he has certainly taken some trouble to acquaint
himself with the ancient. But he can never free himself from
a ruling prejudice against the method of " any Paul or Barnabas rushing about founding Churches " (p. 260).

XIV

THE PAULINE CHRONOLOGY

XIV

THE PAULINE CHRONOLOGY

NEW TESTAMENT chronology in general is exceedingly uncertain and obscure. This is no proof that the history which the New Testament records is unhistorical or uncertain. Owing to a variety of causes ancient chronology as a whole is full of doubtful points; and the reasoning on which the commonly accepted dating depends is in most cases complicated and in many cases very far from certain. But in profane history the uncertainty whether an event commonly assigned to B.C. 301 may not have occurred in 302 or 300, is of little consequence and rouses no strong feelings; and the popular books on history give many dates which are known to the accurate scholar to be mere rough approximations, but which are accepted for want of better. But in New Testament history the issues are of grave importance, and touch the deepest feelings in our minds. No date here is accepted—no date ought to be accepted—without the severest scrutiny. A false chronology often causes apparent inconsistencies in the narrative, which disappear when the chronology is corrected.

It is certain that Pauline chronology has suffered from being generally handled by scholars who had no special training in ancient chronological studies, but merely dipped into the subject for the single purpose of fixing early Christian events. The present writer ventures to think that great

(345)

part of the history of Paul can be dated with a precision and
certainty rare in ancient history, by a series of reasons, drawn
from the most diverse sides, all of which point to the same
result. In ancient history, as a whole, new discoveries are
being constantly made, which sometimes alter an accepted
date, sometimes render precise a date that previously could
be stated only with the saving word "about". Practice in
these questions will enable any one to appreciate the strength
of the arguments by which Pauline chronology can be settled.
Dates on coins or inscriptions, given by the number of years
from an accepted era, are generally the surest form of evidence; but even they can often be cavilled at, for the era has
to be fixed, and this is often possible only by a long and
perhaps uncertain argument. The coin may date an event
in the year 316; but what was the year 1? And what was
the opening day of the year? In ancient times the first day
of the year was placed in different seasons by different
nations, even by different towns. New Year's Day might
be 1st January in one city, while neighbouring cities celebrated
it in spring, or summer, or autumn.

One great cause of difficulty may be at once set aside.
The incidence of the annual Passover has been the subject
of probably more controversy, and elicited more elaborate
and tedious discussion, than any other question in ancient
history. It has been proved repeatedly by the most learned
in Jewish archæology that the day of Passover might vary
between several days of the month, and even between two
months, according to the phases of the moon; and that it
was only fixed by the High-priest after observation of the
appearance of the new moon in the month Nisan, in which
the feast was held. It is contended by these scholars,
and has been almost universally accepted in modern times,

that until about fourteen days before Passover was celebrated
the day and even the month of its incidence were uncertain.
We need not spend time in explaining the causes of this
uncertainty : they have been explained over and over again
without adding one iota to knowledge or advancing in any
degree the solution of the question.[1]

It was possible to be content with about twelve days'
advertisement of the Passover, while the Jews lived only in
Palestine.   But in the Dispersion, when the Jews were
scattered over the Greek and Roman and even the Barbarian
world, this could not be permitted.   It was the common
Passover that held together the scattered nation ; the Jews
came back for the Passover from great distances.   Any uncertainty as to the month would have made this impossible.
Even uncertainty as to the day would have seriously detracted
from the value of the feast as a unifying power.   The feeling that all Jews, even those who could not go to Jerusalem,
celebrated the feast and uttered the sacred words at the
same moment and instructed their children in the mystic and
historic meaning of the ceremonies on the same evening—
that feeling was an essential element in the influence which
the Passover exerted on the whole race.   No one can read
Acts xx. 3-6 without feeling that Paul and his friends knew
the Passover to be the same, whether at Philippi or at
Jerusalem.

With the slow communication of ancient times, it was
necessary that, if the exact incidence of the Passover were
to be known universally to the Jews in the whole world with

[1] The latest and perhaps the clearest exposition of this uncertainty is by
Professor Bacon of Yale in the *Expositor*, 1899 and 1900. Mr. C. H. Turner,
in Hastings' *Dictionary of the Bible*, i., p. 420, takes a more reasonable view,
but even he allows too much for supposed uncertainties, and (as I venture
to think) spoils his chronology thereby.

certainty and in good time, the date must be fixed on
scientific principles during the previous year. The century
before and after Christ was the age of calendar reform.
The required scientific knowledge was available; and no
historian can doubt that it was used for this great purpose
before the time of Paul's journeys.

The old empirical method was not disused. It was a
religious duty that the new moon of Nisan must be observed
and reported to the High-priest. But the ceremony was
now formal, and its results were mapped out and made
known to the Jewish world months beforehand. Later, as
the Christian element in the Empire ill-treated the Jews, the
latter were thrown into opposition; and as the Empire became Christian and anti-Jewish the Jews revolted from the
science that was learned from the outer world; and there
was a resolute ignoring (seen in the Talmud) of all that they
had owed to Greek and Roman science in the happier times
of the early Empire.

The subject is so complicated by many diversities of eras
and of new years, etc., that, to give a brief sketch of it, we
must omit all delicate points of difference and speak throughout roughly in simple terms, according to years of the Christian era beginning on 1st January. Especially the relation
of Eusebius's dates to Jerome's is a complicated question;
and we compare them roughly. As the Eusebian chronology
is fundamental in our sketch, we must explain that Eusebius's
lost *Chronica* is known: (1) through an Armenian translation; (2) through the use of it made by Syncellus and
others; (3) through the Latin translation, expanded and
modified in some cases by Jerome, a learned but not an
accurate man. When we speak of Eusebius's dates we refer
generally to the Armenian translation.

The chronology of Paul is most conveniently treated by regarding the two years' captivity in Cæsarea (Acts xxiv. 27) as the central point. From that most of the rest of his life can be readily reckoned backward or forward. The beginning of the captivity was shortly after Pentecost, in June, two full years before the end of Felix's administration. The end of the captivity coincided with the arrival of Festus to succeed Felix as the Roman governor of Palestine, about June of a certain year.

Among the various chronological systems the following will engage and reward our consideration :—

1. The Eusebian System (so-called).[1] Eusebius places the coming of Festus to Palestine in the last year of Claudius, A.D. 54. Now Eusebius knew perfectly well (as he says in his *History of the Church*) that Festus came after Nero's reign began ; but the explanation of this seeming inconsistency is that the plan of his chronological tables made him call the entire year in which Nero began to reign the fourteenth of Claudius, and the next whole year the first of Nero.[2] Apparently, then, he thought that Festus came after Claudius's death, in October, 54, but before the year ended. Eusebius, however, made some mistake. Even those scholars who cling to what they call the Eusebian dating have had to acknowledge that he was wrong by one or more years.

The prejudices and predilections of the present writer were all in favour of the Eusebian dating ; but the evidence against this date is overwhelming. Must we then conclude that Eusebius committed an inexplicable blunder, making

---

[1] It will be shown in the sequel that this is not the Eusebian system, but a deviation from the Eusebian system, owing to a mistake made by Eusebius himself.

[2] So, *e.g.*, he puts two early acts of Caligula as Emperor in the last year of Tiberius.

his chronology for this period quite untrustworthy? This conclusion long seemed inevitable, until recently a German scholar, Dr. Erbes, gave the explanation—so simple that it seems marvellous how one failed to see it sooner. Eusebius in his reckoning of the kings (which he liked to make continuous, disregarding any *interregnum*), counted A.D. 45 as the first year of Herod Agrippa II. (Acts xxvi.), because his father, Herod Agrippa I. (Acts xii.), died in A.D. 44. From an early authority he learned that Festus came in the tenth year of Agrippa II., and wrongly counting from 45 he set down in his tables the coming of Festus in A.D. 54. But the years of Agrippa were really counted from 50, so that his tenth year was 59.[1]

The supposition that Eusebius made such a mistake in using his authority is quite in accordance with his practice. There are several other cases in which he has failed to observe that his authority reckoned on a different principle from himself, and identified the "tenth year" of a king in his authority with the "tenth year" in his own mistake. For example, he rightly gives fifty-six years six months as the total duration of Augustus's power. That estimate was counted from the spring of 43, when Augustus attained high office. But Eusebius counted Augustus as following Julius Cæsar without any interval, and he thus goes wrong by an entire year; and when we count back from Tiberius to Julius we find that Eusebius has dropped one year. The present writer had repeatedly been baffled by this mistake in Eusebius, until Dr. Erbes's observation about the years of Agrippa set him on the right track.

[1] Dr. Erbes (*Todestage Pauli und Petri* in Gebhardt and Harnack's *Texte und Untersuchungen*, xix., 1), who does not like the plain issue of his own theory, has an elaborate and futile argument to show that the eleventh year was mentioned by Eusebius's authority, making the coming of Festus in 60.

Thus we gather that the coming of Festus to Palestine was placed in A.D. 59 by the early historian, who served Eusebius as the authority for his dating. This authority, who lies behind Eusebius, was probably a first-century historian, and Dr. Erbes suggests that he was Justus of Tiberias (the rival of Josephus). We may for convenience speak of this date as the Justine-Eusebian, recognising that the connection with Justus is only conjectural, but that the date rests on some old and good authority, whose numbers were wrongly understood by Eusebius owing to the mistake above described.

2. Jerome recoiled from the obviously false date given by Eusebius, and in his translation of the *Chronica* he brought down the coming of Festus and some connected dates by two years. With this we may associate other modifications of the Eusebian dating: some German scholars advocate 55 as the year when Festus came; Professor Bacon of Yale advocates 57. The latter date has absolutely no ancient authority in its favour; and it is a mere misnomer to call it Eusebian. These all assume that Eusebius made a blunder, and fail to give any reasonable explanation why he fell into it. He had access to good authorities; and if (as they dated) Festus came under Nero in 56 or 57, it is inexplicable why Eusebius should have carried him back to the last year of Claudius.

3. The great majority of scholars accept the date 60 for Festus; but they confess that it is only an approximate date, and that there is no decisive argument for it. But, being accepted for want of a better, it stands firm and has possession of almost all the books on the New Testament, many of which do not mention that it is admittedly uncertain. We shall prove that it is entirely impossible.

Let us now accept the Justine-Eusebian date, and see where it leads us. We shall find a series of arguments confirming it—arguments which had led the present writer to advocate it for years before Dr. Erbes's discovery. On this system the captivity in Cæsarea lasted from about June, 57, to about midsummer, 59; and Paul must have travelled from Philippi to Jerusalem in March and April, 57. The following arguments confirm this date :—

I. A direct inference from Acts xx. 5 ff. Paul celebrated the Passover of 57, Thursday, 7th April, in Philippi. He remained there through the days of unleavened bread, 7th to 14th April, and then started for Jerusalem. He " was hastening, if it were possible for him, to be at Jerusalem the day of Pentecost"; and Luke is clear that, with the chances of the long journey before him,[1] he stayed only till the feast was ended, and forthwith started on the morning of Friday, 15th April. The journey to Troas lasted "until the fifth day";[2] the time is long (only three days were needed in Acts xvi. 11), but the company had to find a boat at Neapolis. They reached Troas on Tuesday, 19th April, and stayed seven days there. Now the regular custom in ancient reckoning is to include both the day of arrival and the day of departure, even though both were incomplete.[3] The company, therefore, stayed from Tuesday, 19th April, to Monday, 25th April, in Troas, and sailed very early on the Monday morning, as Luke describes.

The year which our ancient authority assigned agrees exactly with Luke's precise statement of days. On the other hand, if we suppose that Paul travelled in 58, Passover

---

[1] At that time travelling was easy and sure to a degree unattained again till this century, but it was very slow.

[2] Such is the exact force of the Greek expression, Acts xx. 6.

[3] See Hastings' *Dictionary of the Bible*, vol. v., p. 474 f.

in that year fell on Monday, 27th March; and Luke's statement of numbers and days is inconsistent with that. Similarly, the other years around 57 are excluded. We come
then, to the conclusion that if Luke is accurate, Paul's journey
to Jerusalem was made in 57.

If Paul was hastening, why did he stay on in Troas till
the following Monday? Either he stayed because he could
not find sooner a convenient ship bound on a rapid voyage
(which is the probable and natural explanation), or because
he wished to make some little stay in Troas, where on his
former visit he had found "an open door" which at the
moment he was not able to take advantage of (2 Cor. ii.
12 f.). In either case it is plain that he dare not linger in
Philippi after the feast; and the supposition of some chrono-
logists that he did not start immediately after the feast
seems mere cavilling at the plain interpretation of Luke, in
defiance of the needs of the situation.

II. Our next argument is founded on Josephus, made
more precise by dates on contemporary coins; and it places
the coming of Festus not later than A.D. 59. Some coins
of Agrippa II. are dated by an era, which has been recognised by numismatists as the foundation and naming of
Neronias (evidently a great event[1] in the career of that
King). The coins show that the foundation occurred in 61-2.
Now Josephus says that the foundation nearly synchronised
with a feast in Jerusalem, some time after Albinus had succeeded Festus as governor of Palestine—probably (as we
shall see) the Feast of Tabernacles, 18th September, A.D. 61.
We put the coming of Albinus in May-June, 61 (see III.).

---

[1] For Agrippa his relations to the Roman government were of critical
importance; and permission to name his capital after the Emperor was a
mark of Imperial favour.

Now Festus had died suddenly in office; news had to be carried to Rome; Albinus was appointed to succeed him; his appointment was known to the Jews in Jerusalem some time before he arrived, so that they could send messengers to Alexandria to meet him; all this occurred in the winter season, when communication was slow; this carries back the death of Festus to the end of 60.

Having now established approximately the end of Festus's procuratorship, we have to fix the beginning, which nearly coincides with the end of Paul's imprisonment. It is certain and agreed that Festus came to Palestine in the course of the summer in some year. The date commonly accepted in modern time is A.D. 60. But between his coming and his death events had occurred implying a much greater lapse of time than between midsummer and December, 60. Not to mention his successful operations against the assassins, he had been involved in an envenomed dispute between his friend, King Agrippa, and the priests at Jerusalem about the King's action in building a tower overlooking the holy precinct of the Temple. After considerable quarrelling Festus allowed the Jews to send an embassy to Rome, including the Highpriest, who certainly would not be able to go away from Jerusalem on such a long journey within a few months before a Passover, as he must necessarily be present at that feast. Taking that fact in conjunction with the necessities of ancient navigation, we have a moral certainty that the embassy would start in late April or in May,[1] for the season of thoroughly safe navigation began only on 15th May. The voyage and the negotiations in Rome must have occupied several months. At last the embassy gained

---

[1] Dr. Erbes regards this as certain, though it forces him to strange shifts.

its cause; but the High-priest was detained in Rome, when the rest were allowed to depart. The news reached Jerusalem; a new High-priest was needed, and Joseph was appointed.

Now these events would occupy the whole summer and part of the autumn : the voyage to Rome, the negotiations, the voyage back to Judæa (a more rapid journey, as was always the case), the proceedings in the election of a new High-priest. The appointment of Joseph may be confidently placed about October. He did not retain office long, but was after a brief tenure deposed. Josephus places the death of Festus after the appointment and before the deposition of Joseph; and, as we have seen, the death of Festus occurred in the end of A.D. 60. Thus the concluding events in the administration of Festus lasted from May to the end of the year 60; and his government cannot have begun later than A.D. 59, as it had been going on for at least several months before the embassy sailed for Rome. As Festus came in summer, we must place his arrival either in 59 or in some earlier year; and his arrival was quickly followed by Paul's trial, his appeal to Cæsar, and his voyage to Rome, which began in the autumn. Thus the commonly accepted date in A.D. 60 is absolutely excluded, if Albinus came in A.D. 61.

After Joseph was deposed Ananus was appointed High-priest in his place (early in March, 61). Ananus held office three months, and was then deposed (late in May, 61), some short time before Albinus came to Palestine.

III. That Albinus came in 61 and not in 62 to govern Palestine as procurator is established with certainty by the following reasoning. Josephus mentions that, some time after Albinus came to Jerusalem, there occurred a feast, and

the city of Cæsareia Philippi was refounded by Herod
Agrippa II. about the time of that feast under the name
Neronias. Now this was a highly important event in the
reign of Herod. Neronias was his capital; and an era was
counted from its foundation. The numismatists have determined this era. The year 1 was A.D. 61-62. The year may
be confidently assumed to have begun in the spring-time, as
was customary in Southern Syria; and the custom with such
new eras was to count the current year as 1 (not to make the
new year start from the day of the foundation). The feast
at which Neronias was founded, therefore, fell in the year
beginning in spring 61 and ending in spring 62; and therefore it was either the Feast of Tabernacles, in autumn 61, or
the Passover, in spring 62. No other feast can possibly be
taken into account. Albinus, therefore, who had been in
Jerusalem some time before the foundation, must have come
to Palestine in the spring or early summer of 61.

In the uncertainty between the Feasts of Tabernacles, 61,
and Passover, 62, several reasons combine to give the preference to the former; but this is unimportant for our purpose. Either of them would give the result that, if Albinus
came in the early summer, he must have come in A.D. 61,
not in A.D. 62. No other year has the slightest claim to
be considered, or has been thought of by any recent
scholar.

Now, as to the time of year when Albinus came, that is
certain. In the first place, it was usual for officials to arrive
to take up office at this season, though sometimes arrival
was delayed till midsummer, and doubtless exceptional cases
of arrival at other seasons occurred.

In the second place, our argument has placed Ananus's
three months' tenure of the high-priesthood between March

and the end of May, 61. Soon after his deposition Albinus arrived ; and after his arrival the tithes were collected from the threshing-floors, as Josephus tells. That would take place about late June or July, and confirms our dating of Ananus's high-priesthood. Later than that Josephus mentions the feast (Tabernacles, 61), and afterwards the foundation of Neronias (fixed by coins in 61-2).

In the third place, the coming of Albinus is fixed in the very end of May or in June by another argument of very illuminative kind, which has never before been observed, and which confirms the previous reasoning in a striking and conclusive way. When the news of the death of Festus reached Rome, Nero nominated Albinus to succeed him. News of this was carried (of course by the Imperial post) to Jerusalem. In the interval King Agrippa deposed Joseph and appointed Ananus High-priest in his place, during February or early March, A.D. 61. Thereafter the news that Albinus was appointed reached the Jews.

In the article on "Roads and Travel" in Hastings' *Dictionary of the Bible*, v., p. 385, I have calculated the post time between Rome and Jerusalem as fifty-two days. We must double this and allow five to fifteen days for Nero to consider and to register and publish the appointment. Now Ananus held office only three months, March-May, and the news about Albinus reached Jerusalem probably about the end of March or the beginning of April, at least a full month before Ananus was deposed.[1] Festus then must have died (as we have already seen) early in December, A.D. 60.

---

[1] It must of course be understood that all these calculations are approximate. The perfectly normal rate of travelling could not be always maintained. But, approximately, this reckoning may be accepted ; the actual facts would not be very far from the reckoning.

IV. Ananus, soon after he became High-priest, brought
James the Just and some other Christians before the Sanhedrin and had them stoned to death. His violent and even
illegal conduct roused strong disapproval even among the
Jews. Some of them sent secretly to King Agrippa, asking
him to forbid such conduct in future. Apparently after
this they learned of Albinus's appointment, and sent messengers to meet him in Alexandria, denouncing the action
of Ananus as illegal inasmuch as it had been carried out
without the procurator's approval (a good and valid ground
of accusation likely to carry great weight with the new
procurator).

Two questions here suggest themselves. In the first
place, why was Ananus's action so strongly disapproved by
the Jews in Jerusalem, who seem to have approved of previous action against the Christians? A Christian historian
gives the answer to this.

Hegesippus, an excellent authority, describes the martyrdom, and says that it occurred while there were in Jerusalem
many persons who had come up for the Passover. Further,
the Hieronymian Martyrology, also an excellent authority,
gives 25th March as the day of the martyrdom. We have
been compelled by the preceding argument to place Ananus's
high-priesthood in the spring of 61, and 24th March was the
Passover in that year. In 62 the Passover was on 12th
April, in 60 on 4th April, in 59 on 15th April, which are all
quite inconsistent with the Martyrology. But in 61 the day
of martyrdom was the day after the Passover; and this
coincidence, justifying both Hegesippus and the Martyrology,
furnishes a strong argument in favour of our dating. It was,
of course, against the law to put a criminal to death during
the feast; but Ananus was bitterly accused by the Jews

themselves (as Josephus tells) for illegal and outrageous conduct on this occasion.

In the second place, why did the Jews send to Alexandria to lodge a complaint with Albinus? Formerly, I supposed that Albinus had been an official in Egypt, and that when Nero appointed him to Palestine, instructions were sent to him, on receipt of which he would hand over his Egyptian office to a successor and travel to Palestine to take up his new duties. The correct answer became clear to me while writing an account of " Roads and Travel in New Testament Times " for Hastings' *Dictionary of the Bible*, vol. v., pp. 375-402. The usual way of travelling from Rome to Syria was by the corn-ships returning from Puteoli to Alexandria, and thence by coasting-vessel to Cæsareia on the coast of Palestine or Berytus (Beirout) on the Syrian coast. So, *e.g.*, went Maecius Celer in A.D. 95, when he was about to assume office in Syria, as Statius, *Silvæ* iii., 2, describes. So the Roman troops destined by Nero to co-operate with the Syrian armies in the proposed Parthian war went first of all to Alexandria, and were thence re-called : they returned by the long voyage *viâ* Cyprus and the south coast of Asia Minor and Crete; and suffered severely from the sea.[1] So when Agrippa in A.D. 38 was going to take possession of his Palestinian kingdom, which Caligula had given him, he was advised to avoid the long, toilsome journey by Brundusium and Syria, and take the quick route by ship from Puteoli to Alexandria. Those ships were large, the sailing-masters were skilful and experienced, and the voyage was regularly performed with speed, ease and certainty.[2] But such voyages were made only during the season of open sea from about 27th May to

---

[1] Tacitus, *Hist.*, i., 31 ; cp. i., 70, and i., 6.   [2] Philo in *Flacc.*, 5.

15th September; and the very best season was while the regular Etesian winds were blowing.[1] Albinus, appointed about the end of January, A.D. 60, waited at Puteoli for the first voyage of the season in the latter part of May. Couriers going by the land road took about fifty-two days from Rome to Jerusalem, and the Jews heard of his appointment about the 1st of April. But officials could not travel like couriers; and Albinus was likely to arrive sooner *vià* Alexandria than *vià* Brundusium, as well as with less fatigue. Thus the Jews were able to send to meet him in Alexandria. His arrival in Palestine may be dated in June, A.D. 61.

V. The Eusebian chronology as a whole confirms our dates. Eusebius makes Albinus succeed Festus in 60, Jerome puts this in 61; we have placed the death of Festus at December, 60, and the coming of Albinus in June, 61. Eusebius makes Florus succeed Albinus in 63, Jerome in 64; the latter date is probably right (the only alternative being January to March, 65). Eusebius and Jerome put the coming of Felix in 51; the true date is 52, but Felix previously had held command in Samaria. Thus Felix had governed Palestine an unusually long time when Paul came before him in 57—"many years," Acts xxiv. 10 (where the word many is understood relatively to the usual duration of procuratorships).

It is established by this concurring series of arguments that Paul came to Jerusalem in May, 57, and sailed for Rome soon after midsummer 59. From this we can calculate backward and forward. He left Ephesus (Acts xx. 1)

---

[1] Perhaps 20th July to 28th Aug.; but there is much doubt about these winds. Modern scholars are apt to forget that each sea has its own Etesian winds, and the rule for the Ægean does not apply to the voyage across Adria (Acts xxvii. 27, Statius, *Silv.* iii., 2, 87) from Italy to Alexandria. Gentle, light westerly winds blow across Adria all summer. See p. 364.

shortly before Pentecost 56, and spent a year in Macedonia and Corinth (writing 2 Corinthians in summer 56 and Romans early in 57). He had spent in Ephesus two years and three months (called three years by Paul after the usual ancient fashion of counting the fraction of a year at the end as a whole year); and must have arrived there about December, 53. He had gone to Jerusalem for Passover, 22nd March, 53 (Acts xviii. 21 f.), and spent the summer and autumn of 53 in Antioch and in revisiting and establishing all his converts in South Galatia. Before going to Jerusalem, he spent eighteen months in Corinth, August, 51, to February, 53.[1] When Paul first came to Corinth, he found there Aquila recently arrived, after being expelled from Rome by Claudius. Now Orosius puts the edict of expulsion in the ninth year of Claudius, and a comparison of his dates with Tacitus shows that he counted the first year of Claudius to begin from 1st January following his accession,[2] so that his first year was 42, and his ninth 50. If Aquila was expelled late in 50, he would come to Corinth perhaps in the spring or summer of 51, some months before Paul.

Gallio came to Corinth when Paul had been there for a considerable time. He would in ordinary course arrive in the summer; and we must therefore conclude that he came to Achaia in the summer 52. While he was in Achaia he took fever and went a voyage for his health.[3] There is no

---

[1] The voyage from Corinth to Palestine does not require a long period, as ships ran specially for the sake of Jewish pilgrims to the Passover, making the voyage rapidly; see article " Corinth " in Hastings' *Dictionary of the Bible*, i., p. 483, and my *St. Paul the Traveller*, pp. 264, 287.

[2] Compare what is said above about the years of Nero.

[3] Seneca, *Epist. Mor.*, 104, 1. Pliny mentions that after his consulship Gallio went on a voyage (from Italy?) to Egypt on account of phthisis (*Hist. Nat.*, 31, 33). He of course governed Achaia before his consulship.

evidence outside Acts as to the date of his government, but his brother Seneca addressed him by his old name Novatus in the treatise *De Ira*, which was probably composed in 49 ;[1] and he had taken his adoptive name, Junius Gallio, before he came to Corinth.

It is less easy to reckon farther back, as the lapse of time is not so well marked in that period. But we may fairly place the beginning of Paul's second missionary journey in early summer 50, allot summer and autumn 50 to the work in South Galatia (Acts xvi. 1-6) with the journey north to the Bithynian frontier and west to Troas. The winter and the summer of 51 were spent in Philippi and Thessalonica and Berœa and Athens. Thus we find that the third visit to Jerusalem (Acts xv. 2) had come to an end not later than the beginning of 50. That visit was evidently brief ; but the residences in Antioch before and after it are of quite uncertain duration. If events hurried rapidly on in Antioch, Paul may have returned from South Galatia about August, 49, and the first missionary journey with all its wide travels and long periods of preaching may have begun after Passover 47. But it is perhaps more probable that the stay in Antioch should be lengthened (Acts xiv. 28), or that the first journey occupied longer time, or both. We may, however, feel fairly confident that the first journey would begin in spring (doubtless after the Passover), either A.D. 46 or 47, more probably the former. The second visit to Jerusalem may be supposed to have occurred in 45 ; but the length of the "ministration" there is uncertain.

As to the conversion, the evidence of a fourth- or fifth-century homily, wrongly ascribed to Chrysostom, is important and probably embodies an early tradition. It states

[1] Lehmann, *Claudius und seine Zeit.*, p. 315 ff.

that St. Paul served God thirty-five years, and died at the age of sixty-eight. Eusebius places his death in 67, Jerome in 68; but they lump together the whole Neronian persecution, from 64 on, in a single entry, not implying that it lasted only one year. In the great political crisis of 68, trials of Christians must have ceased; and the death of Paul must be placed in 65 or 66 or 67. But it seems clear that Paul entered public life after the crucifixion; and if he did so (as was not rare) in his thirtieth year,[1] he must have been under thirty at that event, A.D. 29. This seems to oblige us to place his birth in B.C. 1, his conversion in 32 on 19th January (the traditional day may be certainly accepted), and his death in 67.

When this chronology was first proposed, it was founded solely on the authority of Acts, especially xx. 5 ff.; and it is employed in *St. Paul the Traveller* and later works by the present writer. For years he thought that the Eusebian chronology was opposed to it, and sorrowfully rejected Eusebius. Now, after the acute suggestion of Dr. Erbes, it has been shown that this system is the Eusebian and the traditional chronology. We closely follow Eusebius (or in one case his first-century authority) everywhere; and we see that ancient traditions, rejected by every other chronologist simply because they did not suit his system, fit into it exactly, and confirm its correctness. We have found several of our dates in ancient authorities, and any one proves the others. Not a single positive statement in any ancient author supports the commonly accepted chronology, which is given by its earlier supporters professedly as a makeshift

---

[1] The Greek word *νέος*, a young man, was commonly used of a person from twenty-two to forty years of age; so also *νεανίας*. Hence no stress can be laid on the description of Paul as " a young man ".

in the dearth of positive evidence, and is scouted by many
excellent scholars. Yet it is the accepted system of the
school and college handbooks; and our system is for the
present regarded as an attempt to overturn settled chronology, whereas it is really the old tradition resting on positive
ancient testimony of the highest character.

There is urgent need for a book on Eusebius and the
early Christian chronology, showing his essential accuracy,
and tracing the cause of his occasional mistakes (which are
due to defective method). Here we cannot take up space
in answering some of the objections that are sure to be
brought forward to our system (as, *e.g.*, it has been contended by many that Aretas could not have been in possession of Damascus [2 Cor. xi. 32] before A.D. 37, an objection
which is answered beforehand by Marquardt, *Römische Staat-
salterth*, i., p. 404 f.). We can simply rest on the fact that
ours is the ancient and authoritative chronology.

As to the season of open sea (p. 359 f.), the period is
stated as 27th May to 15th September. These dates are
stated absolutely; but it cannot be supposed that sailors
were absolutely governed by them, regardless of weather in
each year. We may feel quite confident that, if steady settled
weather and an early season occurred in any year, sailors
would take the opportunity and begin to sail earlier than
27th May.

TABLE OF PAULINE DATES

Birth of St. Paul . . . . after Passover, B.C. 1
Entrance on public life in his thirtieth year . . after Passover, A.D. 29
Conversion . . . . January 25, 32
First visit to Jerusalem (in the third year, Gal. i. 18) . . . 34
Second visit to Jerusalem (in the fourteenth year, Gal. ii. 1) . . 45
First missionary journey . . (perhaps March, 47 ; probably) March, 46
Return to Antioch . (perhaps August, 49 ; probably) about August, 48
Third visit to Jerusalem ; the Apostolic Council . . . . early 50
Second missionary journey . . . . begins after Passover, 50
In Corinth (Epistles to Thessalonians) . September, 51, to February, 53
Fourth visit to Jerusalem at the Passover . . . March 22 to 29, 53
Return to Antioch (Epistle to Galatians) . . . . . April, 53
Third missionary journey . . . . . begins early summer, 53
In Ephesus (First Epistle to Corinthians) . December, 53, to March, 56
In Macedonia (Second Epistle to Corinthians) . summer and autumn, 56
In Corinth (Epistle to Romans) . . . . . winter, 56, to 57
At Jerusalem at Pentecost 57
Imprisonment in Cæsarea . . . . . . June, 57, to June, 59
Voyage to Rome . . . . . August, 59, to February, 60
Imprisonment in Rome . . February, 60, to (at latest) February, 62
Later journeys . . . . 62 to 66
Taken prisoner at Nicopolis . . . . . winter of 66 to 67
Execution at Rome 67

XV

LIFE IN THE DAYS OF ST. BASIL THE
GREAT

XV

LIFE IN THE DAYS OF ST. BASIL THE GREAT [1]

THE publication of three volumes of selections from the works of the great Cappadocian Fathers of the fourth century may well attract notice even in this busy time; and the careful and excellent scholarship displayed by the translators and editors thoroughly deserves more generous recognition than it has yet received. The work has been well done; it was well worth doing; and it was by no means easy to do. Gregory of Nyssa is a really difficult author. The style of Basil is, like his own character, direct, vigorous, and much too intense to become so complicated as that of his brother.

[1] *Select Library of Nicene and Post-Nicene Fathers of the Christian Church.* Edited by Dr. Henry Wace, Principal of King's College, London, and Dr. Philip Schaff, Professor of Church History in Union Seminary, New York.

Vol. V., *Select Writings and Letters of Gregory of Nyssa.* Translated with prolegomena, etc., by W. Moore, M.A., Rector of Appleton, late Fellow of Magdalen College, Oxford, and H. A. Wilson, M.A., Fellow and Librarian of Magdalen College, Oxford.

Vol. VII.: Part II., *Select Orations and Letters of S. Gregory Nazianzen.* Translated with prolegomena, etc., by C. G. Browne, M.A., Rector of Lympstone, Devon, and J. E. Swallow, M.A., Chaplain of the House of Mercy, Horbury.

Vol. VIII., *Letters and Select Works of St. Basil.* Translated with prolegomena, etc., by Blomfield Jackson, M.A., Vicar of St. Bartholomew's, Moor Lane, and Fellow of King's College, London.

The variety in the titulature of the three Saints suggests a certain difference of view among the translators.

But even Basil presents numerous difficulties to the comprehension of his readers; and the scholar, who studies an author of this period, with few and poor editions, has a much more difficult task than the translator of some author that has attracted the attention of generations and centuries of learned leisure. Dr. Wace is responsible for the editing of the whole volume of Gregory Nyssen, and part of the volume of Basil; and the many difficulties and questions that confront the translator in every page must all have been weighed anew by him in the execution of a peculiarly thankless, but important task.

It is not our intention to enter into minute questions of translation and criticism, but to attempt to illustrate the usefulness of work like this, by giving some examples of what is to be learned from the selected portions of the three authors. We shall disregard entirely the theological side of their writings, and only quote some of the passages bearing on the condition of society and life at the time and in the land where the three Fathers lived. It is from Basil that we learn most, partly because he had a much more practical and statesmanlike mind than either his brother or his friend, partly because almost the whole collection of his letters, which come into nearer relations to actual life than the theological treatises, is here translated,[1] whereas only a small selection of the letters of Gregory Nazianzen is given (and these seem chosen more for their theological or personal interest than for their bearing on the state of society), and only a very few letters of Gregory Nyssen have been pre-

---

[1] The first 299, with a few specimens of the rest (including the doubtful or spurious correspondence), are included in Mr. Jackson's volume. Our references to *Epist.* are to be understood of Basil's letters, unless another name is mentioned.

served. We shall, as far as possible, narrate each incident in the original words, partly to preserve the true colouring, partly in order to bring out incidentally the success with which the work of translation has been performed.

The modernness of tone that is often perceptible in the literature of the Roman Empire strikes every reader; it corresponds to and expresses a certain precocious ripeness —or, possibly, rottenness—in a too rapidly developed social system. In the Eastern provinces an interesting problem is presented to us; this precocious Western civilisation and education was there impressed upon Oriental races, backward in development and unprogressive in temperament, by the organising genius of Rome and the educative spirit of Greece. It is an interesting process, whereby Western manners and ideas were for a time imposed on, and in a small degree even naturalised among, an Oriental people, and then died out again, either because the circumstances of the Byzantine Empire were uncongenial, or because all civilisation and ideas were destroyed by the Turks. That long process will some time find a historian; a single moment in it is revealed in the pages of the three great Cappadocians.

One of the most interesting passages for our purpose is Gregory Nyssen's satirical sketch of the early life of the two heretics, Ætius and Eunomius. Their history, as told by Gregory, is quite a romance; though it is doubtful how far the account which he gives of theological opponents is to be trusted. Ætius was originally a serf, bound to the soil on a vine-growing estate.

Having escaped—how, I do not wish to say, lest I be thought to be entering on his history in a bad spirit—he became at first a tinker, and had this grimy trade quite at his fingers' end, sitting under a goat's-hair tent,[1] with a small hammer and a diminutive anvil, and so earned a precarious and laborious livelihood.   What income, indeed, of any account could be made by one who mends the shaky places in coppers, and solders holes up, and hammers sheets of tin to pieces, and clamps with lead the legs of pots?

As the story goes, "a certain incident necessitated the next change in his life ".   A woman, attached to a regiment, gave him a gold ornament to mend; he returned to her a similar one of copper, slightly gilt, "for he was clever enough in the tinker's, as in other, arts to mislead his customers with the tricks of trade".   But the gold got rubbed off, and he was detected; "and as some of the soldiers of her family and nation were roused to indignation, she prosecuted," and secured his condemnation.   After undergoing his punish-ment, he "left the trade, swearing that . . . business tempted him to commit this theft".   He then became assistant to a quack doctor, and

made his attack upon the obscurer households and on the most abject of mankind.   Wealth came gradually from his plots against a certain Armenius who, being a foreigner, was easily cheated, and . . . advanced him frequent sums of money.   He next wanted to be styled a physician himself.   Henceforth, therefore, he attended medical congresses, and, consorting with the wrangling controver-sialists there, became one of the ranters, and, just as the scales were turning, always adding his own weight to the argument, he got to be in no small request.

From medicine Ætius turned to theology.   Arius had already started his heresy,

and the schools of medicine resounded then with the disputes about that question.   Accordingly Ætius studied the controversy; and,

---

[1] The translation is certainly right, though "camel's hair " is a commoner sense of the Greek word.   Such tents are, and doubtless always have been, common in the country.

having laid a train of syllogisms from what he remembered of Aristotle, he became notorious for even going beyond Arius in the novel character of his speculations.

At this point the inconsistency of this "veracious" narrative strikes the reader; if the life of Ætius as serf, tinker, quack's assistant, and quack principal is rightly recorded, when had he found time and opportunity to study Aristotle?

Eunomius, the pupil of Ætius, had (according to his theological opponent) an almost equally varied, though much less disreputable, career. He was born at a small village —Oltiseris—of the Korniaspene district, in the north-western part of Cappadocia, near the Galatian frontier. His father was a peasant farmer,—

an excellent man, except that he had such a son. . . . He was one of those farmers who are always bent over the plough, and spend a world of trouble over their little farm; and in the winter, when he was secured from agricultural work, he used to carve out neatly the letters of the alphabet for boys to form syllables with, winning his bread with the money these sold for.

This is an interesting picture of the farmer's life in a remote and obscure corner of Cappadocia; and it suggests that the knowledge of letters and writing had penetrated to a very humble stratum of society, if a peasant farmer could make money in this way during the long winter season, when the ground was covered with snow for months. Facts like these make it all the more remarkable that a bishop who was present at the Council of Constantinople, in 448, had to get a friend to sign on his behalf, *eo quod nesciam literas.* The Phrygian Church, which had been so flourishing in the second and third centuries, was destroyed with fire and sword by Diocletian, and the country never properly recovered from that crushing persecution; education and prosperity were for a time almost annihilated. But Cappadocia had not been so thoroughly Christianised before the time of Diocletian, and hence it escaped more easily. In reading over the *Acta Sanctorum*, every student must observe that a much larger number of Cappadocian than of Phrygian martyrs are recorded under that great persecution ; but the fact is that the destruction in Phrygia was so thorough that the memory of individuals was not preserved. Where a whole city with its population was burned, who would record the martyrdom of any single hero? In Cappadocia many martyrs were tried and condemned, and their memory embalmed in history: in Phrygia the Church in considerable districts was obliterated for the time, and its tone permanently depreciated.

Eunomius, perceiving that his father led

a life of laborious penury, said good-bye to the plough and the mattock and all the paternal instruments, intending never to drudge himself like that ; then he sets himself to learn Prunicus' skill of short-hand writing ; and having perfected himself in that he entered at first, as I believe, the house of one of his own family, receiving his board for his services in writing ; then, while tutoring the boys of his host, he rises to the ambition of becoming an orator.

Here, again, we are struck with the development of education in this obscure district, when a shorthand clerk could be found worth board and lodging in a family, which must have been either rustic or of a small provincial town.

Gregory draws a veil over the subsequent stages in the life of Eunomius, until the epoch when he saw that his toil "was all of little avail, and that nothing which he could amass by such work was adequate to the demands of his ambition ". He accordingly turned to heresy-mongering, and found that this was a much more lucrative profession. " In fact, he toiled not thenceforward, neither did he spin ; for he is certainly clever in what he takes in hand, and knows how to gain the more emotional portion of mankind." He made religion pleasant to his hearers and dupes ; " he got rid of 'the toilsome steep of virtue' altogether "; and Gregory declares that he initiated them in practices and vices which it would not be decent even in an accuser to mention.

Considering the style in which religious controversy was carried on by almost all parties at this time, we cannot attach any special credibility to Gregory's accusation that Eunomius's teaching was so profoundly immoral. But it is of some interest to observe that the charge of appealing to the excitability and to the vices of the public was mutual. Eunomius declared that his great opponent Basil, the brother of Gregory, was " one who wins renown among poor old women, and practises to deceive the sex which naturally falls into every snare, and thinks it a great thing to be admired by the criminal and abandoned ".

In these descriptions of Ætius and Eunomius, and in many other occasional touches in the writings of Basil and Gregory, we observe traces of a certain contempt for the low-born persons who had to make their living by their own work. The family of Basil and Gregory possessed considerable property in land, and their tone is that of the aristocrat, brought up in a position of superiority, and voluntarily accepting a life of asceticism and hardship to which they were not trained. Basil is distinctly a champion of the popular cause against the dominant power of the Emperor and of the wealthier classes; but his position is not that of Cleon and Hyperbolus, claiming rights for the class from which they sprang, and not free from a touch of vulgarity in their speeches and a taint of selfishness in their aspirations.   His spirit and his aims are like those of Tiberius Gracchus, actuated by sincere and Divine sympathy for the wrongs and miseries in which he had no part, and showing perhaps want of judgment, but not selfishness.

From the Apostle Paul onwards it was, as a general rule, the local aristocracy that produced the leading figures in Anatolian history during the Roman period.   Education was indispensable to advancement and influence under the Empire ; and the poorer classes were cut off from the opportunity of getting education by a chasm which very few could cross.   The Imperial system never attempted to spread education more widely ; rather, it almost discouraged any movement of this kind.   Only private individuals,[1] or the cities of the provinces, made some attempt to increase the educational opportunities for their own people.   Basil and Gregory of Nazianzos belonged to the class of landed proprietors whose fortune opened to them the path of education and enabled them to study in Athens or some other of the leading Universities.

Such families belonged originally to a conquering class of land-owners, who dwelt as a country aristocracy amid an older conquered population.   They dwelt in a kind of building which was called Tetraypyrgion or Tetrapyrgia : quadrangular farm steadings enclosing an open courtyard, with towers at the corners and over the gate.   Such buildings were made to be defensible ; and Eumenes found that regular military operations were necessary to reduce them.[2]

---

[1] Pliny the younger may be taken as typical of a class.

[2] Plutarch, *Eum.*, 8 ; *Studies in the Eastern Roman Provinces*, p. 372 f. (Hodder & Stoughton, 1906) ; *Cities and Bishoprics of Phrygia*, ii., p. 419.

Their plan has been preserved to the present day in the great Khans, built along the principal roads by the Seljuk Sultans to defend the trade from the wandering and unruly Nomads.

According to Gregory of Nyssa, Christianity was the nearly universal religion of Cappadocia in the second half of the fourth century. He says in his *Epistle on Pilgrimages* that,

if it is really possible to infer God's presence from visible symbols, one might more justly consider that He dwelt in the Cappadocian nation than in any of the spots outside it. For how many Altars [1] there are there, on which the name of our Lord is glorified. One could hardly count so many in all the rest of the world.

There is, doubtless, some truth in this picture ; but it has been considerably heightened in colour, even setting aside the Oriental hyperbole of the last words, which were not meant to be taken literally. Basil, who is always more trust- worthy than Gregory, because he was more honest and more earnest, and stood closer to real life, gives a somewhat different account. He sees how far the Christian spirit was from hav- ing extirpated the pagan spirit, even where it had triumphed in outward appearance. He gives, for example, an interest- ing account of the Magusæi, a people who were settled in Cappadocia "in considerable numbers, scattered all over the country, settlers having long ago been introduced into these parts from Babylon". Probably they had been transplanted to Asia Minor by the Persian kings, to strengthen their hold on the country ; and they had remained for nearly eight centuries unmixed with the other inhabitants, preserving their own religious customs and separateness of blood. In a recent

---

[1] " Θυσιαστήρια, the sanctuaries (with the Altar), into which at this time no layman except the Emperor might enter."

book on Turkey,[1] it has been pointed out as one of the worst
evils in the country that the different races remain apart,
divided by difference of custom, and by consequent mutual
hatred; and the existence of the same evil in ancient time
might have been stated even more strongly than it is in that
work.   In the fourth century Roman rule and the influence
of the Church had alike failed, as yet, entirely to obliterate
racial differences; but it is only in incidental references like
this to the Magusæans, that the existence of such despised
races is admitted by the Cappadocian Fathers.   As Basil
says, " Their manners are peculiar, as they do not mix with
other men. . . . They have been made the prey of the devil
to do his will.   They have no books; no instructors in
doctrine."   Basil means, of course, Christian books : it is not
improbable that in secret they preserved and used Magian
books.   "They are brought up," as he goes on to say, "in
senseless institutions."   Besides more obvious characteristics,
"they object to the slaying of animals as defilement ; and
they cause the animals they want for their own use to be
slaughtered by other people.   They are wild after illicit
marriages: they consider fire divine," and so on.   These
illicit marriages are described by Eusebius [2] as being between
such near relatives as father and daughter, brother and
sister, son and mother; and the same writer says that the
Magusæi were very numerous in Phrygia and Galatia, and
everywhere retained the social customs and mysterious
religious ritual which they had brought with them from
Persia.

Illicit marriages were not confined to the Magusæi, but
were still admitted among the general population of Cappa-

[1] *Impressions of Turkey*, p. 95.
[2] *Præp. Ev.*, vi., pp. 275, 279, Viger.

docia, as is evident from the Canonical Letters, and from some incidental references.

Apparently, the Magusæi made a superficial pretence of Christianity, but retained their pagan customs almost unaltered ; as at the present day some races in the same country put on an outward appearance of Mohammedanism, though wanting its real character. Such, for example, are the Takhtaji (woodmen), about whom every traveller, who has seen much of Asia Minor, speaks : Dr. Von Luschan, *Reisen in Lykien*, ii., p. 199, vouches on personal knowledge for the survival among them of the custom of marriage between brother and sister, and they are as much despised by the Turks now as the Magusæi were by the Christians of Basil's time. But even among the Cappadocians proper, who had embraced Christianity in a more thorough way, there continued to exist many customs belonging to their pre-Christian state, which the Church had either tacitly acquiesced in, or at least failed to eradicate. Basil belonged to the Puritan party, and waged stern war with many of these customs. His invectives against them have preserved their memory ; and the student of ancient society will turn to these passages with a very different spirit and interest from that which Basil felt.

Marriage by capture was still a common practice, justified and supported by common opinion. In Letter 270 Basil speaks of this " act of unlawfulness and tyranny against human nature and society," and prescribes the treatment which is to be meted out to the offenders. The nature of the punishments shows that he is writing to some church official, probably one of his subordinate bishops, or village-bishops, or presbyters.

Wherever you find the girl, insist on taking her away, and restore her to her parents, shut out the man from the prayers, and make him excommunicate.[1] His accomplices, according to the canon which I have already put forth, cut off, with all their household, from the prayers. The village which received the girl after the abduction and kept her, or even fought against her restitution, shut out with all its inhabitants from the prayers; to the end that all may know that we regard the ravisher as a common foe like a snake or any other wild beast.

It is clear, then, that the whole neighbourhood approved the capture as preliminary to enforced marriage ; and even the clergy to some extent acquiesced in the popular opinion, for Basil says that " if you had all been of one mind in this matter, there would have been nothing to prevent this bad custom from being long ago driven out of your country ".

Basil was not so severe on some superstitions which had clothed themselves in a thoroughly Christian form. He regards it as quite praiseworthy that sick persons should have recourse for cures to the prayers of hermits; and he promises to try to find some relics of martyrs for a new church built by Bishop Arcadius (*Ep.* 49). Gregory Nazianzen declares that the mere visit of Basil almost cured the sick son of the Emperor Valens, and would have done so completely, had not his saving influence been counteracted by the presence of Arian heretics (*Or.* xliii., § 54). Yet Basil writes a noble eulogy of the medical profession : " To put that science at the head and front of life's pursuits is to decide reasonably and rightly" (*Ep.* 189). But the lively interest taken by the physicians of the time in theological controversy, as proved by that very letter, and by the life

---

[1] In the canonical letter to Amphilochius, p. 238, the total duration of the punishment in its various degrees is specified as four years.

of Ætius described above, is not suggestive of good; and, on the whole, we may gather that the medical profession had degenerated seriously from the scientific spirit of the old Greek medical schools.

On the other hand, he was very severe on the *Panegyreis*, or local festivals, which, along with religious observances and sermons, united a good deal of social enjoyment of a kind that was in his opinion objectionable (*Ep.* 42). We should be glad to learn more about these festivals. There can be no doubt that they were a Christianised form of the earlier pagan festivals, celebrated at the places which have continued to be the great centres of religion in all ages of history. The festivals were, in the first place, "spiritual gatherings," where might be heard "expositions of the teaching of the Apostles, lessons in theology," and so on; but, besides, there were presented before the assemblies plays, music, mountebanks, jests and follies, drunken men and—worst of all in Basil's estimation—beautiful women. The most interesting of these festivals took place at Venasa, the old seat of one of the three great temples of Cappadocia; and it corresponds to the modern festival of St. Macrina at Hassa-Keui, a few miles south of Venasa (which is now purely Turkish), to which Mohammedans as well as Christians resort, bringing sick animals to be cured on the holy occasion. The quaint and interesting story of the Deacon Glycerius is associated with that festival (*Ep.* 169 ff.); but it is too long for our space, and, moreover, has been very fully discussed elsewhere.[1]

Again, Basil condemns unsparingly the evils and abuses that existed in the Church of his time. He forbade an old unmarried presbyter of seventy to have a woman living in

[1] *Church in the Roman Empire before* 180, ch. xviii.

his house, and when the presbyter wrote to explain that
there was no evil relation between them, he rebuked him
with growing sternness, ordering him to expel her from his
house and "establish her in a monastery". Basil also
strenuously denounced the practice of taking money from
candidates for ordination : "They think that there is no
sin because they take the money not before but after the
ordination; but to take is to take at whatever time" (*Ep.*
53). He strove to reintroduce "the ancient custom observed
in the Churches," that ministers should be tested by examination as to their moral character and their whole past
life before being admitted, and to put down the ordinary
practice among the village-bishops of allowing "presbyters
and deacons to introduce unworthy persons, without any
previous examination of life and character, by mere favouri-
tism, on the score of relationship or some other tie"(*Ep.* 54).

The clergy had not yet become a distinct order, wholly
separate from the laity : they practised trades in order to
make their living. Basil had difficulty in finding any
clergyman to whom he might entrust a letter to Eusebius,
Bishop of Samosata, "for though our clergy do seem very
numerous, they are men inexperienced in travelling, because
they never traffic and prefer not to live far away from home,
the majority of them plying sedentary crafts, whereby they
get their daily bread " (*Ep.* 198).

From the letter just quoted, and many others, it is clear
that Basil usually tried to find clerical letter-carriers; and we
may understand that in many other cases, where no exact
information is given, this was the case, *e.g.,* in *Epist.* 19 to
Gregory Nazianzen, where he explains that he could not
reply on the spot to Gregory's letter, "because I was away
from home, and the letter-carrier, after he had delivered

the packet to one of my friends, went away". But other convenient opportunities were sometimes used: *e.g.*, magistrates travelling were often asked to carry letters for their friends (*Ep.* 215, 237).

The number of travellers was evidently far greater on the roads leading to Constantinople or Athens than towards Armenia. Basil has "no expectation of finding any one to convey a letter to Colonia in Armenia, which is far out of the way of ordinary routes" (*Ep.* 195). On the other hand, he speaks of a continuous stream of travellers coming from Athens to Cappadocia (*Ep.* 20); and though the letter, addressed to Leontius the Sophist, bears the stamp of the rhetorical style, sacrificing fact to effect, yet it implies that a considerable number of Cappadocian students, like Basil and Gregory Nazianzen, attended the University of Athens.

The important road to Samosata in Syria would be probably well frequented; and, when Basil speaks of difficulty in finding messengers thither, either he is speaking of the winter season, when the passes were blocked by snow, or he requires to find a trustworthy special messenger for an important letter.

On the whole, the impression given by the letters is that the custom of travelling, which had increased under the early Roman Empire to an extent almost unknown until the present century, was fully maintained in the fourth century.

Travelling on pilgrimage to the holy places of Palestine was not very much approved by the Cappadocian Fathers. Basil says here little on the subject. Gregory, having been entrusted with the duty of "visiting the places where the Church in Arabia is on the confines of the Jerusalem district," desires also to "confer with the Heads of the Holy Jerusalem Churches". He describes his journey thus:—

Our most religious Emperor had granted us facilities for the journey, by postal conveyance, so that we had to endure none of those inconveniences which in the case of others we have noticed; our waggon was, in fact, as good as a church or monastery to us, for all of us were singing psalms or fasting in the Lord during the whole journey.

But, though he took advantage of this opportunity of visiting Jerusalem, he did not approve of going on pilgrimage. He thought that there was nothing to be gained, even for men, by pilgrimage, except the more vivid appreciation of the fact "that our own places are far holier than those abroad"; and he considered that people should stay at home till they died, and that it was better for "the brethren to be absent from the body, to go to our Lord, rather than to be absent from Cappadocia, to go to Palestine". As to women going on pilgrimage, the difficulties of travelling made it still more unbecoming and improper.

For instance, it is impossible for a woman to accomplish so long a journey without a conductor; on account of her natural weakness, she has to be put upon her horse and to be lifted down again; she has to be supported[1] in difficult situations. Whichever we suppose, that she has an acquaintance to do this service or a hired attendant to perform it, either way the proceeding cannot escape being reprehensible; whether she leans on the help of a stranger or on that of her own servant, she fails to keep the law of correct conduct; and as the inns and hostelries and cities of the East present many examples of licence and of indifference to vice, how will it be possible for one passing through such smoke to escape without smarting eyes?

The evil reputation of the inns and taverns on the great roads of the Empire, to which Gregory here alludes, is

[1] Gregory seems to have had the lowest possible idea of women's capacity: they could not even sit on a horse, without being held to prevent them falling off.

confirmed by many other testimonies. Under the pagan
Empire, the hostelries were for the most part little better
than houses of ill-fame ; [1] and under the Christian Empire
there seems to have been no serious improvement. The
story of the birth of St. Theodore of Sykea in Galatia,
about A.D. 560, bears witness to a singularly depraved condition of public feeling; and in the Middle Ages matters
seem to have been equally bad for the Pilgrims to the Holy
Land. Felix Fabri of Ulm, about 1480, says that "the inns
on the isles of the sea are houses of ill-fame," and warns
every "good and godly pilgrim" at night to "return to his
galley and sleep therein safe in his berth ".[2] The character
of the public hostelries was, doubtless, one of the reasons
that weighed with Basil in making his great foundation near
Cæsareia, including not merely an almshouse and hospital,
but also

a place of entertainment for strangers, both those who are on a
journey and those who require medical treatment on account of
sickness, and so establishing a means of giving these men the
comfort they want, doctors, means of conveyance, and escort.

A foundation like this shows Basil's practical character ;
he diagnosed the real character of the evil, and struck out
the cure; and, as we believe, his foundation became so
important that it gradually attracted the city to itself, and
the ancient site is now deserted, while Basil's site is the
present Kaisari.[3]

The frequent allusions to the severity of winter weather
will surprise those who do not know the country. Although

---

[1] See Friedländer, *Sittengeschichte Roms*, ii., p. 44.

[2] Translation in *Palest. Pilgrims' Text Society*, i., p. 163; compare p.
21.

[3] A πανδόχειον at Constantina in Osrhoene, *B. C. H.*, 1903, p. 200, was
founded in 514, *hotellerie ecclesiastique pour pelerins.*

Cappadocia does not lie so high, and the winters are not so severe, as in Armenia, yet Cæsareia is 3,500 feet above sea-level, and the border-land between the valleys of the Halys and Sarus and Euphrates is a good deal higher; and at that elevation winter is long and hard. Basil speaks of "such a very heavy fall of snow that we have been buried, houses and all, beneath it, and now for two months have been living in dens and caves" (*i.e.*, under the surface of the snow, like the underground dwellings—dens and caves—used in some parts of Cappadocia) (*Ep.* 48). Even an unusually mild winter "was quite enough to keep me not merely from travelling while it lasted, but even from so much as venturing to put my head out of doors" (*Ep.* 27).[1]

In another letter he mentions that "we have had a winter of such severity that all the roads were blocked till Easter" (*Ep.* 198). Again, "the road to Rome is wholly impracticable in winter" (*Ep.* 215). Even a meeting with the Bishop of Iconium must be arranged "at a season suitable for travelling" (*Ep.* 191), though the road from Cæsareia to Iconium traverses only level country and crosses no hills or passes except that of the Boz-Dagh, about 600 feet above the plain.

As to the state of peace and order in the country, there are many indications that the administration of government was both arbitrary, weak and ineffective. Basil writes to Candidianus, the governor or a high official of the province Pontus,[2] shortly after his return from Athens, probably about A.D. 360, asking redress for a serious wrong: the

[1] Contrast with this the account given of a modern missionary in my *Impressions of Turkey*, p. 222. The winter weather does not prevent travellers of Western origin from going about; but the Eastern people are not great travellers, and regard winter as a closed season.

[2] Not Cappadocia, as editors think, for Annesi was in Pontus.

house on his farm had been broken into, part of the contents stolen, and his servants beaten, by a band of rude persons from the neighbouring village of Annesi. Basil himself seems to have been living at the time in his retreat in the gorge of the river Iris, near the farm. The farm was managed by a steward, who had died ; and a creditor in Annesi had taken this disorderly way of recovering a debt which he claimed. We have, of course, only a statement of one side of the case ; but the main facts cannot be doubted. We are struck, however, by the fact that Basil makes no attempt to get redress by ordinary process of law. He writes direct to a high officer, and asks that, as a punishment, the man be "apprehended by the district magistrate and locked up for a short period in the jail". Basil had too much of the aristocratic tone to take proceedings before the district magistrate against a vulgar rustic. His claim is that the governor should act at once on his representation, and should give a slight lesson to the neighbours that Basil was not a person whose property and house could be lightly insulted, even in his absence. It was probably after this event that Basil gave the use of the estate and the slaves on it for life to his foster-brother, Dorotheos, the presbyter of the village, reserving to himself an annual rent from it for his support. Mr. Blomfield Jackson has rightly brought out that this act had not the character, which has often been attributed to it, of a total renunciation of the property. Basil was not a man to retire wholly from the world and live in pure asceticism. He recognised rightly the duty incumbent on him of action in the world ; and he knew that he could act far more usefully, if he were not in a position of penury. He was used to the position of a country gentleman with means and influence ; and the thought of abandoning this position and entering on a life of real poverty evidently never occurred to him as a serious possibility. When the assessment on the property was raised, he protested vigorously and asked that the ancient system of rating should be retained, as Dorotheos might throw up the property, making Basil himself responsible for the whole of the rate (*Ep.* 36).

Gregory Nazianzen in his *Panegyric on St. Basil*, § 56, tells how "the assessor of a judge was attempting to force into a distasteful marriage a lady of high birth, whose husband was but recently dead," and used all the powers of his position against her and Basil, who was trying to protect her, until the populace rose in defence of their bishop,

especially the men from the small-arms factory and from the imperial weaving-sheds; for men at work in these trades are specially hot-tempered and daring, because of the liberty allowed them. Each man was armed with the tool he was using, or with whatever else came to hand at the moment. Torch in hand, amid showers of stones, with cudgels ready, all ran and shouted together. . . . Nor were the women weaponless; . . . they were by the strength of their eagerness endowed with masculine courage.

In the end Basil's help alone preserved the official from their violence.

The events which called forth Letters 72-73 illustrate this subject. They seem to have been the following, though the allusive way in which Basil refers to what was familiar to his correspondents makes several of the details doubtful. A certain Callisthenes, a man of great influence, probably an official (see p. 403), resided in some city of South-west Cappadocia. At Sasima (the town of which Gregory Nazianzen was made bishop, much against his will, by

Basil), where three great roads met, and where there was, doubtless, a post-station and a vast amount of traffic and travellers, there had occurred a quarrel between Callisthenes and a set of slaves belonging to Eustochius, who was apparently a merchant residing at or near Cæsareia. Some dispute about precedence, or other incident of travelling, caused such angry feeling that the slaves had even used personal violence to Callisthenes; and they had made themselves liable to some serious punishment. Callisthenes seems to have been sole arbiter of their fate; and the owners of the slaves, perhaps a trading company to which Eustochius belonged, had no way of preventing him from exacting the extreme penalty. Eustochius appealed to Basil, who exerted himself to the utmost to secure milder treatment for the slaves. He wrote to Callisthenes a letter (not preserved), and received a very polite reply, couched in that Oriental style of elaborate courtesy which means nothing, professing to leave the decision with Basil, but insisting that the slaves should come to Sasima to submit to punishment, and giving no pledge as to the penalty which would satisfy him. Basil replied, acknowledging the courtesy of the letter, but pointing out clearly that, unless Callisthenes gave some distinct promise before the slaves went to Sasima, the politeness of the letter was merely a matter of words. He allowed that, if Callisthenes insisted, the slaves must go to Sasima; but he hoped and begged that Callisthenes would be satisfied with their appearance there and submission to his will, and would remit further punishment. Especially, he desired a promise that Callisthenes would himself be present at Sasima, and not let himself be detained by business on the road, leaving to others the exaction of the legal penalty. This desire implies that, if Callisthenes were not present to remit the penalty, no other person would have the power to do so ; and that the slaves had been condemned to appear and suffer a certain punishment, unless Callisthenes chose to be satisfied with less.   What the penalty was is not stated by Basil, but his language implies that it was very serious, possibly death. The decree had apparently been pronounced at Cæsareia, whither Callisthenes had sent a soldier to demand satisfaction, and his vigorous complaint at headquarters secured an order in his favour from the governor of the province.

Basil also wrote to Hesychius, who lived in the same city as Callisthenes, and was apparently an official of the Church. He sent a deacon to carry these letters, and instructed him to take other steps in the business.   The amount of trouble which Basil took furnishes a proof of the interest which he felt in the condition of slaves, and of the way in which he was ready to use the whole strength of the Church, as well as his own, to secure milder treatment for them (see p. 403).

Complaints about the burden of taxation were evidently often made.   Thus: "everything nowadays is full of taxes demanded and called in . . . for even the Pythagoreans were not so fond of their Tetractys, as these modern tax-collectors of their four-times-as-much" (a rule imposing quadruple payment for arrears); an estate "is now left and abandoned on account of the weight of the rates imposed on it".   In *Epist.* 110: "give orders that the tax paid by the inhabitants of iron-producing Taurus may be such as it is possible to pay".   A new system, whereby the burdens on the clergy were much increased, is referred to elsewhere. The harsh treatment of the clergy by Maximus, the governor of Cappadocia, is complained of.   The governors seem to have been far from just or good.   We hear of the same

Maximus, persecuted by the next governor of Cappadocia, and of a governor in Africa so bad as to be excommunicated by the Church. The arbitrary conduct of governors, in violation of formal law or of equity, is a frequent subject of complaint.

In *Epist.* 54 we learn that "a large number of persons are presenting themselves for the ministry through fear of the conscription". The strong dislike for military service, by making the mass of the people entirely incapable of self-defence, undoubtedly rendered them an easier prey to the ravages of Parthians and afterwards of Saracens.

As to the conditions of labour, we learn little from the works here translated, though there are materials in the other works for a much more elaborate picture. In *Epist.* 18 Basil mentions the hired labourers engaged on a farm during the heat of summer; in the winter, when all agricultural work was suspended, they would not be needed. He distinguishes these hired farm-servants from the agriculturists proper, some of whom turned to other industry during the winter, like the father of Eunomius. The slaves who cultivated such estates as Basil's at Annesi must be distinguished from both hired labourers and free agriculturists.

Famine-relief operations were organised by the Church officials; for scarcity seems to have been common. Basil says that "the dearth is still with us, and I am therefore compelled to remain where I am, partly by the duty of distribution, and partly out of sympathy for the distressed" (*Ep.* 31). The letter is ordinarily assigned to A.D. 369, and was certainly earlier than the death of Eusebius, Bishop of Cæsareia, in A.D. 370.[1] It was followed by a long and

[1] This famine and the relief operations are also described by Gregory Nazianzen, *Panegyric*, §§ 34-36.

severe scarcity which was raging at Nazianzus in A.D. 373, when Gregory Nazianzen delivered his Oration xvi. to his suffering and terrified congregation.

It is a highly elaborated and artificial civilisation that is set before us in these works; but there are many signs of the bad administration, which went from bad to worse during the following century and a half, until Justinian made a great and noble effort to reform the whole executive. His *Novellæ* present a terrible picture of provincial oppression and misgovernment;[1] but a rigorous diagnosis of the evil, such as is there given, is the first step towards improvement. Whether the changes in the executive which he made were ill-advised, or the evil was too deeply seated to be reached by changes on the surface, little permanent improvement was attained; but the attempt which was made to cure the evil, as well as the unsparing statement of its character and causes, deserve different treatment from the brief paragraph of unlimited condemnation, in which Gibbon sums up the character of the *Novellæ* in his chapter xliv., quoting and apparently endorsing the opinion of Montesquieu, that "these incessant and for the most part trifling alterations can be only explained by the venal spirit of a prince, who sold without shame his judgments and his laws". Change was urgently necessary, both on the surface and at the heart. In St. Basil of Cæsareia we have a great administrator, whose plans of cure for the deeper evils affecting his country were wise and statesmanlike, though, as was natural, too purely ecclesiastical to be complete. But he could make no provision to ensure a succession of Basils. The Roman Empire

---

[1] Entirely confirmed by other evidence, *e.g.*, an inscription recently found in Pisidia of the year 527 (*Bulletin de Corresp. Hellénique*, 1893, p. 501 ff.).

had too much neglected its duty of creating a sufficient educational system for the people; and the society of the Roman Provinces was not fertile and vigorous enough to produce a series of men like Basil.

Twelve years ago, the greatest of living historians, Professor Theodor Mommsen, said to the present writer that, if he were now beginning a new life of scholarship, he would take up the period between Diocletian and Justinian. The scholar who devotes himself to that period will be filled with a growing admiration for Basil; and he will recognise the merits and the scholarly insight of the books which we have taken as the text of this paper. Any ambitious young scholar, who wishes to do real service by increasing our knowledge of past history, will find here an open field; and he could not better begin than by a systematic study of the society presented to us in the pages of the three great Fathers. The voluminous writings of the three contemporary Cappadocians, Basil and the two Gregories, apart from the purely theological and ecclesiastical interest, possess a high value as storing up many facts about the state of society and of education, about the administration and law of the late Roman Empire as practically affecting the people, about the taxpayers' views on taxation, the travellers' views as to the roads and the seasons, the householder's views on the safety of his property, the merchants' and the investors' views on the public credit and the standard of commercial honesty; in short, about the ordinary life of a highly organised community, in which the Oriental style of society and manners was being replaced by the European; and, above all, they show us the views entertained by three men of power and education as to the duties of the Church in its relation to all these various interests. A study of the three great Cappadocians from this point of view would make a most instructive and interesting work.

After this glance at the times and surroundings of Basil, it is fair to look at the man himself.

He was probably the most vigorous, striking and manly figure in the Church of Asia Minor under the Empire of Constantinople, though some blemishes of temper and of pride have combined with a certain hardness and want of sympathy in his nature to render him an object of less interest in history than he deserves. Mr. Jackson's translation is at once pleasant to read as English, and true to the letter and to the spirit of the original; and we may hope that it will succeed (as it deserves) in drawing more attention on the part of classical scholars to the varied interest of the Christian writers of the period in question.

In Mr. Jackson's prolegomena we have a careful account of the life of Basil, and a very full account of the works which are not translated here. In the biography, the results of earlier writers, Tillemont and Maran (the Benedictine editor), are worked up; and there is added to them a much more precise localisation of the scenes, in which recent geographical discoveries are utilised. Naturally, however, the biography is secondary to the translation; and there is still need for a careful study of the life of Basil and for a more exact determination of the dates of his letters as well as of the larger works. Several interesting incidents in his history seem to me not to have been properly understood; and the dates assigned to some letters by the Benedictine editor (and accepted by Mr. Jackson) are in several cases not convincing and even quite unsatisfactory.[1] While we cannot enter on

---

[1] The biography of Basil in *Dictionary of Christian Biography*, meritorious and useful as it is, is too much guided by the earlier modern authorities.

any such wider questions within our narrow limits, we may profitably devote some few pages here to studying, under the guidance of Mr. Jackson, a few passages which bring out some personal characteristics of " St. Basil the Great"; and, at the same time, the quotations will exemplify the spirit and excellence of the translation in this volume.

The letter which faced me, as I first opened the volume, No. 135, may be taken as a specimen, selected at random, of the translation and of Basil's expression. Basil acknowledges two books which Diodorus, Presbyter of Antioch (afterwards Bishop of Tarsus), had sent him for perusal. " With the second," he says, " I was delighted, not only with its brevity . . . but because it is at once full of thought and so arranged that the objections of opponents and the answers to them stand out distinctly. . . . The former work, which has practically the same force, but is much more elaborately adorned with rich diction, many figures, and niceties of dialogue, seems to me to require considerable time to read and much mental labour, both to gather its meaning and retain it in the memory. The abuse of our opponents and the support of our own side, which are thrown in, although they may seem to add some charms of dialectic to the treatise, do yet break the continuity of the thought and weaken the strength of the argument by causing interruption and delay. . . . If the subject of the dialogue be wide and general, digressions against persons interrupt its continuity and tend to no good end. . . . So much I have written to prove that you did not send your work to a flatterer. . . . I have, however, now sent back the larger and earlier of the two volumes, after perusing it as far as I have been able.[1]

---

[1] The effect of this rather suggestive statement is toned down in the original by a sentence here omitted about Basil's weak health.

The second I have retained with the wish to transcribe it, but hitherto without finding any quick writer." [1]

This letter conveys a very favourable impression (and a correct impression) of Basil's tone to his friends, and to those who thought like himself: it is judicious in its criticism, pointed and simple in expression, polite and kindly in tone; it advises without assumption, and encourages without flattering.

Everywhere the warmth of Basil's affection for friends and relatives, and the pleasant recollection of old associations, combined with his good sense and lofty tone, convey a most favourable impression. Take a few examples: " One would rather see his friend, though angry with him, than anybody else, flattering him. Do not, then, cease preferring charges like the last! The very charge will mean a letter; and nothing can be more precious or delightful to me" (*Ep.* 21). Or this: " Now for my sins, I have lost my mother, the only comfort I had in life. Do not smile if, old as I am, I lament my orphanhood. Forgive me if I cannot endure separation from a soul, to compare with whom I see nothing in the future that lies before me. So once more my complaints have come back to me; once more I am confined to my bed, tossing about in my weakness, and every hour all but looking for the end of life" (*Ep.* 30). Or again, these recollections of childhood from *Ep.* 271: " To travel once again in memory to our young days, and to be reminded of old times, when for both of us there was one home, one hearth,

---

[1] This shows a rather low standard of the book-trade in Cæsarea, one of the greatest commercial cities of the East. Without such scribes, the publication of an edition of a book was impossible. A similar statement is made by Gregory Nyss., *Ep.* 15 (Migne).

the same schoolmaster, the same leisure, the same work, the same treats, the same hardships, and everything shared in common! What do you think I would not have given to recall all this by actually meeting you, to rid me of the heavy weight of my old age, and to seem to be turned from an old man into a lad again!"

But it was not pleasant to be on the opposite side from Basil. Speaking of the Arians, he is hardly to be trusted even as to facts. He felt too bitterly; and he exaggerated so rhetorically, that his words cannot be taken literally. Thus in *Ep.* 242 he declares that in the thirteen years of Arian persecution "the Churches have suffered more tribulations than all those that are on record since Christ's gospel was first preached"—an utterly unjustifiable statement (against which Mr. Jackson rightly, perhaps too mildly, protests, as "not to be taken literally"). The harsh and rude invective which Basil uses about his opponents is the fault of his age, and, while we regret it, we cannot wonder at it.

Difficult, however, as it is to appreciate the real character of the Arian controversy as a question of social life, on the whole we gather, I think, that the progressive tendencies were on the side of Basil, and acquiescence in the existing standard of morality characterised the Arian point of view. The "Orthodox" Church was still the champion of higher aspirations, and Basil, however harsh he was to all who differed from him, was an ennobling and upward-struggling force in the life of his time. At a later period the facts changed; and, in the Iconoclast period, the sympathy of the modern student must, I think, be almost wholly against the successors of Basil, and in favour of the maligned and despised heretics.

The contest in which Basil was involved against the
Imperial power in regard to the division of Cappadocia into
two provinces produced the most striking scenes of his life,
and displayed both his strongest qualities and his worst
faults of character. The questions at issue in this contest
seem not to have been correctly apprehended by writers on
the life of Basil. The policy of the Byzantine rule had
been uniformly directed to subdividing the great provinces,
and thus diminishing the power of provincial governors.
Subdivision was the natural result of the centralisation of
authority, the exaggeration of the power of the court, and
the diminishing of the power of officials at a distance from
the court. Cappadocia was by far the largest of the provinces; its turn had now come to be subdivided, and in 371
the Arian Emperor Valens resolved on this step. He may
probably have been roused to it by the fact that the influence of Cæsareia, under its vigorous and uncompromising
"orthodox" bishop, was dead against his ecclesiastical policy.
It was natural that he should wish to diminish that influence;
but in itself the subdivision would naturally have been soon
made even by an orthodox emperor; and at a later time
Justinian divided Cappadocia into three parts. The bias of
Valens was shown, however, by his leaving the smaller part
of Cappadocia to the metropolis Cæsareia, and making the
new province of Secunda Cappadocia decidedly larger. The
officials who lived at Cæsareia, and the business which came
to it, were much diminished, as the province of which it was
the metropolis shrank to less than half its former size. The
city, naturally, regarded the change with dismay, and protested strongly. Basil exerted himself to the utmost; but
the three letters which he wrote intreating the intercession of
certain influential persons with Valens in favour of Cæsareia,

are among the poorest in the collection.[1] They are inflated
and exaggerated in their description of the loss that would
result to Cæsareia; they show no appreciation either on the
one hand of the real causes that recommended the subdivision,
or on the other of the weighty reasons that might have been
urged against the centralising policy.   In fact the whole
system of the Orthodox Church was in favour of centralisation; and Basil himself would have been the most vigorous
supporter of that policy in any case where it did not affect
his own city and his own archbishopric.   He could not argue
on strong grounds against the change, for his whole system
of thought debarred him from those grounds, and his protests
are weak and hysterical.

The true greatness of Basil, however, shone forth immediately afterwards, when Valens came to Cæsareia.   The
archbishop triumphantly resisted the efforts made by the
creatures of Valens to overawe him and bend him to the
will of the Arian Emperor.   Valens himself was not blind to
the nobility and dignity of Basil's character; he left the
archbishop in secure possession of his rank and the freedom
of his opinions; he attended Divine service performed by
him in the cathedral; he held private conference with him;
and he gave land[2] to endow Basil's new foundation, the
hospital, etc., near Cæsareia.   Considering how bitter was

[1] *Epp.* 74, 75, 76. The first is addressed to Martinianus, who had some
personal friendship with Basil; otherwise he is unknown, but he evidently
was not a Cappadocian official.   The profusion of literary allusions in the
letter, and the compliments to the knowledge of history and of mankind that
Martinianus possessed, suggest that he was a philosopher or man of letters.
He evidently lived at some distance both from Constantinople and from Cappadocia. Mr. Jackson's statement that he was an official of Cappadocia
rests on no ancient authority, and seems to me not to suit the letter.

[2] Mr. Jackson's suggestion that they were part of the Imperial estate of
Macellum, beside Cæsareia, is very probable.

the quarrel at this time between the Arian and the orthodox party, Valens deserves more credit in this case than he has generally received. But, as to Basil, every one must say, with Mr. Jackson, that "his attitude seems to have been dignified without personal haughtiness, and to have shown sparks of that quiet humour which is rarely exhibited in great emergencies except by men who are conscious of right and careless of consequences to self".

But, in the following months, the quarrel with Anthimus, Bishop of Tyana, the metropolis of the new province of Cappadocia Secunda, shows Basil at his worst. He struggled to maintain his former rights over the churches and mon- asteries of the new province with undignified pertinacity. He created new bishoprics, not on account of the needs of the Church, but to increase the number of his supporters and their weight; and his old friend Gregory of Nazianzos could hardly forget or forgive the way in which Basil used him for his own purposes by almost forcing him to become Bishop of Sasima, one of these new sees. He went in person to collect the revenues of St. Orestes (what Gregory calls sarcastically his "supply of sucking-pigs and poultry from St. Orestes"), and his servants came almost to a battle with those of his rival. Basil certainly would have justified his action in the same terms that Innocent, Bishop of Rome, used shortly afterwards, about 408, that it was not right that the Church of God should be altered to suit the changes of this world.[1] But every attempt made to maintain that principle, fine as it seems in words, was a failure under the Empire, and must be a failure. The classification of dioceses was not of the essence of the Church; it naturally and pro- perly varied with the changes of society, and prosperity, and

---

[1] See *Historical Geography of Asia Minor*, p. 93.

political arrangement. The reason why Cæsareia had been an ecclesiastical centre lay originally in its being the political capital, and therefore the natural centre from which the province could best be affected and its churches directed. But, when Tyana had become the metropolis of considerable part of Cappadocia, it was merely introducing confusion to maintain that the cities of that province should look to Cæsareia ecclesiastically, when they must look to Tyana in political, legal and social respects. Neither Anthimus nor Basil showed in this case true dignity, or self-respect, or the respect due to a colleague ; but, while no one cares about Anthimus, it is painful to those who respect and admire a great man to read about Basil's action, and above all to read his condemnation in the estrangement of his old friend Gregory, who had at first supported him in the case.

Many touches of the raillery which became rude and unpleasant towards his opponents,[1] appear in a much more pleasant style when he writes to his friends.

He has found out that " there does seem something thinner than I was—I am thinner than ever ".

In *Ep.* 4 he acknowledges a gift under the guise of a complaint that the giver is "evicting from our retreat my dear friend and nurse of philosophy, Poverty ".

Twitting Gregory with the shortness of his letters, he says, " The letter is shown to be yours, not so much by the writing as by the style of the communication : in few words much is expressed ".

The tone of these quotations doubtless gives the key to explain the rather enigmatic *Ep.* 1, where he speaks as if his travels through Syria and Egypt had been undertaken

---

[1] As when (*Ep.* 231) he calls one (perhaps Demosthenes, the agent of Valens) " the fat sea-monster " and " the old muleteer ".

for the single purpose of meeting Eustathius, the philosopher to whom the letter is addressed.

In *Ep*. 56, apologising for leaving a letter unanswered until his correspondent wrote again, he says, "I naturally forget very easily, and I have had lately many things to do, and so my natural infirmity is increased. I have no doubt, therefore, that you wrote to me, although I have no recollection of having received any letter from your excellency. . . . Really this letter of mine, as it is more than twice as bulky (as yours), will fulfil a double purpose. You see to what sophisms my idleness [surely laziness] drives me. . . . But, my dear sir, do not in a few words bring serious charges, indeed the most serious of all. Forgetfulness of one's friends, and neglect of them arising from high place, are faults which involve every kind of wrong. . . . I shall begin to forget you when I cease to know myself. Never, then, think that, because a man is a very busy man he is a man of faulty character."

The dignity, mingled with humility and desire for peace, shown in the two letters to his uncle Gregory, 59, 60, may be referred to as illustrating the graver and loftier side of his character.

As examples of the sound and high judgment, which placed him on the right side in most great social questions, we may quote the opinion which, when he writes to a physician, he states about his profession as being at the head and front of life's pursuits (see p. 380).

He refers in *Ep*. 191 with longing admiration to the hospitable intercourse which "was once the boast of the Church. Brothers from each Church, travelling from one end of the world to the other, were provided with little tokens, and found all men fathers and brothers. But now," he says, "we are confined each in his own city, and every one looks at his neighbour with distrust ".

Basil was ready to defend the weak against the strong. In *Ep.* 73 he uses the whole influence of his position and of the Church to save some slaves from harsh punishment at the hands of Callisthenes, a government official [1] to whom they had behaved rudely. "Though you have sworn to deliver them to execution as the law enjoins, my rebuke is still of no less value, nor is the Divine law of less account than the laws current in the world." See p. 388.

Basil's tone in addressing women lacks the charming ease that generally characterises his letters to his male correspondents. An illustration is supplied in the two letters which he addressed to Nectarius, a noble of Cilicia, and his wife, on the death of their only son. The letter to Nectarius (No. 5), in spite of the rhetorical touch (which may be pardoned, as it stands alone), "if all the streams run tears, they will not adequately weep our woe," is very fine, and the conclusion is charming, "Let us wait a little while, and we shall be once more with him. The time of our separation is not long, for in this life we are all like travellers on a journey, hastening on to the same shelter"; and so on in terms that have now become, through familiarity and repetition, less impressive than they were to Basil's contemporaries. But the letter to the bereaved mother is far inferior. "Alas, for the mighty mischief that the contact with an evil demon was able to wreak. Earth! what a calamity thou hast been compelled to sustain! If the sun had any feeling, one would think he might have shuddered," etc. After these bombastic commonplaces of rhetoric, he

---

[1] He is shown to be an official by his having the power to send a soldier to Cæsareia with a message on the subject.

addresses the bereaved mother in almost equally frigid consolations. "When first you were made a mother, . . . you knew that, a mortal yourself, you had given birth to a mortal. What is there astonishing in the death of a mortal? . . . Look round at all the world in which you live; remember that everything you see is mortal, and all subject to corruption. Look up to heaven, even it shall be dissolved; look at the sun, not even the sun will last for ever. All the stars together," etc., etc., "are subject to decay." In the early part of the letter Basil says, "I know what a mother's heart is"; but Mr. Jackson, in his note on the words, well remarks that the mother might have replied in the words of Constance to Pandulph: "He talks to me that never had a son". A certain externality and hardness of tone characterises the letter, and makes it more of a rhetorical exercise than a spontaneous outburst of sympathy.

A few passages occur to me in which it may be doubted whether Mr. Jackson has fully caught the meaning. For example, *Ep.* 8, 1, when, evidently, Basil is replying to a letter of the people of Cæsareia, asking him to return from his sojourn with Gregory, he says: "Give me, therefore, I beg you, a little time. I am not embracing a city life." Mr. Jackson adds the note: "*i.e.*, the life of the city, presumably Nazianzus, from which he is writing". But surely a person who writes to the great city of Cæsareia from the small town of Nazianzus, and speaks of "city life" (τὴν ἐν ταῖς πόλεσι διατριβήν), must be referring to life in Cæsareia, not life in Nazianzus. Moreover, I cannot doubt, both from the context and the localities, that Basil was at the moment dwelling, not in Nazianzus, but in Carbala or Caprales (still called Gelvere), where Gregory's home was situated, where he was (as he intimates) enjoying the life of retirement and contemplation, and where to this day the memorials of Gregory are preserved, and the rock-cells mark the abode of many hermits in the succeeding ages.[1] I should venture to suggest that a thought has been left unexpressed by Basil from brevity and rapidity, and that the sense is, " a little time, pray, a little time grant me, I beg; [and then I shall come to you,] not welcoming the life of cities (for I am quite well aware of the danger caused to the soul in that life), but judging that the society of the saints [as contrasted with the solitary life of the hermit] is the most practically useful. [But grant me the delay,] for in the constant free interchange of ideas [with ' Gregory, Christ's mouth '] I am acquiring a deep-seated habit of contemplation." Elsewhere, also, Basil declares plainly his opinion that the life of action and public work is the more honourable, as it is the more wearisome and difficult and unpleasant side of the truly religious life.

As another example, take *Ep.* 190, §1 : " The most careless observer must at once perceive that it is in all respects more advantageous for care and anxiety to be divided among several bishops ". This reads like a general maxim intended for wide application; but the Greek seems to me to need a different sense, applying solely to the case of Isaura, now under consideration, " it is more advantageous that the care of the district be divided [2] among several bishops ". The case, which had been referred to Basil by Amphilochius, Arch-

---

[1] The exact localisation of the home of Gregory, on the estate Arianzos, beside the village Carbala (or Caprales, Basil, *Ep.* 308), about eight miles south-west of Nazianzus (now called Nenizi), is made in *Historical Geography of Asia Minor*, p. 286; see also Sir C. Wilson's *Handbook to Asia Minor*, etc. (Murray), p. 169. The modern village of Gelvere is built in the Tiberina, described by Gregory Naz., *Ep.* 6, 7, a narrow, rocky, picturesque glen, like a hole in the plain (4,500 feet above sea-level), " the very pit of the whole earth," as Basil calls it (*Ep.* 14).

[2] εἰς πλείονας ἐπισκόπους καταδιαιρεθῆναι τὴν μέριμναν.

bishop of Iconium, for advice, was a remarkable one. The large district round the great city Isaura had fallen into utter disorganisation (probably owing to the unruly character of the Isaurians, who were frequently in rebellion). Several bishops were needed for the care of so large a district. Basil would prefer that a bishop for the city should first be appointed, who might afterwards associate others with himself, as his experience showed him that they might be most usefully placed. But, owing to the danger that the bishop might be tempted by ambition to rule over a larger diocese, and might not consent to the ordination of others, he felt it safer to appoint in the first place bishops ($\pi\rho o \ddot{\iota}\sigma\tau\alpha\mu\acute{\epsilon}\nu o\upsilon\varsigma$) to the small towns or villages which were formerly the seats of bishops, and thereafter to select the bishop of the city.[1] We have here a good example of the decay of bishoprics in political troubles, of the revival of disused bishoprics, and of the trouble that might be caused by an ambitious prelate.

Some other examples have struck me where opinions as to the meaning are likely to differ. But when we consider how little care has been devoted to the elucidation of Basil, and contrast it with the voluminous studies that have contributed to the long and difficult growth of the interpretation of Horace, or Virgil, or Sophocles, we can better appreciate the difficulties that Mr. Jackson had to face, and better estimate the gratitude we owe him.

---

[1] On the desire of bishops to extend their authority over smaller cities and to diminish the number of bishops, see *Studies in the History and Art of the Eastern Provinces* (Hodder & Stoughton, 1906), p. 28 f.

INDEX

I

Paul—

Age of, 37, 67, 362.
Author of *Colossians*, 302.
Character as painted by Mr. Baring-Gould, 325 ff.
Chronology, 67, 345-65.
Command of money, 336 (*St. Paul the Trav.*, p. 310 ff.).
Comparison of, with John and Peter, 31, 33.
Conversion of, 10, 16 f., 70 ff.; sudden and not gradually prepared, 71, 87; completion, not reversal, of his ideas, 72, 80, 87, 90, 96; variations in story of, 17, 19 f.
Courtesy of, 36 f., 39.
" Critical " theories about, 11, 17, 22, 40 f., 49 f., 301-2.
Dates, 67, 345-65.
Defence before Sanhedrin, 83 ff., 96.
Divine alone is real, 71.
Education, according to Mr. Baring-Gould, 330 f. ; but see also under Curtius and Hicks, and 334 f.
Errors due to over-straining and over-emphasis, 30, 34 f.
Feminine element in his nature, 337.
" Fought with beasts," 316, 332.
" Fulness of time," what this implies about Paul, 335.
Gentiles, theory of position of the, 8 ; commissioned to, 73 f. ; feeling to, 66.
Hellenism, relation of Paul to, 62, 259, 330 ff.
High-Priest, why unknown to Paul, 95.

Paul (*continued*)—

His theory of degeneration in religion, 5, 164 f.
Humanity the secret of his charm for us, 28 ff., 34, 82.
Influence of, on history, 53.
Jealousy ? 38.
Jews and Paul, 89, 308 f.
Journey from Cæsareia to Jerusalem, 266.
Kingdom of God, 81. See Messiah.
Legendary localities at Tarsus, 275, 277.
Letters of, written for the needs of the moment, 82.
Luke and Paul, 44.
Martyr at Derbe, 295.
Messiah, eager from childhood for the coming of, 66 f., 69, 80 f.
Name, 65.
Not married, 68 f.
Olive-tree in Paul, 219-32.
Organiser, an, 53, 64, 78. See Plan.
Pharisee, a, 64, 73, 83-94.
Plan for conquering the Roman Empire, 74, 80, 100, 197 ff., 256 ff.
Rank in society, 37, 376.
Reason for persecuting Christians, 69 f.
Revelation, his belief in, to himself was honest, 10 ; not result of madness, 11.
Revelation, believed in real, 3 f., 8 f., 22, 71 ; perception of it intuitive and certain, 20, 71 f.
Revelation, universal and not confined to Jews, 4.

INDEX

II